Erotic Nihilism in Late Imperial Russia

Erotic Nihilism in Late Imperial Russia

*The Case of
Mikhail Artsybashev's* Sanin

Otto Boele

THE UNIVERSITY OF WISCONSIN PRESS

Publication of this volume has been made possible, in part, through support from
the ANDREW W. MELLON FOUNDATION.

The University of Wisconsin Press
1930 Monroe Street, 3rd Floor
Madison, Wisconsin 53711-2059
uwpress.wisc.edu

3 Henrietta Street
London WC2E 8LU, England
eurospanbookstore.com

Copyright © 2009
The Board of Regents of the University of Wisconsin System
All rights reserved. No part of this publication may be reproduced, stored in a retrieval system, or transmitted, in any format or by any means, digital, electronic, mechanical, photocopying, recording, or otherwise, or conveyed via the Internet or a Web site without written permission of the University of Wisconsin Press, except in the case of brief quotations embedded in critical articles and reviews.

5   4   3   2   1

Printed in the United States of America

Library of Congress Cataloging-in-Publication Data
Boele, Otto.
   Erotic nihilism in late imperial Russia : the case of Mikhail Artsybashev's Sanin / Otto Boele.
   p.   cm.
   Includes bibliographical references and index.
   ISBN 978-0-299-23274-0 (pbk.: alk. paper)
   ISBN 978-0-299-23273-3 (e-book)
   1. Artsybashev, M. (Mikhail), 1878–1927. Sanin.   2. Nihilism in literature.
3. Decadence in literature.   I. Title.
PG3453.A8S393   2009
891.73´3—dc22
                        2009013800

Contents

	List of Illustrations	vii
	Acknowledgments	ix
	A Note on Transliteration, Translation, and Dates	xiii
	Introduction	3
1	From Onegin to Bazarov: The Canon of Epoch-making Heroes	27
2	Sanin: A Hero of Our Time?	51
3	Counterliterature: The Search for Poetic Justice	76
4	The Pornographic *Roman à Thèse*: Publication, Censorship, Ban	97
5	*Sanin* and Its Readers: A Bible for an Entire Generation?	116
6	Hard-core Saninism: The Case of the Free Love Leagues	143
7	Muscles for Money: Sanin as Ex-student	170
	Conclusion	191
	Appendix	195
	Notes	207
	Index	245

Illustrations

Mikhail Artsybashev, 1903	9
Caricature of Ignatii Potapenko	44
Handwritten front page of theater adaptation of *Sanin* entitled *How to Live?*	79
Ad for Friedrich Fehér's 1924 screen version of *Sanin*	114
Caricature of the free love leagues	164
Caricature of Mikhail Artsybashev	180
Writer Nikolai Breshko-Breshkovskii and student-wrestler A. Sh.	185

Acknowledgments

I would like to thank the institutions whose financial support has made this book possible: the Netherlands Organization for Scientific Research, the Royal Netherlands Academy of Arts and Sciences, the Centre for International Mobility in Helsinki, the University of Groningen, and the Institute for Cultural Disciplines of the University of Leiden.

Since 1999, I have published a number of articles, some of which have gone into this book. I thank the publishers for granting me permission to use this material. My discussion of Count Amori's *Sanin's Return* in chapter 3 was part of an article published as "Melodrama as Counter-literature? Count Amori's Response to Three Scandalous Novels" in the collection of essays *Imitations of Life: Two Centuries of Melodrama in Russia*, ed. Louise McReynolds and Joan Neuberger (Durham, NC: Duke University Press, 2002). Part of chapter 2 is reprinted from my introduction to *Sanin*, trans. Michael R. Katz (Ithaca, NY: Cornell University Press, 2001). Part of chapter 1 was published in slightly modified form as "'New Times Require New People': The Demise of the Epochmaking Hero in Late Nineteenth-Century Russian Literature," in *Dutch Contributions to the Fourteenth International Congress of Slavists, Ohrid, September 10–16, 2008* (Amsterdam: Rodopi, 2008).

Many people have played an important part in the writing of this book, and I want to thank them for their encouragement, advice, and practical assistance.

Words cannot express how much I owe to Michael Katz, my friend and colleague of Middlebury College, who invited me to write the introduction to his new English translation of *Sanin*. I thank him for giving me his relentless support, for providing me with various opportunities to present my research, and for helping me with the translation of some of the more awkward Russian quotes. Working on Artsybashev would have been considerably more difficult without Michael's interest and wit. I also wish to thank Nicholas Luker (University of Nottingham), the only true Artsybashev specialist on the planet, who took a keen interest in my work from its inception. I am grateful to my former colleagues at the University of Groningen, my *Doktorvater*, Joost van Baak, and my friend Sander Brouwer, for their support throughout my scholarly career.

In 1997, I had the great good fortune of spending one year as a visiting scholar in the Slavic Department of the University of California at Berkeley. I thank Irina Paperno, whose work has been a source of inspiration to me, for making that stimulating year at Berkeley possible and for commenting on early drafts of my work. I am also grateful to Eric Naiman, who expressed a genuine interest in my research and allowed me to use his office during the summer break. Additionally, I would like to thank Olga Matich for her support and to thank a number of former graduate students who made my year at Berkeley a memorable experience: Evgenii Bershtein, Ingrid Kleespies, Konstantin Klioutchkine, and Robert Wessling.

I owe a great debt to Joachim Klein, professor emeritus at the University of Leiden. He has generously supported my applications for jobs and endowments, and he introduced me to a number of inspirational scholars from Germany, Italy, and the United States. I appreciate his continuing interest in the fate of Slavic studies at Leiden.

In Russia, several people have been invaluable extending to me their professional expertise, hospitality, and friendship. I am extremely grateful to my friends and colleagues Vladimir and Marina Abashev and Elena Vlasova (Perm), Aleksandr Belousov and Elena Dushechkina (St. Petersburg), and Tatiana Tsivian and Vladimir and Masha Kliaus (Moscow). I would like to express my particular appreciation to Dmitrii Ravinskii of the National Library in St. Petersburg, who always complied with my bothersome requests to order copies or check obscure sources.

A great number of people have otherwise contributed to this book, perhaps without even being aware of it. I am grateful to Joe Andrew, Carolyn Ayers, Peter Barta, Mojmír Grygar, Ben Hellman, Pepijn Hendriks, Andrew Kaspryk, Henk Kern, Kirill Kobrin, Arthur Langeveld, Ronald LeBlanc, Louise McReynolds, Peter Ulf Møller, Susan Morrissey, Joan Neuberger, Riccardo Nicolosi, Pekka Pesonen, Galina Rylkova, Igor Smirnov, Willem Weststeijn, Ben Wiegers, and Frederick White.

Acknowledgments xi

    Jos Schaeken, head of the Slavic Department in Leiden, merits special thanks for his support and, particularly, for his patience. I am grateful to Ellen Rutten and Egbert Fortuin for reading part of the manuscript and for simply being great colleagues. For her assistance in the preparation of the final text and her perceptive comments, I should like to thank Thera Giezen. Of course, the responsibility for the final result lies entirely with me.

    Finally, I would like to thank my wife, Sandra, and my parents-in-law, Reint and Sanny Molenkamp, for enabling me to complete this book.

A Note on Transliteration, Translation, and Dates

In the main text, I have relied on the Library of Congress system of transliteration with a few exceptions. The names of Russian rulers and well-known cultural figures are expressed in the more familiar English versions (Nicholas for Nikolai, Tolstoy for Tolstoi). In the notes I adhere strictly to the Library of Congress system (Gippius for Hippius). Dates are expressed in accordance with the Julian calendar. All translations are mine unless otherwise indicated.

Erotic Nihilism in Late Imperial Russia
───────────────────────────────────────

Introduction

In February 1908 Lev Tolstoy received an agitated letter from a certain Moisei Dokshitskii, the seventeen-year-old son of a watchmaker, who claimed to have fallen into a state of utter confusion after reading Mikhail Artsybashev's novel *Sanin* (1907). Always striving for "inner perfection," as he put it, Dokshitskii became convinced that the novel's eponymous hero embodied his ideal: "[He is] the perfect man who you want to become once you have seen him." After acquainting himself with Tolstoy's writings, however, he began to doubt whether the unabashed sensualist Vladimir Sanin was worth emulating: "I simply cannot decide what is better, *saninstvo* or the Christian teaching. . . . If you can understand the state I am in, please, write to me as soon as possible."[1]

For Tolstoy, this letter was an incentive to read Artsybashev's novel himself. In his reply to Dokshitskii, written only a few days later, we learn that *Sanin* has filled him with horror "not so much because of the smut but because of the stupidity, the ignorance, and the self-assurance [of the author]." Apparently not familiar with the works of either Eastern or Western philosophers, Artsybashev seemed to revel in "inverted commonplaces," cheaply stating the opposite of what was generally accepted.[2] To help Dokshitskii overcome his moral agony, Tolstoy promised to send him a copy of his "Reading Circle," his own anthology of thoughts and statements by famous philosophers, and also suggested that Dokshitskii read the Gospel.[3]

Before Tolstoy could even mail his reply, Dokshitskii had managed to write a second and much calmer letter, in which he stated that his infatuation with *saninstvo* was over: "After reading *Sanin* and the like, it seemed to me that I had found my own essence, but gradually I became aware of certain incongruities between *saninstvo* and life."⁴ Although Dokshitskii was still interested in Tolstoy's opinion of *Sanin*, the contest between *saninstvo* and the Gospel in his own life had now clearly been decided in favor of the latter.

Was there really a teaching called *saninstvo* in early twentieth-century Russia, as Dokshitskii's letters suggest? The short answer to this question must be negative. To the best of my knowledge, there are no manifestos or theoretical writings, other than the novel itself, that seriously promoted a coherent ideology under such a heading. And yet, to many of Artsybashev's contemporaries, *saninstvo* or "Saninism" was not only something very real but also even ubiquitous.⁵ Newspapers reported on "Saninists" disturbing public lectures. Critics noted the rise of a pleasure-seeking, "Sanin-like" hero in Russian literature and the widespread imitation of his shameless behavior in everyday life. The main impetus for writing this book was a desire to explain how this notion that *saninstvo* was a popular and widespread ideology came about as well as to trace the echoes of this notion in Russia's cultural memory.

Saninism was never exposed as a false rumor or a concoction of the press, at least not in a manner convincing to everyone. Even today, some consider the story of Saninism to be if not incontestably true, then at least highly plausible. When I recently googled the term "Saninism," one of the hits directed me to a site containing an article on the reception of Russian literature in Japan that not only mentions the Japanese translation of *Sanin* (traditionally advanced as the ultimate proof of its incredible success) but also maintains that early twentieth-century Russia witnessed an entire movement called Saninism.⁶ For all the triviality of this source (an internet site on Russian-Japanese cultural relations), it provides a graphic illustration of how easily and uncritically the notion of an ideology inspired by the character Vladimir Sanin has been perpetuated.

As this study attempts to show, Saninism is not a historical phenomenon such as communism or populism, the main ideas and figureheads of which everyone can name. But it is not a mere chimera either. Saninism, I argue, is a myth that, to many people, "explained" something about life in Russia during the last decade of the tsarist regime and that continues to color our perception of the period in question. Precisely because of this lasting ability to function as a signifier of a perceived moral decline during the twilight of the Russian empire, closer analysis of the myth's assumptions and implications can yield vital insights into early twentieth-century Russian culture. In what circles, for example,

Introduction   5

did Saninism reportedly occur? What was the social and political background of its alleged followers? What genres did writers use to vent their concern? By asking these questions, I hope to show that the myth of Saninism is more than a number of sensationalist reports in the boulevard press and more than simply a catchall term used to designate whatever was felt to be wrong with the nation. The myth of Saninism, I contend, is a system of interlocking discourses on adolescence, sexuality, Russia's system of secondary education, and the legacy of the radical intelligentsia of the 1860s. To many of Artsybashev's contemporaries, Saninism served as an interpretative framework that allowed them to make sense of both the "failed" revolution of 1905, which had nearly toppled the monarchy, and the equally confusing events that immediately followed it. This is not to say, of course, that these issues were necessarily addressed with explicit reference to *Sanin*. Many of them predated the publication of the novel. Yet it *is* the case that, after its publication, *Sanin* was widely acknowledged to be the most outspoken expression of the "spirit of the time," an emblem of the intelligentsia's often bemoaned "egotistic" mentality after the rebellion of 1905. As the influential critic Vladimir Kranikhfel'd put it in 1909, "You may not like Sanin, but you cannot ignore him. He is an undeniable fact of Russian life."[7]

The Ugly Face of the Silver Age

The myth of Saninism inevitably intersects with an even more powerful one in the history of Russian culture. This is the myth of what is now commonly referred to as the Silver Age, a period of aesthetic and spiritual blossoming that is usually situated between the rise of symbolism in the early 1890s and the Bolshevik takeover in October 1917. Although this period is now considered one of the finest in the history of Russian literature and art, its reputation was downright unfavorable in the 1920s and early 1930s, when it was associated with sexual depravity, overt hedonism, and pornographic literature.[8]

Predictably, it is this view that Soviet historiography and literary criticism preferred to uphold, since it allowed for the implication that the October Revolution of 1917 had been both purgative and inevitable. Speaking at the first convention of Soviet writers in 1932, Maxim Gorky set the tone when he characterized the last decade of the old regime as "the most shameful and impudent decade in the history of the Russian intelligentsia."[9] After the revolution of 1905, the intelligentsia had betrayed its traditional ideals of self-abnegation and political activism, Gorky believed, and instead had dedicated itself to the petty pursuit of personal happiness. Literature could not but reflect this mood, and so it was not surprising that novels suffused with themes of sex and suicide enjoyed such enormous success: "Shrewd Vasilii Rozanov propagated eroticism, Leonid Andreev wrote nightmarish stories and plays, Artsybashev chose a lascivious vertical male-goat wearing pants as his hero [i.e., Vladimir Sanin]."[10] For years, this narrative of moral and cultural degeneration, followed by revolutionary salvation, would be the standard Soviet story of the decade 1907-17. Even Elem Klimov's sophisticated, if controversial, film *Agony* (*Agoniia* [1974]) on the murder of the debauched mystic Grigorii Rasputin in December 1916 does not refrain from reproducing this scheme. In the epilogue, a voice-over briefly outlines the historic events that followed the murder of Rasputin, but it deliberately avoids mentioning the February Revolution. Thus, the impression is created that it was the October Revolution, not its "bourgeois precursor," that put an end to the monarchy and liberated the Russian people.[11]

Russian emigrants were less inclined to view the establishment of Bolshevik power in such positive terms, of course, but for a long time they too regarded Russia's fin de siècle as a time of cultural decline and moral corruption. In 1926 Vladislav Khodasevich, an emigrant poet who had collaborated with several figureheads of Russian modernism, described the intellectual climate before the revolution as follows: "We were living in those years that followed the year 1905: these were the years of spiritual fatigue and of pervading aestheticism. In literature [this period was marked] by numerous low-quality imitators of the modernist school, which suddenly became recognized precisely for those aspects [of it] that were bad and insignificant. In society, frail barefoot girls were resurrecting Hellenism. The bourgeoisie, who suddenly discovered an appetite for a 'daring life,' ran up against 'sexual questions.' The *sanintsy* and *ogarki* were multiplying at the lower level. Decadent buildings were built on the streets. And, without being noticed, electric charges were slowly accumulating above it all."[12]

Despite the snobbish overtones in Khodasevich's words, his characterization of the interrevolutionary years does not differ fundamentally from Gorky's. Not only do both men agree on the loathsomeness of much that was published in these years, but, writing from the vantage point of history, they also invest their account with a conspicuous sense of doom suggesting that a dramatic apotheosis was imminent. Regardless of their ideological, political and aesthetic differences, then, Gorky and Khodasevich arrived at rather similar conclusions regarding the moral standards of prerevolutionary Russian culture and the inevitability of its ruin.

This disparaging view of prerevolutionary modernism continued to dominate Soviet scholarship well into the 1970s, but a more positive attitude began to take shape among emigrants in the late 1930s.[13] Turn-of-the-century culture came to represent the pinnacle of modern Russian poetry and religious thought, an inexhaustible source of cultural richness created by the nation's finest minds. As a consequence, the October Revolution came to be remembered as a national disaster that had brutally interrupted the "natural" course of Russian cultural evolution.[14] Even if this process of reappraisal would never completely eradicate the initial vision of Russia's fin de siècle as that of a period of decadence and all-pervasive aestheticism, the image that finally emerged and came to be cherished by members of the emigrant community, and by dissidents in the 1960s, was that of a vital and thriving culture tragically cut short.

The myth of Saninism fit in well with the Soviet narrative of revolutionary salvation. While it would have been inconceivable to devote an individual monograph to either *Sanin* or other "pornographic" literature, historical studies, biographical dictionaries and even memoirs could mention it in passing so as to conjure up a befitting image of the most "shameful and impudent decade in the history of the Russian intelligentsia." It is equally understandable that the myth of Saninism proved incompatible with the lofty image of the Silver Age as a time of cultural revival. This explains why the *sanintsy* figuring in Khodasevich's 1926 article were seemingly erased from cultural memory once the positive reputation of the Silver Age was firmly established.[15] An exile himself and an ardent opponent of the Bolsheviks, Artsybashev is rarely mentioned in emigrant sources after the 1930s; between his death in 1927 and the very end of the Soviet Union, his work was never published again, either in Russia or abroad.[16]

I am not suggesting that *Sanin* and the scandal it created were entirely forgotten in emigrant circles. In his well-known *Contemporary Russian Literature* (1926), D. S. Mirsky devoted a few lines to Artsybashev that have been reproduced in more recent histories of Russian literature (and to which I return in chapter 5). But all in all, it may be fair to say that the myth of the Silver Age, as it was created in memoirs, essays and (auto-)biographies, was purged of names and works that contradicted the perceived essence of that period. One of the goals of this book is to trace the blind spots of this myth by studying the reception of *Sanin* and to restore, as it were, the ugly face of the Silver Age.

Modernism and Neorealism

It could be objected that the connection between Artsybashev and the Silver Age is rather tenuous and that any attempt to make it look more significant must fail. After all, Artsybashev was, and considered himself to be, an exponent of the realist school, precisely the style with which modernism sought to break.[17] In a 1913 interview, he made his views on literature clear: "Common sense, consistency, argumentation, a clear and concrete idea of one's subject that constitutes the plot of the work, a thoughtful evaluation of the phenomena introduced in the novel, clarity and concreteness—these are the things I demand of a literary work."[18] In addition, one could argue that the quality of his work simply proved too poor to stand the test of time and that it was forgotten because it is inferior, not because of some deeply felt need among emigrants or dissidents to create a mythic past that was carefully cleansed of suspicious names.

Echoing Iurii Tynianov's ideas on literary evolution, scholars have often treated Artsybashev's work as a "vulgarization" of a more respectable movement—realism or modernism—already in decline.[19] We find this notion in studies discussing Artsybashev's alleged indebtedness to the work of Ivan Turgenev (see chapter 2) and the ideas of Friedrich Nietzsche. Edith Clowes, for instance, discusses *Sanin* as an example of Nietzsche's "distorted popularization," ranking its author next to other "lowbrow writers" such as Anastasiia Verbitskaia and Anatolii Kamenskii.[20] Using a vaguely defined, but essentially similar, tripartite classification of prerevolutionary fiction, Jeffrey Brooks places *Sanin* not in the lowest but in the middle segment, viewing it as a "male equivalent to the women's fiction [of Verbitskaia]."[21] These and other scholars seem to agree that *Sanin* and Verbitskaia's bestseller *Keys to Happiness* (*Kliuchi schast'ia* [1909–13]) catered to the needs of a semi-intellectual audience, allowing them to appropriate themes and images introduced in the highbrow writings of modernist authors.[22]

This study is not intended to redefine the canon of early twentieth-century Russian literature by claiming *Sanin* as a forgotten masterpiece.

Mikhail Artsybashev, 1903.

On the whole, I agree that Artsybashev was not a particularly original writer. I do think, however, that the relationship between Artsybashev and modernism is more complicated than the traditional distinction between realist and modernist writing, and between high and low literature, suggests. While it is true that many modernist authors thoroughly disliked Artsybashev's work, it is equally true that aesthetic and ideological differences did not prevent them from collaborating with him.[23] Under the editorship of Artsybashev and on his personal initiative, the liberal monthly *Sovremennyi mir* (*Contemporary World*) published several of Aleksandr Blok's poems. Blok, for his part, was one of the very few reviewers who admitted to being impressed with *Sanin*, which he called "Artsybashev's most significant work so far."[24] Symbolist Fiodor Sologub was a regular contributor to the almanac *Zhizn'* (*Life*), which Artsybashev had set up as a counterpoint to Gorky's almanac *Znanie* (*Knowledge*). After the October Revolution, other symbolists, such as Zinaida Hippius and Dmitrii Merezhkovskii, who shared his hatred of the Bolshevik regime, forged political alliances with Artsybashev. Without ignoring the skepticism with which the symbolists treated the realist camp and Artsybashev personally, I propose a more lenient approach to the distinction between realism and symbolism on which literary historiography has traditionally insisted. Artsybashev was not that much of an alien in the eyes of the symbolists that they would refuse to work with him. I would not venture to say the same about Verbitskaia.

Even more important for the purpose of this study: the boundaries that we may be tempted to draw between serious literature and popular fiction, between the experimental and subtle prose of Andrei Bely or Mikhail Kuzmin and the more conservative aesthetics of Artsybashev or Anatolii Kamenskii, were not all that obvious to the popular press and its readership that together played a crucial role in spreading the idea of a massive Saninist movement. Authors as divergent as Artsybashev, Sologub, Kamenskii, Bal'mont, and Kuzmin were often grouped together on the assumption that they all wrote pornography and openly professed sexual license. It is ironic that Artsybashev considered Mikhail Kuzmin's homoerotic novel *Wings* (*Kryl'ia* [1907]) a distortion of his own ideas and that Kuzmin felt equally uncomfortable being associated with Artsybashev.[25] Whatever his actual place in the extremely varied landscape of early twentieth-century Russian literature, Artsybashev was widely perceived as a key figure of "modern" literature with all the ambivalent associations that such an identification entailed.

Finally, it is my contention that when Artsybashev's novel was published in 1907, it lived up to the idea of what many authoritative critics then considered "serious" literature. In terms of style, plot development, and narration, *Sanin* is an extremely traditional novel that never tries to conceal its indebtedness to nineteenth-century realism. From the vantage point of literary history, the novel's conservative aesthetics may be sufficient reason to discard it as a one-time hit of an epigone of the great realist writers; to Artsybashev's contemporaries, however, this traditional orientation may have prompted them to take the novel seriously in the first place and to read it in a "traditional" manner as an important chronicle of contemporary life. Whatever we may think of Artsybashev's lack of innovation, it appears to have been an essential precondition for the emergence of the myth of Saninism.

Sanin: The Scandal

Most students of Russian literature know, even without having read the novel, that *Sanin* caused a huge scandal owing to its "pornographic" or, at least, licentious content and that it was officially banned because of it. By Russian standards, its bawdiness makes it an exceptional book, if we are to believe writer Viktor Erofeev. Overlooking the barren landscape of erotic literature in Russia, Erofeev could not produce any examples of such texts with the exception of a "few stories by Aleksei Tolstoy" and "of course . . . *Sanin*."[26]

When viewed in the international context of fin-de-siècle culture, however, *Sanin* looks anything but unique. At the turn of the century, under the influence of such thinkers as Max Stirner and especially Friedrich Nietzsche, European authors started to challenge the repressive sexual morality of their age, professing a life-affirming and individualistic philosophy of life that legitimized the pursuit of sensual pleasure. Like Artsybashev, some of these authors had difficulties getting their work published or performed. In Germany, Frank Wedekind's notorious play *Spring Awakening* (*Frühlingserwachen*), which openly deals with teenage pregnancy and homosexuality, finally premiered in 1906, fifteen years after it was completed, but with significant cuts.[27] In 1960 the belated publication of D. H. Lawrence's linguistically far more explicit novel *Lady Chatterley's Lover* (first privately printed in Italy in 1928) caused public outrage in England, which resulted in an obscenity trial against its publisher, Penguin Books.[28] *Sanin*, then, we might be tempted to conclude, is simply the Russian version of a literary scandal that other European countries also witnessed.

To a considerable extent, this conclusion is valid. Although Artsybashev stubbornly maintained not to have read Nietzsche, in *Sanin* and some of his other stories, the German philosopher looms large. If anything, the felt presence of Nietzsche illustrates the extent to which his ideas must have been "in the air" in Russia (as is now commonly accepted) and, consequently, how unoriginal *Sanin* really is.[29] Yet, just as *Spring Awakening* and *Lady Chatterley's Lover* have unique reception histories that were determined by the literary traditions and moral sensitivities of German and British readers respectively, so too the *Sanin* scandal cannot be reduced to a "general European" clash between the competing value systems of the nineteenth century and modernity. The question remains how this general clash manifested itself in Russia and what uniquely political, religious, and social connotations it acquired in the perception of various groups of Russian readers. Far from advocating an approach that posits the uniqueness of Russian history as opposed to a supposedly unified path of development in "the" West, I nonetheless explore the scandal of *Sanin* with an eye toward its cultural and national specificity. Thus, I hope to show that the erotic descriptions in the novel (which are tame by any standard) cannot fully account for the indignation it caused, even if it was eventually banned by the 1001st statute, popularly known as the "statute on pornography."

But what about the Russian context? Is Artsybashev's novel really that exceptional, as Erofeev seems to think? Despite Erofeev's apparent inability to name any erotic texts in Russian literature besides a "few stories by Aleksei Tolstoy" and *Sanin*, the fact that the latter was widely regarded as a "sign of the times" would suggest that there were other texts professing similar ideas, albeit in a less outspoken manner. In their introduction to the abridged translation of Verbitskaia's novel *Keys to Happiness*, Beth Holmgren and Helena Goscilo speak of a "canonically neglected fund of racy *fin-de-siècle* texts," which includes, among others, Kuzmin's aforementioned *Wings*, Lidiia Zinov'eva-Annibal's "Thirty-Three Abominations" ("Tridstat'-tri uroda" [1907]), Evdokiia Nagrodskaia's *Wrath of Dionysus* (*Gnev Dionisa* [1910]), Verbitskaia's *Keys to Happiness*, and, of course, *Sanin*. What these texts have in common, according to Holmgren and Goscilo, is that they "blend philosophy and pseudo-science with melodrama, to promote individual freedom through sexual nonconformism or transgression."[30] Inasmuch as this list could easily be extended, we might want to ask whether *Sanin*

Introduction

is really that unique, even when viewed within the narrower context of turn-of-the-century Russian literature.

Here again, I should stress that I am not in any way attempting to "save" *Sanin*, for example, by claiming that Artsybashev was the first to promote sexual nonconformism or by arguing that, as a writer, he should still be ranked above Verbitskaia, the creator of "Sanin in a skirt."[31] I fully acknowledge that, apart from reflecting a more general preoccupation with sexuality that manifested itself in late-tsarist Russia, the novel is indeed one of many fictional texts written around that time in which traditional sexual morality is challenged.[32] The reason to restrict myself to *Sanin* is that I do believe its reception history to be quite exceptional. By studying its reception, we can learn not only about Russia's appropriation of alternative models of sexuality or about the emancipation of the middle-class reader but also about the way in which the paradigm of nineteenth-century realism continued to inform the tastes of readers and critics alike. I contend that it was not so much the novel's promise of unbridled sex as the paradox of an "egotistical" and "rapacious" ideology being expressed in a work that was stylistically of a piece with the tradition of the nineteenth-century novel that unsettled Artsybashev's contemporaries. Because critics on the left invariably associated realism with democratic sympathies and the struggle for social improvement (opposing it to the supposedly escapist literature of modernist writers), a traditional but "antihumanistic" novel such as *Sanin* was likely to leave a bewildering impression. Like Nikolai Chernyshevsky and Tolstoy, Artsybashev employed an omniscient narrator who regularly interrupts the story with pedantic digressions on man's moral hypocrisy and self-deceit. Yet, *Sanin*'s often quoted maxim that man should strive to "satisfy his natural needs, even if they are evil" was obviously at odds with Chernyshevsky's concept of egotistical rationalism, not to mention with Tolstoy's insistence on the need for total abstinence.[33]

In terms of the public outcry it generated, *Sanin* may well be compared to other notorious texts in Russian literature, such as the first letter of Piotr Chaadaev's *Lettres philosophiques* (*Filosofischeskie pis'ma*), first published in 1836; *Selected Passages from Correspondence with Friends* (*Vybrannye mesta iz perepiski s druziami* [1847]), Nikolai Gogol's reactionary collection of reflections and exhortations; and *What Is to Be Done?* (*Chto delat'?* [1863]), Nikolai Chernyshevsky's utopian novel. Even if the cultural and historical significance of these works is much greater than that of *Sanin*, the vehemence of the debate that Artsybashev's novel provoked suggests that it had contemporary significance. Interestingly, the case of *Sanin* resembles in some respects the three earlier scandals. Like Gogol, who was widely considered the champion of socially critical literature until he spoke out in favor of serfdom and autocracy, Artsybashev lost his reputation as a progressive writer the moment he published *Sanin*. Henceforth, leftist critics and Soviet scholars would consider him a "reactionary" and "decadent" writer who unresistingly recorded the debauched spirit of late-tsarist Russia. Artsybashev's falling into disfavor with the left did not redeem him in the eyes of the authorities, however. To them, his novel was a politically suspect work that was likely to conduce to the corruption of youth and the spread of revolutionary ideas. In this respect, the brouhaha over *Sanin* recalls the publication history of *What Is to Be Done?* Indeed, the censor explicitly compared the reception of the two books.[34] Artsybashev was spared the lamentable fate of Chaadaev, who was placed in an asylum for allegedly besmirching his fatherland in his "philosophical letters," but he was nearly turned into an outcast as well when, in 1910, Bishop Germogen threatened to anathematize him.[35] Perhaps *Sanin* may even be regarded as the ultimate scandal in the history of prerevolutionary literature for contriving to evoke simultaneously the wrath of the authorities, the church, and the intelligentsia.

Mikhail Artsybashev

This study is not primarily concerned with either the life and career of Mikhail Artsybashev or with his complete oeuvre. It discusses a relatively small part of his literary output and completely ignores the postrevolutionary years, which he spent for the most part as an emigrant in Poland. Finally, I do not attempt to present a coherent picture of Artsybashev's ideas or of his development as a writer and thinker, nor do I present new interpretations of the novel itself (although I do make a gesture in the direction of an alternative reading of it in chapter 7). However, a brief outline of the main landmarks in Artsybashev's life and work will certainly help to place this writer in his proper literary-historical context.

Prior to the publication of *Sanin*, Mikhail Artsybashev enjoyed a modest but relatively sound reputation as a talented writer with appropriately liberal ideas. Born in 1878 into a family of minor landowners in the Ukraine, Artsybashev seems to have wavered for some time between literature and the visual arts as possible future careers. At sixteen, without having completed his formal education, he started working as a clerk for an insurance agent and in 1897 he enrolled at the Kharkov School of Arts, where he made a favorable impression on his teachers. His plans to enter the Academy of Fine Arts in St. Petersburg never materialized, however. After his move to the capital in 1900, he soon gained recognition as a writer and gave up professional painting.[36]

Artsybashev's first major stories appeared in periodicals like *Mir bozhii* (*God's World*), *Russkoe bogatstvo* (*Russian Wealth*), and *Zhurnal dlia vsekh* (*Journal for All*), prestigious monthly journals with an outspoken preference for solid realist fiction. They presented an obvious platform for an author like Artsybashev, who showed little affinity for modernist experiments. Just like Gorky, Leonid Andreev, and Aleksandr Kuprin, other regular contributors to the aforementioned journals, Artsybashev was hailed as a promising author following in the footsteps of the socially engaged writers of the nineteenth century.[37]

Artsybashev's first "mature" product (according to the author himself) was the short story "Pasha Tumanov." It was accepted for publication in *Russkoe bogatstvo* by no one less than Nikolai Mikhailovskii, one of the most influential and radical critics of his time. The story revolves around a boy who fails a crucial exam, is expelled from the gymnasium, and eventually shoots the headmaster for refusing to readmit him. Although the expulsion is formally justified, the narrator does not place the blame for the tragedy with the victim or with the good-natured headmaster who tries to comfort the boy but with the impersonal school system, which is held responsible for ignoring pupils' real needs and thus taken to account for Pasha's violent protest. One of numerous turn-of-the-century stories to attack the classical gymnasium, "Pasha Tumanov" seemed to meet all the criteria by which critics like Mikhailovskii judged a literary work. The censor's decision to ban the story only added to Artsybashev's profile as an author radically opposed to the existing order.[38]

One would have expected Artsybashev's worldview to have thoroughly changed during the years between "Pasha Tumanov," with its explicit social criticism, and *Sanin*, after the publication of which Artsybashev garnered the reputation of a reactionary writer. On closer inspection, however, his oeuvre shows remarkably little development in style and philosophical outlook. Although his work would eventually become gloomier, the themes of suicide, marriage versus "free love," and life's economic struggle, with which he was familiar from personal experience, would continue to occupy him throughout his career.[39] Speaking in more general terms, most of Artsybashev's work deals with the "timeless" notion of man's vanity and his proclivity for self-deceit. The lines from Ecclesiastes that serve as the epigraph to *Sanin* may well serve as a motto for his entire oeuvre: "This alone have I found: that God, when he made man, made him straightforward, but men invent endless subtleties of their own."[40] Time and again, Artsybashev drives home the message that there is a fundamental discrepancy between the way in which people behave as socially conditioned beings and how they *would* behave if they followed their own instincts. This discrepancy can manifest itself in education ("Pasha Tumanov"), man's living conditions (urban as opposed to rural), and erotic love. But the very suggestion of some disturbing incongruity between inner essence and outer appearance is always sustained. Borrowing Peter Ulf Møller's characterization of Tolstoy's method, we can say that, in Artsybashev's work, reality is usually presented "in a form of the comparative, that is, it is presented as *more real* or *truer* than something else that is also given in the text."[41]

The autobiographical story "The Wife" ("Zhena" [1906]), Artsybashev's first published work to explore the theme of free love, reads as a textbook example of this comparative method. The "I" falls passionately in love with a woman but immediately loses interest as soon as he marries her. Once he is forced to play the official role of loving husband, he feels estranged from his wife who, in contrast, entirely lives up to her obligations as a married woman and becomes ever more jealous. At the end of the story, when they have already broken up, she comes to appreciate her husband's unorthodox ideas about complete sexual freedom. In a rather implausible scene, he convinces her that their separation is for the best and that lovers should never commit themselves to one another for life. When she timidly remarks that their son will now grow up without his father, he removes the last traces of her doubt by casually replying that it is more natural for children to be brought up by their mothers.

In "The Wife," as in *Sanin*, marriage is rejected precisely because it is an institutionalized form of erotic love. It restricts man in his natural pursuit of sexual satisfaction. Characteristically, the hero gains this understanding only after a long period of delusion and a number of painful confrontations with society. When he finally discovers the "truth" about marriage (about sexual relationships, about life in general), it turns out to be something surprisingly simple and accessible to all. The only precondition for internalizing this truth is a willingness to give in to one's "natural" inclinations and ignore the social conventions, which cripple man's life.

Artsybashev's disgust with rules and conventions and his eagerness to expose their "absurdity" found their ultimate expression in *Sanin*. In addition to ridiculing such petty bourgeois values as strict monogamy (or monandry) and social respectability, the novel also attacks the antibourgeois, yet equally dogmatic and "petrified," morality of the radical intelligentsia that insisted on political commitment and complete self-abnegation. Artsybashev was not the only author to criticize the revolutionary movement on these grounds, of course, but the unfortunate timing of the novel's publication, which coincided with Prime Minister Stolypin's coup d'état, and the narrator's undivided sympathy for the main character, who treats the behavioral imperative of the revolutionaries as yet another "invention," contributed to the novel's being perceived as a direct assault on the most sacred ideals of the intelligentsia.[42]

Sanin: A Synopsis

Although there have been several new editions of *Sanin* since the early 1990s, when the Russian book market opened up and became inundated with forgotten masterpieces, its place in Russian literary history has remained fairly marginal. Whatever modern readers expected to find in *Sanin*, perhaps tempted by its reputation as a pornographic work, its rediscovery has not led scholars or critics to reassess Artsybashev's standing; he is still viewed as no more than a second-rate writer. Because of its lasting obscurity, I provide a short synopsis of the novel, highlighting only those characters and episodes that provoked the strongest reactions from the critics. A true novel of ideas, *Sanin* offers a plethora of secondary characters and subplots, which we can safely ignore for the purpose of the present discussion.

Sanin tells the story of the former student Vladimir Petrovich Sanin, an unruffled and muscular young man who, after an extended period of absence, returns to his native town somewhere in the provinces. A former political activist who has become "bored" with the revolutionary movement, Sanin spends three months with his mother and his younger sister, Lida. His carefree behavior and hedonistic philosophy of life clearly set him apart from the local intelligentsia, whose ostentatious devotion to the revolutionary cause he observes with a mixture of bewilderment and amusement.

During his stay in the nameless provincial town, Sanin only reluctantly interferes with other people's business, and yet he plays a crucial role in their lives. He drives his sister's intended fiancé, the conceited officer Zarudin, to suicide by knocking him to the ground in public. He also unwittingly drives Soloveichik, a far from steadfast Tolstoyan who cannot accept the meaninglessness of life, to suicide. Yet, if Sanin is technically responsible for these two deaths, the reader is left with no doubt that he functions only as a catalyst, accelerating a process that had already begun in both men. If Soloveichik is mentally unfit for life, then Zarudin becomes the victim of his own foolish pride, as he cannot imagine going on with his life after the humiliating scuffle with Sanin (who was merely acting out of self-defense). Even when Sanin forces the attractive school teacher Zinaida Karsavina to have sex with him in a rowboat (perhaps the novel's most notorious scene), the implied author manipulates us into believing that what we are witnessing is not rape but a young woman's initiation into a happier and more natural way of life.

The novel also features a suicide attempt by Sanin's pregnant sister, who tries to drown herself (but is saved by her brother), and a successful suicide by the student Iurii Svarozhich, an intelligent yet self-preoccupied young man whose vicissitudes mirror Sanin's in the negative. Expelled from Moscow University on the suspicion of revolutionary activities, Iurii moves in with his father and sister Lialia, who introduces him to her friend Karsavina. A romance develops but, when he is about to make love to Karsavina for the first time, Iurii suddenly recoils from her, convincing himself that he is above such bestial desires. Sanin then takes advantage of the situation and deflowers her on the same evening.

After some three months of relaxing, drinking, and discussing, Sanin decides it is time to move on. Tired of his meddlesome family and narrow-minded revolutionaries, he leaves without saying goodbye and boards a train for an unknown destination. The last chapter describes how Sanin, sitting in a third-class railway carriage, takes umbrage at the coarseness of his fellow travelers, leaves the compartment, and finally jumps off of the train. He stands up unharmed and gives a cry of pleasure marveling at the vastness of the steppe around him. The last paragraph is worth quoting in full: "Sanin breathed easily and gazed cheerfully at the endless expanse of earth, advancing with powerful, broad steps farther and farther toward the bright, joyous light of dawn. And when the steppe awoke, its distant fields blazing blue and green, when it spread itself beneath the immense vault of the sky, and when the sun rose sparkling and shining ahead of him, it seemed as if Sanin were striding forth to meet it."[43]

I return to certain episodes in more detail in the course of this study but, for the moment, I draw the reader's attention to the conspicuous idealization of the hero, of which the final paragraph is a telling example. Not only is Sanin given ample opportunity to expound his ideas in eloquent fashion and to demonstrate their supposed soundness throughout the novel, but, in contrast to most other characters, who are forced to reconsider and give up their strongest convictions, he also does not change at all. In other words, Sanin is "right," whatever ideological or physical opposition he meets. It was this suggestion that outraged Artsybashev's readers, even if they differed fundamentally on the question of Sanin's larger historical and political significance.

The Problem and the Method

Inasmuch as the subject of this book is indissolubly connected with the fate and reception of a single novel, it would seem only logical to use an approach that draws at least some of its inspiration from the theoretical insights of reader response criticism, which emerged in the United States and Germany (the so-called Konstanz school) in the 1960s and early 1970s. Through the course of this book, we will come across numerous reactions of and references to professional critics and ordinary readers alike who were offended by Artsybashev, mocked his hero, or simply bemoaned the state of affairs in Russia, which they believed to be epitomized by the publication of a licentious work like *Sanin*. Surely, a theory that posits the importance of the "addressee's active contribution" for the "historical life of a literary work" would have much to offer.[44] But how exactly could this study benefit from reader-response criticism or the "aesthetics of reception" (*Rezeptionsästhetik*), as it is usually called in continental Europe?

First of all, the reception of *Sanin* constitutes somewhat of a special case in that it can hardly be studied from a diachronic perspective. The novel was banned less than a year after its serialization in the journal *Sovremennyi mir* and would not be reprinted in Russia until 1990.[45]

Inasmuch as the novel virtually did not exist for the Russian reader for over seventy years (except for a handful of scholars), the idea of its "historical life" becomes problematic. Yet, it is precisely this assumption of a work being read by a number of consecutive generations (i.e., diachronically) that lies at the heart of reader-response criticism. Concentrating on the canon of Western literature, it disregards works that last only for one generation or works whose historical lives are abruptly ended by the censor's interference.

A more important drawback of reader-response criticism concerns its practical applicability. The more experimental approaches do seek to collect empirical data among contemporary readers, but reader-response theorists such as Wolfgang Iser and Hans-Robert Jauss are primarily interested in reconstructing the assumed reception of a text by the implied reader. Their goal is not to develop a method for the documentation and analysis of historical readers' reactions but to theorize how *the* reader must have interpreted text X *back then.* Jauss's famous concept of "horizon of expectation" (*Erwartungshorizont*) may be useful for establishing in what way a canonical text proved to be innovative (for example, Pushkin's "Station Master" against the tradition of the sentimental novella), but it shows that his primary concern lies with the evolution of literature rather than with the actual role of the addressee.[46] Since *Sanin* is anything but innovative, applying a method designed to evince artistically more progressive tendencies does not seem to be very productive.

This study does focus on the immediate reactions of professional critics and anonymous readers (as far as recorded). The aim is not so much to take stock of these reactions and determine their underlying political agendas as to contest two widely held notions: first, that *Sanin* primarily appealed to readers insufficiently equipped to digest the "real thing"; and second, that the response of these readers was both massive and uncritical. Trying to explain what she believes to be the source of the "popularity" of *Sanin,* Neia Zorkaia, for example, refers to the novel's "formulaic monotony" and its use of clichés, especially in the "deindividualized" portrayal of the female characters—devices that betray its proximity to the literary style of the boulevard.[47] Zorkaia's condescending observations conjure up the hackneyed image of nonprofessional readers as passive consumers who happily content themselves with the vulgarized leftovers of highbrow modernism. Such a notion of reading as mass consumption is misleading, as Michel de Certeau has persuasively argued, for it denies the highly diverse and individual ways in which a reader appropriates a literary text.[48] For obvious reasons, it is impossible to describe the reactions of all anonymous readers who lived over a hundred years ago (if it were possible, it would bring us close to reaching de Certeau's ideal of a "science of singularity"), but from what is available, we can infer that, even if readers agreed that the general drift of *Sanin* was reprehensible and pernicious, they could still disagree on the novel's deeper significance adducing "telling" details and "characteristic" episodes to buttress their own interpretations. In short, this study will argue that the reception of *Sanin* was far less passive and homogeneous than has been assumed thus far.

As important as literary reviews of and immediate reactions to *Sanin* are, I intend to go beyond reception history proper by describing how the main character came to be perceived as a collective portrait of a generation, a "hero of our time" who gradually began to function independently from the novel. Thus, it became possible to use the term "Saninism" or refer to its assumed practitioners without explicitly mentioning its source of inspiration. Broadening the scope of my study in this way implies that I pay specific attention to the interaction between *Sanin* and perceived forms of behavior or, to put it in more general terms, between literature and daily life. Here I am not so much referring to the politically subversive function that has often been attributed to Russian literature but rather to its potential to provide readers with an interpretative matrix for framing occurrences and events in reality. Realist texts, especially if they purport to "chronicle" contemporary life, can provide a label for a certain type of behavior that exists, as Iurii Lotman has argued, "spontaneously and subconsciously in the masses of a given culture." They "designate" behavior whereas romantic texts seem to offer a behavioral *program* to be adopted by the reader.[49]

Lotman's distinction between romantic and realist texts in relation to the semiotics of behavior is an important one that can help us to analyze Saninism not as an ideology that sought to inspire a certain type of comportment but as a construct that allowed Artsybashev's contemporaries to "make sense" of certain forms of behavior (including their own), such as alcohol abuse, juvenile sex, and a perceived lack of interest in political matters. It is one of this book's central theses that the stir caused by *Sanin* was a corollary of the semiotic mechanism of "designation," as described by Lotman, rather than of its supposed functioning as a manual for living, as has often been claimed.

The decade 1907–17 was one of the most dynamic but also one of the most confusing periods in Russia's prerevolutionary history. The empire boasted a multiparty system as well as a national parliament (which would remain virtually powerless until the February Revolution of 1917) and was going through an unprecedented economic boom that further stimulated the formation of a middle class and a modern consumer-oriented market. This development eroded existing social hierarchies and considerably undermined the prestige of institutions traditionally endowed with moral authority, such as the church and the intelligentsia. Yet, the feeling of cultural and moral disorientation that many people experienced during these years stemmed not only from profound changes in society and political life but also from the virtually unrestrained way in which these events were covered in the press. As a result of their proliferation, newspapers were often involved in a fierce competition and vied for the reader's attention by printing sensational reports of suicide and juvenile debauchery. The seemingly endless flood of editorials, columns, and other articles on secret sex clubs, allegedly inspired by Artsybashev's writing, illustrates this point very well. Whereas before the revolution of 1905, the controversy over *Sanin* would have been confined to a relatively small circle of writers, critics, and pedagogues, after the censorship reforms of that year it was likely to be exploited by journalists outside of the literary establishment who were targeting a semi-educated audience.

The often juicy articles about the allegedly corrupting influence of *Sanin* that I analyze will no doubt create the impression that these reports were only based on "rumors" that were unscrupulously exploited or perhaps even fabricated by the press for reasons just outlined above. Yet, it is here that we must watch our step. To treat these stories as mere inventions of the gutter press would be to underestimate the veracity that these rumors apparently possessed at the time. Rumors, as the French sociologist Jean-Noël Kapferer has pointed out, can only be disseminated if they are of some interest to a group of people prepared to accept them as "news," that is as *potentially* true. Even if a rumor later turns out to be false and "obviously absurd," this obviousness arises only in *retrospect* after the rumor has been ultimately refuted. Moreover, as long as a rumor circulates in a given community, its members feel tempted to reduce various disconnected phenomena to a common denominator and assimilate them into a scheme "assigned" by the rumor.[50] This process of "sensitization," to use Stanley Cohen's term, explains why some rumors die hard.[51] Once an overarching narrative is supplied, it takes little effort to discover additional clues and arguments that can make the initial rumor look even more plausible.

The main conclusion to be drawn from this is that although the most sensational reports on Saninism probably have to be discarded as false, Artsybashev's contemporaries clearly believed in the effect of a novel that openly challenged traditional sexual morality in the aftermath of the revolution of 1905. To them, Saninism was not a hoax, even if they sometimes mistrusted its coverage in the press. All in all, this study is less about establishing the historical "facts" than recreating the whole spectrum of anxieties and expectations that Artsybashev's hero aroused among professional critics, ordinary readers, and even those who had not read the novel at all.

Survey of Chapters

One of the things that fascinated me from the outset of my research was the decisiveness with which Artsybashev's readers regarded Vladimir Sanin as a collective portrait of an entire generation or, to use a nineteenth-century expression then still very popular, as a "hero of our time." Paradoxically enough, however, while the expression is deeply ironic, connoting social superfluity and spiritual estrangement, the obvious idealization of Sanin's comportment and bodily features reminded Artsybashev's audience of a more optimistic figure introduced in the 1860s: the new man. Indeed, at times, Vladimir Sanin looks like a bizarre montage of characters randomly sampled from the works of the romantic poet Mikhail Lermontov, the radical critic and novelist Nikolai Chernyshevsky and, above all, one of the champions of Russian realism, Ivan Turgenev.

It is not my intention to dissect Vladimir Sanin as a literary character by identifying his possible prefigurations in Russian literature. Still, the numerous attempts undertaken by Artsybashev's critics to draw up Sanin's genealogy with the aim of establishing his "real" nature are certainly worth investigating. In order to appreciate these interpretations, however, we need to take a closer look at the historical context in which *Sanin* was received. Spanning a period of more than sixty years, chapter 1 focuses on the nineteenth-century tradition of conceiving of literary characters as representatives of a specific generation. I briefly rehearse the main concepts of "real criticism," which was largely responsible for the emergence of this tradition, but pay more specific attention to the "character crisis" of the 1880s and the ways in which critics sought to account for the apparent disappearance of epoch-making heroes from

Russian literature. After this historical overview, I turn to the publication history of *Sanin* (which had an immediate effect on its reputation as a chronicle of contemporary life) and its reception by critics and readers who were well versed in nineteenth-century literature. How could Artsybashev's hero generate a feeling of déjà vu and, at the same time, be construed as the most convincing personification of the post-1905 mentality? To what extent did the historic dispute between the radicals and the liberals of the 1860s inform the debate on Saninism? These are the questions I ask in chapter 2.

Chapter 3 shifts the analysis from the reactions of professional critics, writers, and other opinion makers to the reception by marginal writers and anonymous readers who could not immediately articulate their views in the printed media. Drawing on parodies, mock sequels, adaptations for the stage, and fictional diaries (many of which were never published), I attempt to demonstrate that the novel was appropriated in a far more critical way than is generally believed to be the case.

Sanin's reputation as a pornographic bestseller forms the subject of chapter 4. Here I discuss the formal grounds on which the novel was banned as well as the political considerations that led radical critics to stigmatize *Sanin* as pornographic (as opposed to "principled," that is, politically correct) literature. Relying on criteria that were vaguely defined at best, participants in the debate on *Sanin*, including the censor, made surprisingly little effort to pinpoint exactly what constituted its pornographic nature. In contrast to Germany, where the court lifted the ban on *Sanin* after a committee of experts established its historical and literary value, Russia never abandoned the idea that the novel was one of the most lurid texts in the history of Russian literature.

The "average, gray reader," to borrow an expression from the populist critic Iakov Danilin, is the main hero of chapter 5 in which I argue against the popular notion that Artsybashev's hero was widely adopted as a role model. The main focus, however, lies with the social and political profiles of the "typical" *Sanin* reader as they were drawn up by critics of Marxist, populist, and liberal persuasions.

The subject of chapter 6 is the crossroads of literature, rumor, and the yellow press. It analyzes reports on the mysterious free love leagues, which supposedly mushroomed in the spring of 1908. Although Artsybashev was not the only author who was held responsible for this deplorable craze, it is his name that most frequently appears in connection with it. Using amateur plays, police reports, and other unpublished materials, I attempt to excavate the voices of the assumed victims of Saninism: adolescents and, more specifically, gymnasium students. Thus, I hope to show that the reported enthusiasm for Saninism affected young people's self-image in that it left them with a sense of guilt about their own debasement. The discourse these young people employed was often couched in rhetoric that echoed much older frustrations, such as aggravation with the "police regime" of the classical gymnasium and concern over the perceived crisis of Russian family life.

Situating *Sanin* in the context of Prime Minister Stolypin's economic reforms, chapter 7 offers, among other things, a reading of Artsybashev's novel as a narrative of economic self-determination. Contrary to what many critics have argued in reference to Sanin's carefree attitude toward life, I argue that the novel allows us to glimpse the contours of a new behavioral ideal that is based on self-reliance, physical strength, and an "American" work ethos (as Artsybashev described it in an interview). In promoting this ideal, Artsybashev was attacking the impoverished student community for its prejudices against physical labor. This chapter also discusses a few stories by the lowbrow writer Nikolai Breshko-Breshkovskii and wrestling legend Ivan Lebedev, in which the economic metaphor of "the struggle for life" (still implicit in Artsybashev's work) is further developed.

In the first section of this introduction, I asked whether Russia had really known a teaching called Saninism in the years leading up to the revolution of 1917. To avoid arousing expectations that this book cannot fulfill, I immediately expressed a categorical "no." Yet the very writing of this study suggests that it is possible and indeed necessary to come up with a more extensive and nuanced answer. I therefore pose a number of additional questions that can help us to come to grips with the elusive nature of this book's central subject. How exactly did the myth of Saninism emerge and how did it shape people's perception of political and social reality after the events of 1905? What was its effect on the collective self-image of school-aged youth? What were the consequences of Stolypin's conclusion that there "could not be smoke without fire," even if the rumors about the mysterious free love leagues turned out to be exaggerated? More generally, what is the role of literature and its reception in creating the reputation of a historical period? By addressing these questions, I hope not only to lay bare some of the mechanisms responsible for producing the unfavorable reputation of the years 1907–17 but also to show how Russians were expressing their greater freedom after the "failed" revolution of 1905. Briefly, I use the fascinating reception history of *Sanin* as a lens through which to look at some of the profound changes that occurred in Russian society on the eve of World War I, particularly in the field of literature, popular culture, and youth identity.

1

From Onegin to Bazarov
The Canon of Epoch-making Heroes

Although *Sanin* has enjoyed the reputation of a pornographic potboiler, the stir it created cannot be understood properly without taking into account two other aspects that most critics found even more unnerving: the striking timing of its publication and the literary genealogy of the eponymous hero. By "timing" I mean that the novel was published at a moment that compelled readers and critics to perceive it as a "sign of times," a disturbing milestone in the history of Russian literature that could have occurred only at "this" particular moment. What exactly the novel was believed to be characteristic of is discussed in chapter 2, where I turn to Artsybashev's contemporary critics and their often contradictory readings of the novel. Yet, in order to grasp how they could arrive at these interpretations, we first need to examine some of the most common hermeneutic practices and strategies in nineteenth-century literary criticism, specifically those that were based on the concepts of "typicality" and "contemporary type." Since Artsybashev's hero was received in this tradition, a critical survey of its origins and evolution will allow us to understand better the heated and sometimes hysterical reactions that the novel provoked.

In this chapter, I cannot avoid using two of the most ideologically charged concepts that nineteenth-century criticism has produced: the "hero of our time" and the "superfluous man." I share the suspicion that these expressions have come to arouse—not too long ago they were treated as "real" historical phenomena rather than as the discursive and gendered constructs they in fact are.[1] However, for the purpose of this study, we cannot do without them, if only because they *defined* the very problems they were supposed to designate. Paraphrasing Foucault, we can say that what is at issue is the "over-all discursive fact," the way in which political agendas and feelings of social alienation were encoded into discourse.[2] In using the expressions "hero of our time" and "superfluous man" I remain aware that they were part of the discursive practice and self-image of a predominantly male intelligentsia.

In what follows, I do not pretend to give an exhaustive inventory of the contemporary types and characteristic heroes that Russian critics discovered over a period of more than fifty years. I may ignore relatively well-known heroes, discussing instead rather obscure characters who simply better serve my argument, which is that the search for contemporary types, or "heroes of our time," continued well into the twentieth century, despite the fact that it was felt that the "canon" of epoch-making heroes had already come to a close in the 1860s and that Russian literature had been afflicted by a "character crisis." Put simply, in the last quarter of the nineteenth century, there emerged a gap (or so it was felt) between what critics were looking for and what literature had to offer.

Contemporary Types, Superfluous Men

The concept of typicality was introduced by the feared critic Vissarion Belinskii in order to solve a problem that lies at the heart of realist literature: the reconciliation of the demand for verisimilitude with the necessity of achieving a level of general statement. According to Belinskii, a talented writer was capable of depicting particular characters or events truthfully while investing them with some broader meaning. Although the concept of typicality has much older origins, reaching back to the aesthetics of Aristotle, with Belinskii it became one of the key criteria for judging the social significance of a literary text. Literature that did not attain the desired level of generalization failed to fulfill its role as an agent for social and political change.

Since Russian novels were hero centered from the earliest moments of realism, the belief in literature's capacity to make general statements about contemporary society manifested itself, first and foremost, in the search for "typical" protagonists, characters who were believed to represent a particular mentality or a specific social movement. In a famous review of Mikhail Lermontov's novel *A Hero of Our Time* (*Geroi nashego vremeni* [1838–40]), Belinskii laid the foundation of this tradition by construing the central character, Grigorii Pechorin, as a truthful image of a Russian contemporary type: the disillusioned man of the 1830s. In so doing, Belinskii followed the author's own suggestion, stated explicitly in the introduction, that the novel was intended as a "portrait composed of the vices of our entire generation."[3] Referring to the title character of *Evgenii Onegin*, Aleksandr Pushkin's novel in verse, Belinskii called Pechorin the "Onegin of our time" and thus introduced an enduring interpretive strategy that consisted of comparing literary heroes from a diachronic perspective with the aim of grasping the direction in which society was moving.[4]

Ivan Turgenev is traditionally credited for having created the "successor" of the spleeny man of the thirties: the (aristocratic) idealist of the 1840s whose considerable talents go to waste, arguably as a result of the regime's repressive policy. Turgenev's work features a number of such characters, but none of them acquired as much symbolic significance as did Dmitrii Rudin, the eponymous hero of his debut novel (*Rudin* [1856]). A handsome and talented young man with an almost cosmopolitan aura, Rudin nonetheless proves incapable of realizing any of his ambitious plans and fails as a lover. This double failure is not a unique feature of Rudin, nor even of Turgenev's male heroes in general, but the combination of his romantic leanings, rooted in German idealist philosophy, and the overall fiasco of his life made Rudin the fictional figurehead of an entire generation.

It was also Turgenev who coined the heavily charged and often ridiculed term "superfluous man" that would have a lasting effect on the interpretation of nineteenth-century Russian literature and its characters. As in a number of other stories featuring feeble intellectuals, in "Diary of a Superfluous Man" ("Dnevnik lishnego cheloveka" [1850]) Turgenev appears to have been primarily interested in exploring his hero's sense of superfluity from a philosophical perspective rather than in defining it as a social or political problem. His fascination with the character of Hamlet as a more or less timeless personality type seems to indicate likewise. However, the superfluous man's proclivity to self-analysis that paralyzes him and deprives him of the ability to act in Turgenev's work was soon construed politically as implying a critique of the stultifying atmosphere under Tsar Nicholas I. Thus, gradually the superfluous man acquired a potentially heroic or martyrlike air, even though the concept was at odds with the very notion of agency.

Critics were divided over the question of whether or not Rudin belonged to the category of the superfluous men. The radical left believed he did, contrasting him unfavorably with the supposedly more level-headed type of "new man" that began to manifest itself in Russian literature at the beginning of the 1860s (see the next section). To a critic like Nikolai Chernyshevsky, Rudin was a typical representative of the 1840s; his idealism and eloquence, Chernyshevsky believed, were only surpassed by his fundamental ineffectiveness.[5] More liberal-minded critics, such as Mikhail Avdeev, construed Rudin's seemingly heroic death on the barricades of Paris not as a desperate, theatrical gesture of someone who has reached the end of his tether, but as proof of his willingness to turn his words into deeds.[6] To Avdeev, Rudin was the first social activist in Russian literature.[7]

As futile as this dispute over Rudin may seem, it shows that, for all the casualness with which the term was used, *the* type of the superfluous man never existed, not even in the writings of Russian critics. Whether or not character X qualified as such was a matter of continuous debate and reappraisal, as were the grounds on which this question was being decided. Hence, there arose the equally elusive distinction in late nineteenth-century criticism between the "heroically superfluous" and the "genuinely superfluous" (that is, the useless), a distinction that was particularly applied to the work of Anton Chekhov. Once the term "superfluous" gained currency, fictional characters who, technically speaking, predated the appearance of Turgenev's superfluous man, such as Onegin and Pechorin, could also acquire the label. Thus, whereas the signifier remained more or less the same, lending the debate on the superfluous man a treacherous kind of transparency, the narratives behind this signifier were always changing.

The Search for the New Man

The concept of the superfluous man acquired a new level of abstraction in the writings of Nikolai Dobroliubov, who was heavily influenced by Belinskii, particularly by his ideas on the utilitarian role of literature. Drawing on a number of widely debated novels published after Belinskii's death in 1848, Dobroliubov signaled the emergence of a new "contemporary Russian type," the embodiment of whom, he believed, was the eponymous hero of Ivan Goncharov's novel *Oblomov* (1859). Though certainly congenial with such "phrasemongers" as Pechorin and Rudin, Oblomov was nonetheless different in that he did not try to conceal his true character behind a façade of eloquence and high-flying idealism. Unlike his predecessors, he revealed his true colors, openly acknowledging his utter impotence and uselessness to society. Oblomov's idleness, then, Dobroliubov thought, should be seen as a hopeful sign indicating that "phrases no longer counted" and that society demanded real deeds.[8] Although he feared that superfluous men such as Oblomov would still be around for a while, they were rapidly losing their appeal and moral authority.

Dobroliubov's optimistic article on *Oblomov* was published on the eve of the Great Reforms, almost twenty years after Belinskii's review of *A Hero of Our Time*. In the course of that period, the gallery of superfluous men had expanded considerably, now spanning not two, but at least four decades: the spoiled dandy of the 1820s (Onegin), the restless and disillusioned men of the 1830s (Pechorin), the romantic idealists of the 1840s (Rudin), and the idlers of the 1850s (Oblomov).[9] Every ten years, a new contemporary type had emerged, each one even more ineffective and alienated from society than his predecessor. For Dobroliubov, as we have seen, this succession of superfluous men was not a random but a more or less teleological process reflecting the teleological evolution of society as a whole. Being the last and ultimate representative of his ilk, Oblomov could have emerged only in the 1850s, when the whole nation was preparing for fundamental change. For these reasons, Dobroliubov—and many radical critics with him—expected that the near future would generate yet another type, only this time the type would be a genuine hero who would have the will and determination to overcome the paralysis of the previous generations. This type was usually referred to as the "new man," a species in which, according to Dmitrii Pisarev, another leading critic of the radical camp, "thought and action blended into a solid whole."[10] The new man was, as Rufus Mathewson has put it, "in one sense a development beyond his predecessors, and in another sense—notably in his thirst for action—a direct antithesis to them."[11]

At the threshold of the 1860s, Russian literature boasted two characters who could, at least in theory, lay some claim to representing that new type of man: Oblomov's friend and counterpart, the energetic and level-headed businessman Shtolts, and Insarov, the heroic Bulgarian freedom fighter in Turgenev's third novel *On the Eve* (*Nakanune* [1860]). In contrast to the superfluous men, these characters turned their words into deeds, Shtolts by helping out Oblomov and Insarov by dedicating himself fully to the liberation of his fatherland. Initially, Pisarev seems to have been impressed with Shtolts, a type "still extremely rare in Russia," but one that would eventually become more widespread "as a result of the present course of ideas."[12] Soon after the publication of Chernyshevsky's novel *What Is to Be Done?*, however, he dismissed Shtolts as a "wooden figure" and called Insarov "absurd" and "fictitious."[13] Dobroliubov went to some lengths to explain why Turgenev had made Insarov a Bulgarian, not a Russian, asserting that the occupation of one's fatherland was more conducive to heroic behavior than the pettiness and vulgarity of Russia's social environment. He was nonetheless confident that this very environment would also help the Russian Insarov to step forward and cleanse society of its dark forces.[14] The Russified German Shtolts, on the other hand, was too vague as a type and hardly a personality that would incite Russians to action.[15]

This reluctance to accept the only two energetic and positive heroes of Russian literature as accurate representations of the new man is indicative of the basic dilemma underlying the concept of "contemporary type." On the one hand, the concept called for the representation of a member of a social group in as objective and precise a manner as possible (what Belinskii called "truthful"). On the other hand, in order to be artistically convincing, the representation needed to render the identifying characteristics with an intensity or, indeed, "typicality" that one would never encounter in real life. If the author succeeded in maintaining the precarious balance between particularity and generalization, he could not only shed light on the social tendencies and types of the existing order but also anticipate the genesis of *new* types, even if such new types were beyond his own intention or awareness. It was the critic's task to scrutinize the literary text for glimpses of new historic personalities and then explain the full implications of the work to the public. With the critic's assistance, literature could "predict" the near future by truthfully depicting the present.

It was precisely because Shtolts was not a true representative of the present but rather ahead of his time that Dobroliubov rejected Shtolts as a candidate for the new man. Literature could not "run ahead of things too much" by depicting future types for which the time had not yet come.[16] A "Russian Insarov" was more likely to appear, Dobroliubov maintained, even though, at present, Russian literature could only show the Bulgarian prototype. With ever more people beginning to understand the unsoundness of the existing order in Russia, a climate was developing that would soon generate men (and women) of action. The courageous and selfless behavior of the heroines in *Oblomov* and *On the Eve* were particularly encouraging signs. Although it was too early for the diligent and sober-minded businessman Shtolts, the nation seemed ready for an activist like Insarov.

Thus, by 1860, the concept of the contemporary type had acquired a conspicuously programmatic charge that set it apart from its earlier manifestations. Literature could not content itself any longer with simply diagnosing society and portraying superfluous men; it had to offer some vision of the near future and the new types that were about to emerge.[17] At the same time, it could not "run ahead of things too much," as Dobroliubov stressed time and again, for this would violate the primacy of truthfulness. As we will see in due course, the contradiction generated by these demands would manifest itself in all its immediacy in the debate on *Sanin,* leaving critics wondering whether the hero represented the status quo or a new type of man worthy of imitation.

Fathers and Children

In the 1860s the new man finally made his appearance in Russian literature, supplying generations of radicals with a model of behavior and a clearly defined program for action. Chernyshevsky's notorious *roman à thèse What Is to Be Done?* featured several characters who led purposeful lives and attained personal happiness. Unlike the phrasemongers of the 1840s, or the idle Oblomovs of the early 1850s, who all belonged to the gentry, these were pragmatic and truly positive personalities from the lower middle class, the so-called *raznochintsy,* who were using their knowledge and education to build a better society. As if the message was not clear enough already, Chernyshevsky decided to give his novel the evocative subtitle, "Tales about the New People," thus removing all doubt as to the revolutionary identity of the main characters.[18]

As Dobroliubov had already anticipated in his reflections on Turgenev's *On the Eve,* the "new man" might just as well be a "new woman." Vera Pavlovna, the central character of *What Is to Be Done?*, is the most striking example of the social and spiritual renewal that the novel purports to depict. Thanks to a fictitious marriage with the student and "rational egotist" Lopukhov, she not only evolves from a commoner's daughter into an energetic and astute manager of a profitable sewing workshop for former prostitutes but also finds fulfillment in her personal life by eventually marrying Lopukhov's more sociable friend Kirsanov (after the fake suicide of Lopukhov). Characteristically, her story subverts the paradigm of failure that structured the life of the superfluous man. If the latter was an alienated misfit, incapable of having a successful relationship and a decent career, then Vera Pavlovna and her comrades represent the opposite extreme in their ability to combine communal life with cooperative work.[19]

The enormous effect of Chernyshevsky's novel on its readers is well documented and sufficiently studied by now.[20] All over Russia, young women followed Vera Pavlovna's example and fled their parents' homes to pursue the ideal of education and self-development. Under pressure of a strict code of honor, young men offered their services as fictitious husbands, agreeing to relinquish their conjugal rights. In short, *What Is to Be Done?* enjoyed the status of a sacrosanct text, a "guide to life," like the Bible, with which Chernyshevsky's admirers and enemies alike often compared it. Its influence extended even beyond the radical circles of the 1860s and was absorbed into the ethos of the nonradical intelligentsia as well.[21] Yet, no matter how influential the novel actually was, its reception history did not engender an emblematic hero such as Pechorin or Rudin. In spite of the enduring behavioral paradigm that they helped to establish, none of the new people in *What Is to Be Done?* became invested with the symbolic significance that distinguished the superfluous men they were supposed to replace. In the obligatory listing of "types" that became a stock element in the debate on the Russian intelligentsia after the revolution of 1905, Chernyshevsky's heroes are notably absent.

There are likely several reasons why the new people of *What Is to Be Done?* never came to enjoy any currency as historical personalities. The novel features a mysterious, weight-lifting ascetic by the name of Rakhmetov, who is more convincing as a timeless moral example than a full-fledged literary hero. Even the less idealized characters are disturbingly lacking in individuality. Although this is presented as a conscious choice by the narrator, who declares to be interested only in depicting the "general traits" of a new type, not the peculiarities of individuals, the characters of *What Is to Be Done?* may simply have proven too flat to serve as typical representatives of their generation, as "heroes of our time."

An equally important factor, however, must have been the emergence of a genuinely epoch-making hero two years before the publication of *What Is to Be Done?* Evgenii Bazarov, the vigorous and charismatic protagonist of *Fathers and Children* (*Ottsy i deti* [1861]), Turgenev's best-known novel, was the literary character who came to embody the mentality of the 1860s. A scientific materialist with a ready tongue who was almost provocatively ill-mannered, he soon came to be regarded as a collective portrait of the nihilists—nonaristocratic intellectuals, such as Chernyshevsky and Dobroliubov, who rejected the idealism of the previous generation with its "superstitions" and "petty lies" and instead espoused the more rigid methods of the natural sciences.[22] In *Fathers and Children*, this radical attitude is apparent in Bazarov's contempt for literature and art, and in his hostility toward any form of decorum, notably in what some contemporaries considered his "cynical" treatment of women.

As is well known, *Fathers and Children* infuriated the radical critics of the monthly *Sovremennik* (*The Contemporary*), who perceived the novel as a malicious attempt to discredit the younger generation. The editors, Maksim Antonovich and Iulii Zhukovskii, reacted with sarcastic reviews. Conservative and liberal reviewers were more positive, though they disagreed over whether Turgenev had accurately rendered the psychology of his hero. Evgeniia Tur and Aleksandr Herzen found insufficient motivation for Bazarov's extreme coarseness; Mikhail Katkov, chief editor of *Russkii vestnik* (*The Russian Herald*), which had published *Fathers and Children*, accepted Bazarov as a convincing portrait of the nihilist and even devoted a series of articles to the "Bazarovs in Russian reality."[23]

An unexpected reaction came from Dmitrii Pisarev, who saluted Bazarov as a "new man" and a heroic figure. In a lengthy essay that would also have a lasting effect on the standard Soviet view of *Fathers and Children*, Pisarev argued that the novel's polemical intent was not half as important as its "objective story." Whatever Turgenev had wanted to convey, the final result was an accurate portrait of an "evolving general type": the man of action in whom the will (*volia*) of Pechorin and the knowledge of Rudin converged.[24] In another famous article, written a few years later, Pisarev had no qualms about grouping Bazarov with Rakhmetov on the grounds that both were hard-working "realists."[25]

Although some members of the radical camp never forgave Turgenev for writing what they considered a lampoon, eventually Pisarev's favorable interpretation of Bazarov as an emerging progressive historical type gained wide acceptance among the left. Writing in the 1890s, Piotr Kropotkin remembered how he had been initially dissatisfied with Bazarov for his callousness toward his parents and his all-pervading negativism. Toward the end of the 1870s, when he became friendly with Turgenev, he began speaking more benignly of Bazarov, calling him an "admirable painting of the nihilist."[26] At the turn of the century, populist and Marxist critics were almost unanimous in viewing Bazarov as a worthy representative of the Russian intelligentsia who had ruthlessly exposed the falsehood of the existing order.[27]

Pisarev's article on Bazarov also had a more pessimistic strand that later commentators preferred to ignore. Precisely because of his heroic stature, Bazarov was a spiritually lonely man who was misunderstood by his environment and, in effect, destined not to live up to his full potential. No matter how refreshing and cleansing his appearance on the historical scene was, under the present circumstances, his sphere of action would remain limited: "Everything around him is petty, shallow, and weak, while he himself is fresh, intelligent, and strong."[28] In Pisarev's final analysis, Bazarov was a tragic hero who had to fight forces larger than himself, just like Russia's youth, whose far from enviable fate he embodied. With this conclusion, Pisarev came dangerously close to declaring Bazarov a superfluous rather than a new man, a suggestion that would have been blasphemy to early twentieth-century opinion makers on the left such as Vatslav Vorovskii and Fiodor Dan.[29] Even Dmitrii Ovsianiko-Kulikovskii, one of the very few turn-of-the-century commentators to discuss Bazarov's possible superfluity in some detail, dismissed Pisarev's implications as fundamentally wrong. Instead of taking into account the psychological traits of the *raznochinets,* Pisarev (an aristocrat!) had ascribed to Turgenev's hero the characteristics of his own spiritual and social forefathers: "Bazarov, as Pisarev sees him, is a *gentrified* Bazarov."[30]

Despite Pisarev's remarks on Bazarov's "spiritual loneliness," his articles on *Fathers and Children* were instrumental in establishing Turgenev's hero as a contemporary type. He not only upheld him as a model for emulation to the radical youth but also defended the latter by parading Bazarov as their most typical and radiant representative. By carefully analyzing Bazarov's relationship with women, for example, Pisarev hoped to debunk the myth that the nihilists were all sexually depraved.[31] In other words, to understand Bazarov was to understand the younger generation.

In her well-known study *Chernyshevsky and the Age of Realism,* Irina Paperno has shown in vivid detail how Bazarov soon acquired a second life outside Turgenev's novel. Refashioned by Pisarev in accordance with the radical agenda, he became a model for imitation that inspired the youth in its intellectual endeavors (leading it to reject the humanities in favor of the natural sciences), as well as in its daily conduct. Unpolished manners and a sloppy appearance acquired a symbolic value, which thus became part of a specific behavioral paradigm.[32] As Paperno has observed: "The awkwardness and lack of social skills characteristic of the original *raznochintsy*, who came from lower strata and had not received instruction in manners (an important part of the upbringing of the gentry), were deliberately cultivated, both by those who were naturally ungracious and by those trained in the social graces. Rudeness and curt manners, negligent styles of dress and even untidiness became meaningful, ideologically weighted signs, which immediately distinguished the nihilists both from the members of the opposing camp (the traditionalists, the reactionaries) and from ordinary people."[33]

The reception history of *Fathers and Children* is a telling example of the complicated ways in which literature and reality can interact. Turgenev's novel was used to explain a social phenomenon in a manner that not only affected the perception of it but also had an effect on that phenomenon itself. Whether a similarly intense semiosis occurred in the case of *Sanin* will become clear in the course of the next chapters. For the moment, it is crucial to bear in mind the ambivalent status of Bazarov as a contemporary type and a model for imitation, that is, as the personification of an existing mentality *and* as a "new man." With *Sanin*, this discrepancy between reality and ideal would manifest itself again, giving rise to a debate that was strikingly reminiscent of the controversy over *Fathers and Children*.

Beyond Bazarov

In 1874 the liberal critic Mikhail Avdeev published a book-length study, *Our Society (1820–1870) as Reflected in Literary Heroes and Heroines*.[34] It was a generally well-received overview that purported to sketch society's evolution by examining the ideological and mental make-up of Russian literature's best-known characters. The book is not particularly original in its approach, even if Avdeev's decision to devote half of it to women characters seems to suggest otherwise. Mildly criticizing Belinskii for disregarding Chatskii, the main character in Griboedov's comedy *Woe from Wit* (*Gore ot uma* [1822]), in his search for historical types, Avdeev mostly confined himself to repeating received notions on the usual suspects: Chatskii, Onegin, Pechorin, Rudin, Insarov and Bazarov (all of whom have their own chapters). Two other chapters deal with "superfluous people and Russian Hamlets" and "people of the 1860s." Predictably, the women's section is an almost exact mirror of the preceding part on the male heroes, featuring, among others, Tatyana

(*Evgenii Onegin*), Bela, Princess Mary, and Vera (*A Hero of Our Time*), Natalia (*Rudin*), and Elena (*On the Eve*). For all its lack of originality, however, the publication of *Our Society* was a significant event in the history of Russian criticism. To my knowledge, it is the first attempt to present a nearly exhaustive inventory of historical types and thus to define a "hall of fame" for Russian literature's epoch-making heroes.[35] Apparently, the topicality of Avdeev's book was felt to be such as to merit a new edition as late as 1907.

Given the year of publication, the historical scope of Avdeev's book was necessarily limited. The concluding chapters are dedicated to the "people of the 1860s" and contained little speculation on the next generation that was already emerging at the time of writing. Because he died in 1876, Avdeev never had a chance to revise his work or to expand his gallery of literary characters by including historical types of later origin. And yet, it does not seem likely that he would have done so had he lived another twenty years. A brief look at the writings of early twentieth-century critics shows that the obligatory listing of historical types in articles dealing with the Russian intelligentsia usually avoided mentioning fictional *intelligenty* from the "post-Bazarov" period. As Il'ia Ignatov, a leading critic working for the national daily *Russkie vedomosti* (*Russian Announcements*) and one of the first critics to review *Sanin,* observed in 1907: "Chatskii, Evgenii Onegin, Pechorin, Bel'tov, Rudin, Bazarov—this is the ladder of types of the Russian intelligentsia that everybody is familiar with. . . . With Bazarov it all seems to have ended."[36]

What exactly caused the demise of the epoch-making hero in late nineteenth-century Russian literature is open to debate. It seems feasible that the intelligentsia's ideological fragmentation played a considerable role. By the 1870s the cultural paradigm of the generation of the 1860s had blurred and dissolved into a spectrum of discrete paradigms, ranging from the moderate opposition of liberals to the violent resistance advocated by the more radical elements.[37] All in all, it must have become even harder than before to agree on what a generation's "typical" representative looked like.

But if it is impossible to point out with certainty the deeper causes behind the decline of the epoch-making hero, we still may ask how critics explained this development and what deeper significance they attributed to it. Did it really signal a loss to them and, if so, was it permanent or only temporary? Had Russian society entered a new stage requiring new role models or were the old ones still valid? To provide the beginning of an answer to these questions, we must turn to a largely forgotten polemic between the "men of the 1860s" and the next generation, which was often referred to as the "men of the 1880s" (*vos'midesiatniki*). The former group and a number of Marxist critics proved unwilling to recognize a legitimate successor to Bazarov; literary characters that were pushed forward as possible new "heroes of our time" (by the men of the 1880s) were discarded as historically irrelevant by the men of the 1860s. Drawing on two longer stories by the once immensely popular author Ignatii Potapenko, the remainder of this chapter seeks to reconstruct the "hero of our time" of the 1880s, the would-be successor to Bazarov, who was not admitted to the canon of epoch-making heroes.

Fathers, Children, and Grandchildren

Although the issue of Russian literature's "de-heroization" did not become acute before the 1880s, it was again Avdeev who seems to have suspected that such a development would eventually occur. A true optimist, Avdeev believed that since intellectual thought and social activism were rapidly spreading among the lower strata of society, Russia was inevitably moving away from the times of strong and lonely men. In effect, literature featuring heroic figures would soon belong to the past, as the time for ordinary workers had come.[38]

Writing in the relatively liberal times of Tsar Alexander II, Avdeev could not foresee how the absence of a successor to Bazarov would be construed during the reactionary reign of Alexander III (1881–94). The penultimate tsar revoked many of the liberties that his father had introduced, tightening censorship again and restricting access to higher education. This political course not only was at odds with Avdeev's rosy projections of Russia's unstoppable enlightenment but also turned the demise of the epoch-making hero into a question of some urgency. Was it inevitable and really a sign of progress, as Avdeev had surmised, or did it point to a moral crisis of the intelligentsia, which apparently had stopped producing characters of the same caliber as Bazarov? To what extent was contemporary literature responsible for deepening the sense of stagnation that pervaded Russian society under Alexander III?

One of the first to address these issues was Roman Disterlo, a minor critic who contributed to the moderately populist periodical *Nedelia* (*The Week*). In a number of articles published in 1888–89, he argued that in Russia a new type of writer had come to the fore who differed fundamentally from the writers of previous generations. If earlier writers had declared war on the existing order or, at least, had attempted to expose its shortcomings, then the writer of the 1880s seemed to accept Russian society as it was. Instead of offering new vistas of future happiness or designing new heroic types, as the authors of the 1840s and the 1860s had done, the writer of the 1880s felt at home exploiting more prosaic themes and creating less elevated characters: "[The younger generation] does not feel hate or contempt for man's ordinary life, he does not appreciate and recognize man's duty to be a hero at all costs, he does not believe in the possibility of ideal people."[39]

This more pliable attitude of the new writer led Disterlo to differentiate between the "younger generation" on the one hand, and the "fathers" (the radicals of the 1860s) and the "grandfathers" (the idealists of the 1840s), on the other. What set the new writers apart from the two previous generations, in Disterlo's view, was not the way in which they resisted the status quo but the fact that they did not resist at all. For someone raised on the novels of the fathers, reading a work by a young writer was like being moved from a world of serious thought and deep suffering to a company of naive and carefree tourists.[40] Although a number of writers continued to disseminate the ideals of the past, most of Russia's latest literature exuded a sort of equanimity and skepticism that had previously not been experienced.[41]

By replacing the "traditional" fathers and children paradigm of the 1860s with a ternary generational model, Disterlo provoked the indignation of a number of older critics, such as Nikolai Shelgunov and Nikolai Mikhailovskii. Shelgunov had been a close ally of the radical critics Chernyshevsky and Dobroliubov and had written extensively on the ideological divide between the men of the 1840s and the 1860s.[42] Much to his dismay, he now found himself relegated to the category of the "fathers." Shelgunov did not contest Disterlo's characterization of the "young writers" as skeptics who had distanced themselves from their fathers' and grandfathers' ideals, but he very much doubted their historical significance and therefore rejected the idea of a new generation conflict. Authors continuing the traditions of the past, such as Korolenko, Garshin, and Nadson, were, he maintained, far more popular than Disterlo's "new writers," whose shallow success remained restricted to St. Petersburg.[43]

The influential populist critic Mikhailovskii considered the application of the "fathers and children" formula to the 1880s simply ludicrous. Deprived of any real talent and knowledge, the so-called children of

Nedelia were a deeply reactionary phenomenon that would disappear again once the stagnant years were over. To illustrate the "children's" self-overestimation, Mikhailovskii angrily quoted a letter from an anonymous reader to Shelgunov in which the latter was urged to "clear the road" and yield to the "man of the eighties."[44] Such claims not only testified to a lack of respect for what the men of the 1860s had accomplished, Mikhailovskii argued, but also created the erroneous impression that the youngest generation was a formidable political force. In Mikhailovskii's opinion, the *vos'midesiatnik* was hype that could easily be debunked by simply scrutinizing his moral and intellectual fabric: "Let us take a good look at you and count how many there are of you, let us evaluate your talents and power, which you manage to hide so meticulously that one begins to suspect you haven't got any."[45] In short, the "children" of the 1880s were such a "petty phenomenon" that they only deserved to be mentioned in connection with the prevailing mood in society.[46]

At first sight, Mikhailovskii's exasperation may seem disproportionate. Why did the arguably most feared and authoritative critic of late nineteenth-century literature take umbrage at the writings of a minor colleague? The very suggestion of a new generation having taken over may have hurt Mikhailovskii's pride, of course, but an injured ego seems to be only part of the answer. To appreciate Mikhailovskii's aggravation, we need to take into account that Disterlo's articles were published in *Nedelia*, a weekly that promoted a brand of populism of which Mikhailovskii did not approve. The journal not only advanced the ideal of social improvement through constructive work and gradual enlightenment, an ideal that became popularly known as the "theory of small deeds," but it also introduced a new behavioral model via the theory's ideal adherent: the law-abiding "nonheroic" intellectual who shuns the reckless heroism of the previous generation and modestly serves the people.

The most explicit attempt to formulate this behavioral model came from one of *Nedelia*'s main editors, the journalist and critic Iakov Abramov (1858–1906), who is generally regarded as the spiritual father of the theory of small deeds and gradualism (*postepenstvo*). Contrary to Avdeev, Abramov did not think the role of the intelligentsia had decreased in significance; rather, he claimed, its representatives now just had other, less spectacular, obligations to fulfill, and this considerably diminished their heroic stature. Still, he maintained, the intelligentsia should not slide back into the desperation and inertia of the superfluous men, for this would set Russian society back even further. The point was to find a third way, an escape route that would lead the sons away from the deadlock of the fathers and the grandfathers: "Our intelligentsia considers itself to be either too heroic or else incapable of doing anything. [In this country], everybody is either a hero or a wimp. Isn't it about time that a middle type started to emerge—a man capable of doing simple, honest work? Such a man we need very badly and the future belongs to him."[47]

By proposing an alternative and supposedly more effective type of behavior, Abramov implicitly pronounced a verdict on the radical legacy of the 1860s, more specifically on the imperative of violent resistance and self-denial advanced by the terrorist Sergei Nechaev in his infamous *Catechism of a Revolutionary* (*Katekhizis revolutsionera* [1869]). Instead of openly confronting the regime by killing its main figureheads, the intelligentsia could be more productive by providing the common people with medical care and raising their educational level. While no one could object to such a line of action per se, and while Mikhailovskii was also opposed to violence, it was the lack of any political demands in Abramov's program that radical thinkers, including Mikhailovskii and Shelgunov, found disturbing. To them, it smacked of defeatism. According to Lenin, Abramov's theory of small deeds distracted society's progressive forces from the revolution.[48]

Even if Marxist criticism attempted to discredit the theory of small deeds as a reactionary phenomenon, its practical successes were considerable. Despite the deception of the going-to-the-people campaign of the mid 1870s, between the mid-1880s and the start of World War I, thousands of young men and women flocked to the countryside to work as doctors, teachers, and engineers and, in many cases, made an important contribution to the improvement of life in the provinces.[49] Russian literature of this period offers numerous fictional portraits of intellectuals who serve the people in this unspectacular manner. Quite often, their mission is depicted as unsuccessful, if not entirely hopeless, as in the work of Vikentii Veresaev (who gave up the theory of small deeds in favor of Marxism) and Mikhail Artsybashev (a declared opponent of any kind of philanthropy).[50] Sometimes the message is ambiguous, as in the work of Anton Chekhov. Yet, there were also attempts to present a more positive view of the theory of small deeds in literature, attempts that literary historians, for artistic as well as ideological reasons, have largely overlooked. Key to these texts is the idealized image of the central hero who is not simply better or more effective than the other characters but who is presented as adumbrating a "new" historical type. It is here that we can discern the contours of the would-be successor (or one of the successors) to Bazarov, the positive hero of the 1880s.

No More Heroes

A particularly optimistic account of the theory of small deeds and its practitioners can be found in the work of Ignatii Potapenko (1856–1929), one of the most popular authors of the 1890s. In the almost hagiographical story "In Real Service" ("Na deistvitel'noi sluzhbe"), probably his best-known work, an extremely gifted graduate of the Theological Academy by the name of Obnovlenskii gives up a guaranteed career in the highest circles of the Eastern Orthodox church for a modest position as an ordinary priest in the provinces. Though his attempts to purify the relations between the clergy and the members of the parish are initially met with hostility, in the end the saintly Obnovlenskii exults over the moral corruption surrounding him. At the expense of his personal life (his wife leaves him with their son), he guides the local population through a terrible famine and thus brings about nothing less than the village's spiritual renaissance.[51]

Perhaps because he felt he had idealized Obnovlenskii's behavior too much, in his next long story, "Not a Hero" ("Ne geroi" [1891]), Potapenko offered a second-best option for those incapable of complete self-denial. Firmly grounded in the tradition of the Russian *roman à thèse*, "Not a Hero" consists mainly of lengthy conversations; it lacks a proper plot. The protagonist, a convinced populist by the name of Racheev, returns to St. Petersburg after a seven-year absence. He visits his friend Baklanov, a fashionable but shallow writer of populist stories, who introduces him to his uptight wife and his equally stressed-out friends and colleagues. The outsider Racheev is different in every respect. Once a moony student with a pasty complexion, he is now a level-headed, broad-shouldered estate manager who "does what he says," as Baklanov's younger sister remarks admiringly. Racheev repeatedly lectures the other characters, but his behavior is not perceived as provocative. Driven by a genuine desire to help his friends to lead more purposeful lives, Racheev assures them that he himself is a "mediocre person," "not a hero," a man who has learned to curb his once unrealistic ambitions: "During this period of restless impulses [when still a university student], I imagined how I would make the entire

"A Graphic Review of Ivan [sic] Potapenko." The caption, referring to his enormous literary output, reads: "Who said it is impossible to live? Write with your hands and feet, and [you will see] it is possible." (*Satirikon* 13 [1908]. International Institute of Social History, Amsterdam)

Russian people happy, if not the whole world. But once I had acquired a practical base, I modestly limited the region of my activities to the small neighborhood where my estate is located.... And if you are going to ask me now about my program or my system, then I won't be able to give you an answer. I don't have a program. I fathom all details of life in my small region and I try to relieve and improve its existence."[52]

"Not a Hero" also describes the endeavors of three other characters who dedicate themselves to the enlightenment of the common people. Baklanov is introduced as an author of "populist" fiction, but he sells himself to the popular press, only to be punished with burnout when faced with an impossible deadline. He recovers, however, and retreats from the literary rat race, moving to the countryside with his family.

Less straightforward is the case of Evgeniia Vysotskaia, an attractive and wealthy widow who acknowledges her unwillingness to give up her comfortable life in the capital but tries to relieve her conscience by publishing and disseminating edifying reading matter. In what is probably the most crucial dialogue in the whole story, Racheev urges her to stop her dilettante activities and use her beauty and social respectability instead to advance the same cause with more success: "There is work to be done in each and every place, all corners crave for light."[53] Eventually, Vysotskaia learns to appreciate that she can be more effective promoting progressive ideas in the highest circles of St. Petersburg than by toiling in the Russian countryside, which she does not understand.

A third character looking for an opportunity to serve the people is Kalymov, a professional and dedicated publisher who hesitates to supply the country population with his modern and sophisticated primers because of his own unfamiliarity with the rural reader. It is only after Racheev has agreed to serve as an adviser that he considers the enterprise sufficiently well prepared to go ahead with it. Thus, Kalymov's case is yet another example of an educated person who contributes his mite not by rushing into the countryside but by applying his talents and expertise in his own environment.

Abram Reitblat has characterized "Not a Hero" as a "novel of literary bankruptcy," a genre that reflected the intelligentsia's anxiety over the growing popularity of cheap popular fiction and the ensuing marginalization of the "serious" writer at the turn of the century.[54] Baklanov's fate and the novel's extensive deliberations on the literary climate certainly lend support to such a reading. Yet, if we confine ourselves to a more straightforward interpretation that seeks to do justice to the story's purported message, then it becomes clear that Potapenko tried to depict the "middle" type of *intelligent* as Abramov envisioned him. This "middle type" did not have to possess any extraordinary qualities in order to be useful to society and was even entitled to a personal life (Racheev himself is a happily married father). Therefore, the title "Not a Hero" is equally appropriate for Vysotskaia and Kalymov (who can be said to represent the establishment) as for the "true" populist Racheev.

Did any of Potapenko's supposedly mediocre characters attain the stature of an epoch-making hero? Obviously not. Their names were quickly forgotten, even if Potapenko remained active as a writer in the 1900s. Still, for some time, the name of Obnovlenskii did pop up in reviews and other critical writing that reproduced the inevitable listing of Russian literature's most typical heroes. In 1891 the critic Dmitrii Strunin contended that "the type of Obnovlenskii has so firmly impressed itself on the minds of the readers that it can easily stand on an equal footing with the classical types of Russian literature, such as Onegin, Chatskii, Pechorin, Rudin, Bazarov, Insarov, Levin, Oblomov, and a few others."[55] Statements like these are extremely rare, however, demonstrating that the name of Obnovlenskii never really caught on and that, while the search continued, Bazarov remained the last character to be canonized as a "hero of our time."

The Character Analogy

It is unknown whether Abramov, or one of the other theoreticians behind the theory of small deeds, was impressed with the positive "non-heroes" in Potapenko's work, but he discovered a worthy role model in what he regarded as the "positive characters" of Anton Chekhov, particularly in Dr. Astrov, one of the main figures in the play *Uncle Vania* (*Diadia Vania* [1899]). An overworked and currish alcoholic, Astrov does not immediately command sympathy from the viewer but, in Abramov's eyes, it was precisely the combination of his idealism and his human shortcomings that made him such a plausible figure. Despite his rudeness and bad temper, Astrov is a dedicated physician who also tries to improve life in his district by fighting deforestation.[56]

Abramov's attempt to "save" Astrov (as Dmitrii Pisarev had once saved Bazarov) convinced very few people. To the influential Marxist critic Vatslav Vorovskii, Astrov was just one of Chekhov's proverbially disillusioned heroes whose pedigree ultimately led back to the superfluous men of the 1840s. Chekhov's heroes, Vorovskii argued, were mere epigones of these "heroic" superfluous men who had once played a historic role in Russian society but now had nothing more to offer.[57] What Abramov regarded as a new and effective "middle" type of *intelligent*, was in Vorovskii's eyes a watered-down version of a historical type that was rapidly disappearing: "New times require new people. And they will come, . . . proudly challenging fate à la Bazarov with his zest for action."[58]

What is remarkable, if not surprising, about Vorovskii's almost bellicose conclusion, drawn amid the chaotic events of 1905, is the mythic aura with which the 1860s are invested. Even if history can never really repeat itself, according to Marxist thought, and the superfluous man is believed to have developed, too (or degenerated from "heroically superfluous" to "uselessly superfluous"), the years of the Great Reforms stand apart as a model of truly revolutionary times. Other historical periods are evaluated in accordance with the extent to which they approximate this model. In effect, the fictional representatives of these various periods tend to fall into two classes: they are either "new people," like Bazarov, or they are not, in which case they display some kind of superfluity.[59] Abramov's posing of the alternative type of *intelligent*, the nonheroic toiler, was an attempt to avoid the rigorous dichotomy of new and superfluous people, but the fictional portraits of this third type were either quickly grouped in the latter category (Astrov) or else simply ignored (Potapenko's nonheroes).

Given his Marxist convictions, the rigor with which Vorovskii discarded Astrov as a devalued type from the past may not come as a complete surprise. Apparently willing to work under the restraints of the tsarist regime, Astrov (in Vorovskii's view) unwittingly supported the existing order. Yet, Vorovskii was not the only critic to hark back to the binary categories of "romantic" or "pragmatic" and "superfluous" or "new" people. A similar approach pervades the critical writings of Dmitrii Ovsianiko-Kulikovskii, a linguist and literary scholar who is mainly remembered for his study *The History of the Russian Intelligentsia* (1903–14). In this multivolume work, Ovsianiko-Kulikovskii departed from the notion that what Turgenev had termed the conflict between fathers and children was, in fact, a perpetual fight between two psychologically different types—the one more subdued and level-headed (the "new and fresh people," as Ovsianiko-Kulikovskii referred to them), and the other more romantic and exalted ("good people"). Although Ovsianiko-Kulikovskii could not explain, as he admitted himself, why these types succeeded each other every generation, the fact was that they precluded the possibility of their mutual understanding. The continuing dissension between fathers and children did not stem so much from their ideological convictions as from the "fundamental difference in their spiritual organization."[60] As a corollary of this difference, the children always rejected the programs of their fathers, and, in so doing, came to resemble their grandfathers.[61]

Applying this evolutionary model to the last decades of the nineteenth century, Ovsianiko-Kulikovskii was able to draw a parallel between the "men of the 1840s" and the generation of the 1880s. Typical representatives of the latter were three other characters of Chekhov's, Ivanov, Asorin, and Laevskii, who seemed to descend directly from the superfluous men.[62] Although the decade had also seen adumbrations of more uplifting types, the overall picture was one of disillusionment and spiritual paralysis. The 1890s, by contrast, seemed reminiscent of the time of the Great Reforms.[63] The popularization of Nietzsche, the nation's industrial development, and the ensuing growth of a capitalist economy—all this testified to a heightened energy and a thirst for life that Russia had not seen since the 1860s.[64]

What makes Ovsianiko-Kulikovskii's *History of the Russian Intelligentsia* so instructive is that it builds—even more so than Vorovskii's writings—on what I propose to call the device of the "character analogy." Instead of simply positing a parallel between two periods, the device seeks to establish an analogy between two fictional characters (or between a fictional character and a historical personality) that belong to different generations. Thus, Piotr Boborykin's Nietzsche-admirer Kostritsyn is "like Bazarov" thirty years earlier; the populists are spiritually closer to "Ogarev, Herzen and Turgenev than to Pisarev and Bazarov"; the disillusioned village doctor in Veresaev's story "Off the Road" ("Bez dorogi" [1895]) resembles Rudin.[65] Accepting the possibility of a third option (Abramov's middle type of *intelligent* capable of doing simple, honest work) was incompatible with this evolutionary model. It assumed that the uselessly superfluous man of the 1880s would eventually yield to a new kind of Bazarov, which would signal a further stage in the evolution of Russian society. Just as history did not repeat itself, so too the succession of contemporary types, or "heroes of our time," followed a progressive, dialectical pattern.

The device of the character analogy leaves us with a seemingly paradoxical situation. Ovsianiko-Kulikovskii and other late-nineteenth-century critics were relatively successful in identifying typical representatives of the intelligentsia from the "post-Bazarov era." Reviewing Chekhov's play *Ivanov,* Disterlo wondered whether the name of the title character would last in the pedigree of Russia's "heroes of [our] time," but having just seen the play, he was convinced that it was the "most accurate expression of the reigning mood."[66] Obviously, then, the concept of the "hero of our time" proved surprisingly viable, even though the heyday of realism had passed and Russian society had fundamentally changed.

At the same time, critics could only identify these heroes by falling back on the old dichotomy of superfluous and new people, the classical types of which were only too well known (Onegin, Pechorin, Rudin, Bazarov). Discovering new versions of these heroes in the last two decades of the nineteenth century only had the effect of confirming the status of the canonized characters—the names of contemporary superfluous and new people did not take root. Ivanov, let alone Potapenko's positive hero Obnovlenskii, never acquired a truly unassailable position similar to that enjoyed by Rudin or Bazarov. Even if critics temporarily recognized them as the new heroes of our time, they never figured for a longer period in the standard listing of "classical types." As for Abramov's third way—this simply did not fit the dominant paradigm of late nineteenth-century criticism. Despite the promise of a new role model (which in practice was highly successful), the alternative type of *intelligent* was simply overlooked or rejected as another manifestation of social and political superfluity.

It is ironic that, while Vorovskii predicted the emergence of a "new man" challenging fate "à la Bazarov," the only literary character that could lay some claim to this role was received with general suspicion. As I show in the next chapter, Vladimir Sanin does seem to be endowed with all the characteristics that distinguished Ovsianiko-Kulikovskii's "new and fresh people." Moreover, the eagerness with which critics juxtaposed Sanin to Bazarov indicates that the device of the character analogy was an important instrument, even in early twentieth-century criticism, and that the canon of epoch-making heroes remained hermetically sealed.

At the beginning of the twentieth century, then, the concept of the contemporary type was still seen as providing a medium through which social change and the role of the Russian intelligentsia in particular could be approached. Even if highbrow realism was increasingly marginalized by the growing output of cheap popular fiction and, to a lesser extent, by the advent of modernist literature, there still was a widely shared belief that it was literature's task to signal and depict today's heroes, thus keeping the reader abreast of the latest social and intellectual tendencies in society. *Sanin* certainly conformed to this concept, even if many perceived it as a break with the most venerated traditions of Russian literature.

2

Sanin
A Hero of Our Time?

On Sunday morning, January 9, 1905, a massive crowd of demonstrators from various parts of St. Petersburg set off in the direction of the Winter Palace with the aim of presenting the tsar with a petition. The document contained far-reaching economic and political demands, but they were formulated as a humble request in which the tsar was respectfully addressed as the "father." To demonstrate their peaceful intentions, the marchers carried icons, portraits of the tsar, and a large banner urging the soldiers not to open fire. As an ultimate deterrent, women and children were placed in the front ranks of the procession. Despite these signals of appeasement, the crowd would never reach its destination. At Narva Gate and other places in the city, soldiers were quick to open fire on the demonstrators, leaving two hundred people dead and eight hundred wounded.[1]

"Bloody Sunday" marked the beginning of what later became known as the Revolution of 1905. It sparked a wave of strikes, demonstrations, mutinies, and riots that would cripple the country for nearly two years. The famous October manifesto, which initially provided for a considerable extension of the franchise and granted freedom of speech, was welcomed with elation but did not stop the more radical factions from continuing to oppose the regime. Violence sprang up in the countryside as well, where looting became common. The turbulence did not subside until 1907, when Prime Minister Stolypin's repressive measures began to prove successful. By August 1907 it was clear that order had been restored and that the revolution was over.

This brief summary of the main events of Russia's "failed" revolution is essential to an understanding of why *Sanin* was considered such a topical novel and its protagonist a new "hero of our time." While the various factions across the political spectrum disagreed as to the deeper meaning of the "Saninist" mentality, many of them agreed that the events of 1905–7 were instrumental in producing it. To elucidate the nexus between the political events and the perceived mentality that Artsybashev's hero came to embody, I begin with a detailed account of the novel's publication history and the implications this history proved to have for its reception as a "reactionary" text (intervention by the censor is discussed in chapter 4). After a brief excursion into the generic specificity of the tendentious novel, I continue the discussion of "superfluous men" and "heroes of our time" from chapter 1, paying close attention to the writings of critics who relied on the device of the literary analogy. The name that stands out, particularly in this connection, is that of Turgenev's fictitious character Evgenii Bazarov. Subsequently, I turn to observers who did not believe Saninism to be a vestige of the 1860s but, on the contrary, saw Artsybashev's hero as a typical representative of the "new" capitalist Russia that Stolypin was trying to create. An analysis of Zinaida Hippius's "anti-Saninist" novel *A Devil's Doll* concludes this chapter.

Concentrating mainly on the reactions of the literary establishment (writers of highbrow literature, critics publishing in the prestigious "thick" journals), this chapter argues that, for all the variety of interpretations that were put forward, there was also a common tendency to cast Vladimir Sanin in the role of social or political Other. Allegedly a mouthpiece for an entire generation, Sanin was never "claimed" by any group as its main figurehead. This leaves us with a paradox: "Saninism" was supposedly rampant among the intelligentsia but the Saninist himself was hardly ever heard. The embeddedness of the Saninist's voice in the disapproving discourse of his critics is a peculiarity overlooked by many commentators and scholars.

Publication and First Reactions

The period following the events of 1905–7, which virtually lasted until the collapse of the monarchy in 1917, has often been referred to as the "stagnant years" (*bezvremen'e*) or the "years of reaction." Qualifications such as these articulate the frustration of those, such as the Bolshevists and the Socialist-Revolutionaries, who had placed their hopes on the immediate elimination of the tsarist regime. And yet, for all the tendentiousness of these labels, the very reality of a political reaction cannot be denied. Even if the tsar had technically ceased to be an autocrat by granting parliament legislative functions, he was highly reluctant to accept the new reality and had no qualms about dissolving the first two elected Dumas (1906 and 1907). In the summer of 1907 Prime Minister Stolypin had the election law changed, excluding large numbers of voters who had previously participated. This as well as a number of additional measures intended to discourage even eligible voters from registering for the elections of the third Duma in October sealed the fate of the political reforms of 1905. Although Russia now had a multiparty system and the press enjoyed considerably more freedom, there was a widespread feeling among the intelligentsia that Russia had come full circle and that the political struggle had been in vain.[2]

Placing the political developments of 1907 alongside the months in which Artsybashev's novel was published, we begin to understand how, in the perception of the public, the two became intertwined. *Sanin* was serialized in the monthly *Sovremennyi mir* from January through May 1907, but then its last installment wasn't published until September of that year. The cause of this four-month gap was probably police interference. In a personal letter to the writer Anastasiia Krandievskaia, Artsybashev explained that the delay was caused by, among other things, his detention by the Yalta police and confiscation of the manuscript.[3] This is also the official explanation given by *Sovremennyi mir* in the combined issue of July and August: "The end of M. P. Artsybashev's novel "Sanin" cannot be published due to confiscation of the manuscript during a search of the writer's house."[4] As a consequence of the delay, the serialization of *Sanin* was spread over the first nine rather than six months of 1907, and during the four-month gap between the publication of the penultimate and final installment, Russia's political landscape changed radically. Ironically, while the publication of *Sanin* had been made possible by the abolition of prepublication censorship (one of the reforms that was not reversed), the simultaneity of its serialization and Stolypin's coup d'état was perceived as anything but fortuitous.

There is little we know for sure about the reception of the novel in its uncompleted form, that is, in the course of its serialization. According to Aleksandr Blok, who devoted a few favorable lines to *Sanin* in a literary overview of 1907, the novel immediately met with sharp disapproval.[5] One critic concluded, after only one installment, that *Sanin* "introduced into literature the beginnings of complete and absolute anarchy."[6] In light of the temporary confiscation of the manuscript and Artsybashev's suspicion that the Yalta police acted on some sensational reports in the boulevard press, it seems likely that early criticism of *Sanin* was directed primarily against its allegedly pornographic content.

It was only after the serialization was completed in the fall of 1907 and *Sanin* was published separately in two editions of ten thousand copies each that the novel began to arouse the ideological controversy for which it is remembered.[7] Condemned for condoning political defeatism and for encouraging sexual license, no book expressed the spirit of the times better than *Sanin* in the eyes of the critics. In a symptomatic statement, the critic Vladimir Votsianovskii argued that whereas not too long ago Sanin's philosophy of life would have been rejected as philistinism, under the present circumstances he was admired for it.[8]

Artsybashev himself protested against the tendency to reduce *Sanin* to a political statement on postrevolutionary Russia, claiming that he had completed the novel as early as 1903.[9] Yet this defense made little impression on his reviewers. The well-known critic Piotr Pil'skii, a vehement polemicist of leftist persuasions, pointed out that even if the novel had been written before the events of 1905, it was not published until 1907. This could not be mere coincidence, Pil'skii insisted, and did not in any way exonerate the author.[10] The populist Iakov Danilin reminded his readers of Artsybashev's initial intention to make Iurii Svarozhich the main character of the novel.[11] According to Danilin, the decision to redirect the work's focus from Svarozhich, a current revolutionary, to Sanin, a former revolutionary, and to portray the latter as vastly superior to all other characters could have been reached only in light of the events of 1905–7.[12] According to a more conservative critic, Artsybashev's "merry hooligan" was the legitimate son of the Russian revolution, the logical result of its degeneration. Sanin was, above all, a disappointed revolutionary.[13] Thus Artsybashev's attempts to defend his novel against a narrowly political reading seemed only to incriminate him further.

Sanin and the Tendentious Novel of the "New People"

The canon of epoch-making heroes seemed to have exhausted itself, as we have seen, with Turgenev's nihilist, Evgenii Bazarov. Whether this development was explained by the growing role of the masses, the repression of exceptional individuals by the state, or a consciously "nonheroic" political agenda advanced by proponents of the theory of small deeds, Russian literature appeared to have run out of monumental and truly inspiring characters, foreshadowing the direction in which society was moving. At the same time, writers and critics continued to conceive of literary characters as "types" who, as representatives of a specific generation, embodied a certain mood or ideological orientation. Except for those opinion makers who believed that the time of strong and lonely individuals as agents of social change was over, critics remained on the lookout for signs announcing the arrival of a new hero or "positive type." Vatslav Vorovskii, for example, the Marxist critic who regarded Chekhov's characters as mere epigones of the superfluous men of the 1840s, was confident that a new time was about to arrive that would bring with it new people proudly challenging fate, as Bazarov had once done.[14]

Although Artsybashev eventually acquired the reputation of a pessimistic writer obsessed with death and suicide, he must have shared some of the optimism that Vorovskii and other enemies of the existing order were expressing in the early 1900s. The conspicuous idealization of his hero makes it clear that Artsybashev, too, was looking for the "new man" whose appearance would, it was believed, usher in a new historic era. Artsybashev repeated this idea in the press on several occasions, saying that Sanin was indeed to be understood as a "type," a type that "in its pure form was still new and rare" but whose spirit nevertheless could be found "in every frank, bold and strong representative of the new Russia."[15] Steeped in the principles and rhetoric of nineteenth-century realist criticism, Artsybashev consciously drew on a literary tradition that was rapidly becoming obsolete but that continued to inform the purview of many a critic.

In its plot development and polemical intent, *Sanin* is clearly patterned on the "tendentious" novel that examined the ideological clash between the idealists of the 1840s and the nihilists of the 1860s. A member of the radical intelligentsia enters an "alien" community such as a family, an estate managed by "liberals," or, in the case of Sanin, his hometown that the hero has not visited for many years. The hero's appearance has a profound effect on the lives of the community members. Some are shocked by his unconventional behavior; others are fascinated by his ideas. In some cases, the protagonist has a love affair with a high-minded young woman who is chafing to escape her oppressive environment. At the end of the story, the hero disappears again, his eventual fate depending on the author's political stance. In the antinihilistic novel, in which radicals are attacked, he usually dies (Turgenev's *Fathers and Children*, Dostoevsky's *The Possessed* [*Besy* (1871–72)]) or suffers defeat in some other way. In more sympathetic works, however, the so-called stories about new people, the hero convincingly debunks the outdated ideas of the older generation or successfully puts his own ideas into practice. Examples of the latter sort are Chernyshevsky's *What Is to Be Done?*, Vasilii Sleptsov's "Hard Times" ("Trudnoe vremia" [1865]), and, to mention a later exponent, Ignatii Potapenko's story "Not a Hero."[16]

Sanin recalls the leftist subgenre of the tendentious novel, the stories about new people. The hero's hedonistic philosophy is presented as a refreshingly new, viable ideology, whereas the value systems of the other characters appear both dated and untenable. Functionally speaking, then, Sanin is only an instrument designed to demonstrate the superiority of a higher truth. His unpretentious enjoyment of life is clearly presented as an example to all. Paradoxically, just as the populist Racheev in Potapenko's novel "Not a Hero," Artsybashev's seemingly ordinary protagonist acquires something truly heroic in his capacity as a lonely trailblazer. One of the first representatives of the "new" type that was only just emerging, he is capable of evoking our admiration.

In stories about the new people, a distinctive feature of the hero is his uncompromising willingness to question uncontested truths and their ensuing norms of behavior. The new man's worldview posits a fundamental dichotomy between "reality as such" and the conventions and superstitions that tradition has imposed on it. To debunk the "conventional lies of civilized mankind," as Piotr Kropotkin formulated it in his *Memoirs of a Revolutionist* (1899), absolute sincerity was required.[17] The radicals of the 1860s were expected to behave in a way that was fully consistent with their convictions and to condemn in all openness the prejudices and petty habits they encountered. It takes little imagination to see how the nihilist imperative of complete frankness also informed the behavior of Artsybashev's new man. Sanin shuns no topic, including those deemed sacred by the radical intelligentsia, and defies the laws of common decency on several occasions as, for example, at the funeral of Iurii Svarozhich, when he publicly calls the deceased a fool.[18]

In the 1860s, according to Kropotkin's account, the demand for complete sincerity manifested itself, above all, in a critical attitude toward the establishment. Frankness was understood as a mighty weapon with which to expose society's hypocrisy and undermine the authority of those in power. With *Sanin*, the imperative for sincerity acquired an explicitly personal dimension. Not only is Sanin "sincere" about pursuing his own pleasure instead of the common good (a serious deviation from the behavioral norm of revolutionary activism), but, in what was generally seen as one of the most outrageous scenes of the novel, he also consciously violates the taboo of incest by looking at his sister as a potential sexual object. To appreciate how this detail refracts the nihilist demand for sincerity, we need to return to the mythology of the 1860s once more. In my opinion, Sanin's incestuous feelings for his sister are meant as an intentional subversion of the sexual paradigm that dominated radical thought in the nineteenth century.

In its striving for social and spiritual renewal, the radical intelligentsia of the 1860s placed special emphasis on the need to reform the relationship between the sexes. Women should participate in all spheres of social life, and men ought to treat them as comrades rather than as sexual objects or as the idealized creatures of some higher order. Some authors even speculated that the future equality of the sexes would somehow diminish or neutralize their physical differences. In Chernyshevsky's vision of the Crystal Palace, for example, women are dressed in "very light and loose-fitting" attire, while the men wear "long, wide tunics without waists, like cloaks or togas."[19] Though still dressed somewhat differently from each other, Chernyshevsky's new men and women wear clothes that tend to conceal the shape of the body rather than accentuate it.

The apparent *in*equality of men and women in nineteenth-century Russia made many radicals ambivalent about erotic love and the degree to which sexual relationships could be pursued in an imperfect society. The behavioral ideal that Chernyshevsky had helped to establish obliged the socially conscious *intelligent* to marry a girl from the commonalty and then give up his legitimate rights as a husband so as to help his wife gain independence. Though sex was regarded as a normal physiological need, its satisfaction was problematic given the fictitious character of such a marriage. The ideal relationship between husband and wife—at least in theory—would, it was believed, resemble that between brother and sister and be founded on equality, mutual respect, and "pure" noncarnal affection.

In *What Is to Be Done?* the relationship between the heroine and her first husband is explicitly compared to that of siblings in several scenes.[20] Although Lopukhov is in love with Vera Pavlovna, he watches her with a "look more pure than that of a brother watching his sister."[21]

In Aleksandr Kuprin's pessimistic novel *The Pit* (*Iama* [1909–15]), which describes a similar yet unsuccessful experiment, the student Likhonin sees himself as a "father and a brother" to Liuba, a prostitute whom he is determined to save and educate. When he has sex with her after all, he apologizes for his "weakness," assuring her that he wants to see her not as a mistress but as a "friend, a sister, a comrade."[22] Having just violated the principles he is supposed to uphold, Likhonin quickly recovers by reaffirming the politically correct brother-sister model.

In a grotesque way, the erotically charged scene between Sanin and his sister is meant to convey a similar message. It exposes the superficiality of the brother-sister model by hinting at the opposite extreme of unconsummated love: sexual desire between siblings. In so doing, Artsybashev casts doubt on the sincerity of those radicals, such as Iurii Svarozhich or Kuprin's Likhonin, who claim to consider all women "sisters" and thereby deny their own physical needs. The new nihilist Vladimir Sanin not only debunks such old-fashioned conventions as respectability (by not pursuing a career) or male honor (by refusing to fight a duel); he also exposes the typical behavior of the male intellectual as lacking in sincerity.[23]

As we are about to see, *Sanin* proved a confusing novel to the majority of critics. Drawing on the "leftist" subgenre of the stories of the new people, the novel simultaneously took issue with the political ideals and behavioral norms usually associated with it. Was *Sanin* therefore a "reactionary" novel or did it, in an unexpected way, continue to disseminate the revolutionary ethos of "progressive" realist literature? Finally, how should the figure of Vladimir Sanin be interpreted? The various answers to these questions, offered by Artsybashev's contemporaries, are taken up in the remainder of this chapter.

The Character Analogy: Legacy of the 1860s?

In keeping with the interpretative practice described in chapter 1, the majority of critics immediately recognized Vladimir Sanin as a new type. The progressive nature of this type was open to debate, however. Did Sanin really announce the coming of a new age, or did he merely express the cynical "live-for-the-moment" mentality of postrevolutionary Russia that would disappear again once history resumed its natural "progressive" course? The answer to this question is not straightforward, but it is clear that Artsybashev's hero was generally seen as the most convincing portrait of the contemporary *intelligent* after 1905. There were other characters in Russian fiction who embodied this mood, it was conceded, but none possessed the typicality that distinguished Vladimir Sanin.[24] Hence, it became possible to speak of the "Sanin-type" (*tip sanintsa*) in Russian literature, which critics discovered in the work of a number of other authors, such as Zinaida Hippius, Volodymyr Vynnychenko, Vikentii Veresaev, Boris Savinkov, and Nikolai Timkovskii.[25]

Once Sanin was established as a specific contemporary type, commentators were quick to trace his genealogy to the well-known superfluous or "new" men of nineteenth-century literature. As one critic put it, in typical fashion, "Sanin is just as much a hero of his time as Pechorin or Bazarov. In him we find the light and darkness of a new direction."[26] The well-known reactionary critic Viktor Burenin called Sanin a "hero of our time" and even a "villainous Pechorin."[27] This logic was so self-evident to many of Artsybashev's contemporaries that even a reactionary scribbler like Count Amori labeled Sanin a "hero of his time" in the introduction to his sequel to *Sanin*, *Sanin's Return* (*Vozvrashchenie Sanina* [1914])—a purely commercial rip-off. Count Amori also repeated the standard listing of earlier "heroes" in Russian literature, mentioning Chatskii, Pechorin, and Onegin, only to conclude that "unfortunately, every intellectual is a bit like Sanin, and that is a fact" (for a discussion of this sequel see chapter 3).[28]

This tendency to assess Sanin's social significance from a diachronic perspective by comparing him to other fictional characters can also be detected in a confidential report of the St. Petersburg Committee on Press Affairs that drew specific attention to the novel's "radical" slant. According to the anonymous author of the report, *Sanin* was as successful as it was because it depicted with "merciless objectivity" a new type of nihilist that had only just emerged in Russia. Artsybashev was simply the chronicler of contemporary radicalism, which was having such a devastating effect on the educated youth. Characteristically, the censor found the most persuasive argument for reading the novel in this manner not in social reality, but in the classics of Russian literature. Sanin's apparent kinship with other well-known nihilists, he suggested, meant people like him probably did exist: "For someone who does not associate with our revolutionary environment it is difficult to tell to what extent one can encounter Sanins in real life. However, there are reasons to assume that Mr. Artsybashev did not make up this type but copied it from nature, because Sanin is definitely related to our old nihilists (such as Rakhmet'ev [sic], Bazarov, Mark Volokhov, and others) and is a further development of this type."[29]

This passage is remarkable for no less than three reasons. First, it reveals the persuasiveness of the character analogy (or analogy in literature) as a means for understanding contemporary reality and the types that were supposed to inhabit it. Instead of judging *Sanin*'s significance directly against the background of recent events, the censor takes a heuristic detour by comparing it, above all, with earlier novels. Only then does he venture to speculate on the likelihood of encountering such types in real life. Second, it shows how thin the line between fiction and reality sometimes was. Although the concept of "contemporary type" was originally a discursive construct designed to identify particular social and political phenomena, it also came to be understood as a measure of reality rather than just as a generalized portrait of a generation. As Peter Pozefsky has remarked with respect to the time of the Great Reforms, "just as radicals looked to novels to better understand themselves, so officials sometimes found in the abundant images of radicals in literature the most accessible evidence of a nihilist threat and drew conclusions from them."[30] Finally, the fact that the censor completely disregards the authors' ideological stance in the debate on nihilism, grouping together the positive hero Rakhmetov,[31] Turgenev's more ambiguous protagonist, Bazarov, and the truly negative nihilist Mark Volokhov (in Ivan Goncharov's novel *The Precipice* [*Obryv* (1869)]), is indicative of a persistent inclination among commentators on both sides of the political divide to assign Sanin to the opposite camp, that is, to regard him as the champion of the political or social Other. In this case, the enemy is the "radical on the left," who has been a threat to the existing order for more than fifty years.

If the censor shared with professional (and predominantly leftist) critics a tendency to establish *Sanin*'s significance through literary analogies, he differed from them in that he confined himself to comparing it to the tendentious novel of the 1860s and to the nihilists or "new people" appearing in it. In the censor's opinion, Sanin was not so much a new type as a further development of a type that already existed. Academic as the matter may appear at first sight, the notion of Sanin's seeming newness also led other observers to interpret his individualism in a more timeless key as a form of unabashed rapacity, if not pure villainy. There was nothing new about Sanin, these commentators claimed; the circumstances of postrevolutionary Russia were simply more favorable to him. One critic argued that lascivious men like Sanin were a "fact of life" and that, consequently, every woman was likely to run into one at some point in time. What was new about Vladimir Sanin was the fact that he sought to justify his behavior with an elaborate philosophy: "Artsybashev has created [for all those "ordinary" Sanins] Sanin the moralist [*Sanina-rezonera*] and has developed in him a philosophy of sexual license and vice."[32] What characterized the nation's social climate, then, was not the egotism but the lack of any considerable counterforce fighting it.[33]

When we turn to the counterliterature that *Sanin* provoked, we will see more of this urge to "decontextualize" the novel's perceived message and to refashion the hero into a timeless scoundrel. In general, however, the image that dominated the debate on *Sanin* was that of the postrevolutionary "hero of our time."

Sanin and Bazarov

Among the earlier historical types usually listed in articles on *Sanin*, the name that stood out in particular was that of Turgenev's charismatic rebel-hero, the nihilist Evgenii Bazarov. A mere glance at his and Sanin's physical and psychological traits is sufficient to explain why.[34] Sanin and Bazarov share an impressive physique and a casual but self-assured demeanor. Both have a way with ordinary people, although they belong to the intelligentsia. There is also a certain rigor about them that makes them both frightening and sympathetic at the same time. As one critic noted: "If you take a good look at Sanin's features and you remove the make-up [then you'll see that] he is a reproduction of Bazarov."[35] The prominent Menshevik Fiodor Dan made a similar observation: "A comparison [between Sanin and Bazarov] is all the more justified as Sanin himself is in many respects a copy, or, if you like, a caricature of the famous 'nihilist.'"[36]

When comparing *Sanin* with *Fathers and Children*, critics generally raised two questions. First, what was the true nature of Sanin's nihilism, and how should it be assessed (as "progressive" or "reactionary"?) in the political context of postrevolutionary Russia? Second, was the emergence of "Saninism" in keeping with the tradition of the radical intelligentsia, or did it signal a dramatic departure from it? Precisely because the image of Bazarov as an undaunted revolutionary represented the most sacred ideals of the radicals, the striking similarities between Turgenev's hero and Sanin presented a problem that was too serious to be ignored.

Attempting to play down Sanin's social and historical significance, the Marxist critic Vatslav Vorovskii argued against the notion that Artsybashev had depicted an existing type. Sanin was clearly idealized by his creator, Vorovskii believed; he was a "product of the author's fantasy." Bazarov, by contrast, was "drawn directly from nature" and contained the features of a "real social type."[37] As this juxtaposition threatened to undercut the very point he was trying to make, Vorovskii then contended that Artsybashev's nihilist was also based on a real phenomenon—the current escapist mood of the Russian intelligentsia. Since Sanin exemplified that mood in its most outspoken and characteristic form, he too, in addition to "real social types," provided the critic with "rewarding material."[38]

But other than that Bazarov was a "living historic personality" and Sanin was not, what was the difference between the two nihilists? Here Vorovskii pointed to Bazarov's zest for hard work and thirst for knowledge, which stood in sharp contrast with Sanin's shallow enjoyment of life. If Bazarov's individualism was not only understandable, given his spiritual isolation in mid-nineteenth-century Russia, but even productive because it served the common good, then Sanin's individualistic comportment verged on pure egotism. All in all, his mentality signified the rejection of the intelligentsia's most revered ideals: service to the people in social life and the "duty imperative" in one's personal life.[39]

In his bulky study *The Pornographic Element in Russian Literature*, another Marxist critic, Grigorii Novopolin, also acknowledged that Sanin and Bazarov had a good deal in common. He went so far as to point out the philosophical similarities in their respective worldviews. Sanin's shocking remark that "my life consists of pleasant and unpleasant sensations" was certainly reminiscent of Bazarov's pronouncement that "there are no principles, only sensations."[40] But, Novopolin insisted, on closer inspection, Sanin turned out to be nothing more than a vulgarized look-alike of Bazarov. True enough—though Bazarov also had an appetite for the fairer sex, he could only love an intelligent woman, not any woman, as Sanin apparently could.[41]

Across the political divide, the philosopher Semion Frank reached an entirely different conclusion in his essay "The Ethics of Nihilism." Included in the notorious volume *Signposts* (1909), in which a number of prominent opinion makers (often ex-Marxists) attacked the left-wing intelligentsia for its political bigotry and strict adherence to positivistic materialism, the essay argued that Saninism was firmly rooted in the legacy of the 1860s. The egotistic hedonism of the present generation did not break with the spirit of Bazarov. On the contrary, it was its logical extension. In Frank's view, the present crisis exposed the ideological bankruptcy of the radical intelligentsia, which was now confronted with the ultimate consequences of a worldview bereft of moral principles.[42] Like the censor, Frank was convinced that Sanin and Bazarov were kindred spirits.

The Wager on the Strong

Critics of leftist persuasions often linked Sanin's individualism to the economic reforms introduced by Stolypin in the aftermath of the revolution of 1905. The idealization of a hero pursuing his own desires, even at the expense of his fellow human beings, was seen as symptomatic of the rapacity that Stolypin's encouragement of entrepreneurship and economic expansion were supposed to have ignited.

Key among the many ambitious plans Stolypin introduced was his solution to the so-called agrarian question. Broadly, what he hoped to do was to replace the unprofitable communal system of individual homesteads so as to enable the more energetic and enterprising peasants to develop into a class of private proprietors. The government, as Stolypin himself expressed it, "put the wager not on the wretched and the drunk, but on the strong."[43] Though the agrarian reform came into effect in the fall of 1906 with the enactment of three successive ukases, the bill was discussed and amended in the Duma and the State Council during the next three years, receiving the tsar's final signature only in 1911. Thus, the debate on the agrarian problem, one of the most hotly discussed topics in Russian politics, largely coincided with and was often linked to the controversy over *Sanin*.

Pondering the larger significance of Vladimir Sanin as a contemporary type, commentators often resorted to language strikingly similar to that employed in the agrarian debate and sometimes openly referred to Stolypin's reforms. To them, the "wager on the strong" was an appropriately grim motto for postrevolutionary reality, which, in their opinion, witnessed a massive abandonment of revolutionary and communal ideals. Vladimir Kranikhfel'd, who we briefly encountered in the introduction, expressed this view in its most typical form. After a brief overview of the nation's social climate and its celebration of private initiative, the critic immediately proceeded to discuss *Sanin,* which he considered the "most outstanding literary work over the last years": "Sanin is an incontestable fact of our life. You can hate him, you can have a burning desire to throw him down the stairs at the first possible opportunity, but you cannot deny him, because he is a natural and necessary product of our epoch that favors the 'strong,' people of 'bold initiative,' as another politician, Count Witte, put it prior to Stolypin."[44] Quoting Piotr Struve, who, in a 1903 article, had called for more individualism and a concern for the "material foundations of life," Kranikhfel'd surmised that what the liberal historian and economist had in mind was exactly the sort of man Sanin represented: "The sun of dawn will shine for the Sanins, because they are the victors of that dawn. They can count on a festive welcome wherever the strong are favored. They are now the 'sought-after' people and it is them, the Sanins, whom Struve must have thought of."[45]

Kranikhfel'd was not the only one to view Sanin as a herald of the new capitalist Russia that was emerging under Stolypin. B. Kaplan, a marginal critic, was struck by the frequent use of the word "strong" in *Sanin* and by the author's incessant praise of the hero's well-developed muscles. According to Kaplan, who identified himself as a Jew and was uncomfortable with Artsybashev's idealization of physical power, the novel's main purpose was to announce the arrival of the "new man" in Russia: the predatory capitalist and bourgeois. Whereas the "strong and egotistical type" was firmly rooted in the United States and Western Europe, it was relatively new in Russia. Judging by the enthusiastic reception of *Sanin* by the intelligentsia—"society's barometer," as Kaplan emphasized—one could tell that the bourgeoisie would soon take over and run the country "in the American way."[46]

Far-fetched as the connection between Sanin's muscular power and the "embourgeoisement" of Russian society may seem, it reveals how even the hero's physical attributes invited politically charged readings of the novel, adding yet another layer to the semiotic density of the contemporary type. Sanin *was* a "new man," Kaplan insisted with ill-concealed sarcasm, because never before in the history of the Russian intelligentsia had egotism and sheer force in the pursuit of one's petty desires played such a prominent role. Sanin's use of physical power in the notorious rape scene with Karsavina was to be understood as a telling illustration of capitalism's "enslavement of women," Kaplan argued; on a more abstract level, it was a metaphor for the violent avarice underlying the bourgeois mentality (chapter 7 explores this linkage of physical power and economic self-reliance in more detail). Another commentator contended that, after 1905, the intelligentsia had broken into two different groups: a democratic and a bourgeois camp. It was the bourgeois intelligentsia that had "immediately understood and appreciated Sanin, had recognized in him their hero, their philosophy, and religion of life."[47]

The emergence of Sanin the "bourgeois" confronted Marxists with a paradox that required some sociohistorical juggling before it could be resolved. Despite his being invested with many exterior characteristics that had distinguished the "true" *homo novus*, Bazarov, Sanin did seem to personify a mentality that was still new in Russia: the egotistical individualism of the bourgeois. In that sense, he could be viewed as a more or less progressive phenomenon. On the other hand, since the bourgeoisie was supposed to be disappearing, according to Marxist theory, it was problematic to welcome the spread of its "rapacious" mentality in Russia as an unambiguously positive development.

Fiodor Dan tried to account for this paradox by first of all juxtaposing Bazarov's "heroic, pure" individualism to Sanin's bourgeois morality of "free competition." Bazarov Dan considered a socially active and therefore productive force; Sanin's individualism, however, was antisocial because it transferred the free-market principle from the economy to the field of social and personal relations.[48] Such individualism distracted from the social struggle and, in effect, would only perpetuate the yoke of the masses.[49] To explain the relative newness of Sanin as a social type, Dan fell back on the traditional argument of Russia's youthfulness. Whereas the European bourgeoisie had been familiar with the morality of free competition for a long time, it appeared fresh and new to men like Sanin, whose appropriation of it immediately rendered it more primitive: "Once again it becomes clear that we are not dealing simply with a European bourgeois in a time of decay, but with a Russian Mitrofan perceiving bourgeois morality for the first time."[50] A rebelling child of bourgeois decadence, Sanin as a social phenomenon in Russia was still young.[51] Despite its barbaric primitiveness and joy of boldness, as Dan characterized it, Sanin's individualism signaled a retrogressive tendency among the intelligentsia that, as it turned out, lacked the stamina to continue the political struggle of previous generations. Instead it had turned away from the masses and devoted itself to its "own bourgeois business." Thus, in Dan's final analysis of the

"Sanin cult," the decadent element dominated the primitive one, leading him to conclude that the revolutionary role of the intelligentsia was ultimately exhausted.

The inclination of these critics to link individualism to the "exploiting avarice" of the bourgeoisie may not come as a complete surprise, especially considering that they were Marxists. Ever since Herzen's scathing criticism of the middle classes in Western Europe, any value system remotely associated with the bourgeoisie had been, by definition, suspect in the eyes of the radical intelligentsia.[52] As we will see in the next section, however, a minority of leftist critics refused to accept Sanin's bourgeois identity as a given. More important still, if the hostility among the educated classes toward the formation of a bourgeoisie was prevalent during the second half of the nineteenth century, the intelligentsia's fear of its *own* embourgoisement became acute only after the revolt of 1905. The expression of this fear can be found in the image of Sanin as a bourgeois—an image clearly informed by Stolypin's "wager on the strong."

Saving Sanin?

Given the many similarities that critics discovered between Sanin and Bazarov, we may wonder whether any attempts were made to save Artsybashev's hero, as Turgenev's charismatic rebel had once been saved by Dmitrii Pisarev. Did not Sanin also possess certain positive traits that could redeem him in the eyes of the critics?

Paradoxically, perhaps, the fact that Sanin seemed to have so much in common with Bazarov made it difficult, if not impossible, to save him. If he really was Bazarov's legitimate successor, then the values that he challenged would have to be as rotten as those against which Bazarov had rebelled. But, since Sanin's provocative behavior was directed as much against traditional sexual morality as against the ideals and social conventions of the radical intelligentsia, accepting Sanin as the "new" Bazarov would discredit the "old" Bazarov and everything he represented. This was unacceptable to critics on the left, who therefore repeatedly stressed that the similarities between the two heroes were merely superficial. A new and refreshing type was about to emerge, but Sanin was a false prophet.

While an overwhelming majority of critics and opinion makers condemned Sanin's deeds or considered his appearance in the historical arena a worrying phenomenon at best, a very small number of dissenting critics did speak out in favor of Artsybashev's hero, albeit not without certain reservations. In general, what these critics valued about Sanin was his revolt against the morality of the establishment rather than the philosophy of life that he offered in exchange.

One such dissenting voice in the leftist camp came from the little-known critic Kol-Oman, who suggested that Vladimir Sanin was the "ideologue of a whole army of intellectual proletarians."[53] Deprived of the financial means required by the capitalist system to marry and start a family, these men and women were exploring alternative forms of sexual relationships and cohabitation based not on economic considerations but on their own preferences for a particular partner. A threat to the traditional bourgeois family, Sanin's philosophy of free love appealed to both men and women, who now had to choose between a marriage of convenience or staying single. As an orthodox Marxist, however, Kol-Oman found fault with Artsybashev for pursuing his ideal of free love at the level of the social superstructure. Family life could only be reformed if the economic basis changed first. Artsybashev had raised an important issue, Kol-Oman concluded, but in order to solve it, he was well advised to devote himself to the creation of a new and just society.[54]

Another minor critic, a certain M. Greidenberg, went even further and welcomed Artsybashev's hero as a radiant specimen of the future man. Society was going through one of the most important turnovers in world history, Greidenberg argued: the transition from a system of oppressive social relations to complete liberty of conscience and enjoyment of life.[55] *Sanin* reflected this development featuring two opposite characters, Svarozhich, who represented the fading past, and Vladimir Sanin, the "impassioned image of the future man who is only just emerging."[56] Greidenberg's remarkable eulogy on *Sanin*—probably the only review to defend every aspect of its purported message—concluded with an enraptured vision of the future "when all will be equal and free, when all people will be brothers and there will be only free labor and free love, and one shrine of total happiness."[57] Though he was only an adumbration of this new man, Sanin was to be considered a progressive force at this stage of human history. Perhaps the best known critic to discover something positive in *Sanin* was Arskii (pseudonym of Nikolai Abramovich), who approved of the novel's life-affirming tendency: "Sanin's truth is enormous. Under it [there is] the strong and mighty foundation of the earth itself."[58]

These reactions stand out from the rest in that they give a positive assessment of some aspect of the hero's personality. Greidenberg accepted Sanin without any reservations. However, the obscurity of the authors and the very sparsity of such optimistic readings confirm the general picture that emerges from the thick journals: whether *Sanin* was seen only as a trendy novel or as an alarming but accurate diagnosis of Russia's postrevolutionary trauma, the hero was almost unanimously condemned and relegated to the camp of the political opponent. Despite the novel's reported popularity, virtually no one spoke out in favor of its main character.

Zinaida Hippius's *A Devil's Doll*

As I have argued, *Sanin* continued the tradition of the stories about the new people in contradictory fashion. The hero's superiority to the other characters evokes the impression that the author condones his actions and is determined to present him as a new and truly positive type. But the ideas that are put forward seem at odds with those of the radical intelligentsia, as a result of which the "revolutionary" worldview is discredited. *Sanin* thus combines features of the "leftist" stories about the new people and elements of the "reactionary" antinihilist novel, a genre that attracted the likes of Dostoevsky, Pisemskii, and Leskov.[59]

Given the wave of critical reactions that *Sanin* elicited, writing a fictional countertext designed to disparage the novel's perceived message may seem a superfluous enterprise.[60] Yet with so many critics and readers being convinced of its pernicious influence, the need to warn and enlighten the unsuspecting public was widely and acutely felt. Chapter 3 is devoted to the numerous countertexts, sequels, and parodies that were written in reaction to *Sanin*, texts that allow us to reexperience some of the outrage that was felt beyond the literary establishment. For now, I confine myself to discussing one countertext of a highly accomplished author who used the genre of the antinihilist novel in order to expose the dangers of the Saninist mentality, if not of the novel itself. Zinaida Hippius's *A Devil's Doll* (*Chertova kukla* [1911]) is therefore not about the "new man" (an originally Christian concept that she valued very much) but about his impostor: the "contemporary hero of nonexistence" (*sovremennyi geroi nebytiia*), as she called him.

It is a matter of common agreement that *A Devil's Doll* was the product of Hippius's preoccupation with the figure of the revolutionary and of her friendship with the terrorist Boris Savinkov—a prominent member of the militant organization of the Socialist-Revolutionary Party and one of the masterminds behind the assassination of the Grand Duke Sergei Aleksandrovich in 1906. During the years 1906-8, when they were living in Paris, Hippius and her husband Dmitrii Merezhkovskii discussed politics and religion with Savinkov, hoping to win his support for what they referred to as the "Cause": the creation of a new religious consciousness prompted by a spiritual revolution. When Savinkov's autobiographical novel *The Pale Horse* (*Kon' blednyi*), a fictional diary that draws heavily on apocalyptic symbolism, was published in 1909, some critics suspected that the stated author, a certain V. Ropshin, was just another of Hippius's pseudonyms.[61] Conversely, *A Devil's Doll*, published two years later, was generally regarded as a tame rehash of *The Pale Horse*, flawed by the author's apparent unfamiliarity with the revolutionary milieu.[62]

The Savinkov connection does not exhaust the significance of *A Devil's Doll*, however, and I think there are good reasons for reading it as a venomous reaction against everything that *Sanin* represented in Hippius's eyes. Although some critics regarded the protagonist, Iurii Dvoekurov, as a "hero of our time" and even explicitly compared him to Vladimir Sanin, it is worth noting that, as a literary critic, Hippius repeatedly attacked Artsybashev for his style and what she saw as the spiritual aridity of his work.[63] Moreover, Hippius voiced her most devastating critique of Artsybashev's prose—including *Sanin*—in an article published under the pseudonym Anton Krainii in the fall of 1910 when work on *A Devil's Doll* was still in progress.[64] Clearly, *Sanin* must have been on Hippius's mind when she was creating the title character "Iurulia" (Iurii) Dvoekurov.

That *A Devil's Doll* was intended as a sort of "antiportrait" of the contemporary type also follows from the comments Hippius made directly after the novel was serialized in *Russkaia mysl'* (*Russian Thought*). In the introduction to the book edition, she emphasized that her novel was "not about the revolution," as her readers might be tempted to think, but "about the reaction."[65] Her objective had been to lay bare the deeply rooted regressive forces in Russian society by depicting them in concentrated form in one person—the "contemporary hero of nonexistence." To illustrate his spiritual ossification, Hippius produced a sort of political credo that this hero was likely to support. In it, we can easily recognize the "escapist" spirit that Sanin was believed to embody: crude materialism, sexual license, and a willful disregard for more serious and lofty matters: "'What do I believe in?'—this is the mocking question posed by almost every single letter of the thousands received in reply to opinion polls that attempt to sound out the ideological and religious mood among our contemporaries. 'What do I believe in?' I believe in rose-colored cheeks, in a girl's bosom, in youth, and in life, as long as I live.... Thinking about death is a disease, though there are all sorts of moods. With our dear dreamers and idealists I would simply shake hands and, perhaps, have a cup of tea with them."⁶⁶ Though perhaps not a countertext in the strictest sense of the word, *A Devil's Doll* is certainly designed to discredit the sort of mentality that many contemporaries associated with Artsybashev's novel.

Set in various locations and in different social milieus, *A Devil's Doll* is constructed—like *Sanin*—around its title character, the handsome student and nobleman Iurii Dvoekurov. A former revolutionary, he now pursues a career as a scientist, finding more "enjoyment" in chemistry than in the political struggle or in philosophy—the subject he studied when he enrolled at university. Iurii's apparent dislike of questions about the meaning of life and his impatience with people tormented by such questions do not prevent his surroundings from loving and even admiring him. Handsome, eloquent, and oozing self-confidence, he enjoys the undivided sympathy of his meddling grandmother, his grumpy father, his relatives, and his many acquaintances, who all confide in him as an expert in the art of living. With his good looks and silver tongue, Iurii is also popular with the commonalty. Posing as a shop assistant, he smoothly seduces the kitchen maid, Masha, and takes special delight in kissing her at the postern where it "smells of heavy, cold cats."⁶⁷

With this carefree attitude toward life, Iurii makes a remarkable figure among his former comrades, who are desperately trying to come to terms with the failure of the revolution of 1905. Whereas he enjoys himself with Masha or swiftly traverses St. Petersburg on his bicycle (a signifier of his irresponsible frivolity), they try to keep a low profile hiding in Paris or in ramshackle dachas.⁶⁸ Iurii is nonetheless willing to help his friends, provided it does not interfere with his frivolous pleasures. Whenever the occasion arises, however, he lectures them on their inability to take care of themselves and simply enjoy life. Thus Mikhail Rzhevskii, a searching soul and Iurii's counterpart in every respect, is a "prisoner" of his ideals, refusing to acknowledge that he has lost faith in the revolution. Equally unhappy is Knorr, a gloomy fellow student who is hopelessly in love with Khesia, one of Iurii's many one-night stands.

Though Iurii claims not to "preach" anything, like Sanin he is an ideologue with an outspoken philosophy and a corresponding model of behavior. At a literary evening at which the participants discuss "The Verdict," an excerpt from Dostoevsky's *Diary of a Writer* (*Dnevnik pistelia* [1876]) based on an authentic suicide note, Iurii steps forward and takes issue with the victim for arriving at her fatal decision. Man is a selfish creature, Iurii concedes, being interested only in his own welfare. Yet the acknowledgment of this sober truth is not a reason to kill oneself, as Dostoevsky's suicide believes; rather, it should be an incentive to stop worrying about the salvation of mankind and find enjoyment in life. Iurii explains: "I'm striving for happiness, enjoyment, pleasure, amusement, while trying to harm and trouble other people as little as possible. I wish everyone what he wishes for himself, but let him obtain that on his own. . . . I live by my own truth, that is, without worrying about others, without trying to find the meaning of life, without love, without particular fear; I'm only pursuing my own happiness and I'm constantly successful in finding it."[69]

At first sight, it may seem that Iurii's egotistical individualism is less ruthless than Sanin's. If the latter insists that man satisfy his natural desires, even if they happen to be evil, Hippius's hero adds a restriction that stipulates that one should try not to harm others. Yet the difference between the two positions turns out to be marginal. Since harming *oneself* is the worst thing a man can do, according to Iurii, one should not have scruples about letting one's own interest prevail over those of others. In practice, this is indeed the only maxim that Iurii respects. His moral "rule about the minimization of harm done to others" does not prevent him from getting Masha pregnant, as a result of which she loses her job.

There are more parallels between Iurii Dvoekurov and Sanin that serve to expose the former's treacherous charm. Though Sanin is more instinctive than Iurii, who, on the contrary, emphasizes the need for moderation, for both men the pursuit of happiness is an entirely conscious and rational endeavor. The literary evening at which Iurii elucidates his worldview clearly echoes chapter 32 of Artsybashev's novel in which Sanin, Ivanov, and Svarozhich discuss the meaning of life. Like Iurii Dvoekurov, who deduces the value of life from its "meaninglessness," that is, accepts the meaningless of life as an incentive to embrace life, Sanin formulates his philosophy by dint of a negative argumentation. To Svarozhich's question, "Why go on living?" he replies with a simple counterquestion: "Why die?"[70] Convinced that life may be just as well enjoyed if it lacks some higher meaning, both Dvoekurov and Sanin argue for the adoption of a "new" attitude consciously directed at the realization of one's own happiness.[71]

Underlying Dvoekurov's "conscious" hedonism, like Sanin's, is the assumption of its universal validity. The wisdom of not seeking the meaning of life but simply indulging in the pleasures it offers is accessible to everyone, Iurii believes, and will eventually become common knowledge: "With time all this will become clear and will be understood correctly. After all I have understood it—others will too."[72] With this presumptuous prediction, Iurii becomes a pastiche of the "new man"—a tag with which other characters actually label him a few times though, significantly, without being really convinced themselves. Hippius makes sure to have her most tormented and noble characters reject the idea of Iurii's "newness" and expose him as what he really is: an "uninteresting student" and a "devil's doll." The deceptive image of Iurii Dvoekurov as a more advanced type of man already familiar with the sensual bliss of the future can therefore be interpreted as a mocking allusion to the figure of Vladimir Sanin who likewise "dreams of a better time," when man can devote himself to "all attainable forms of enjoyment."[73]

As in the countertexts to be examined in the next chapter, it is the story's denouement that entirely discredits the hero and his shallow *savoir vivre*. When Khesia is arrested and dies in prison, an agent provocateur deludes a devastated Knorr into believing that Iurii has denounced her in exchange for his own release (Iurii is briefly detained for his previous dealings with the revolutionary movement). Sick with grief, Knorr takes revenge by shooting Iurii, thus putting an appropriately absurd end to what Hippius wants us to view as a meaningless and wasted life. Even more significant is the fate of the child whom Iurii has begotten with Masha. In the final chapter, we learn that little Yegorushka was born and died without his father ever knowing he existed—a telling detail symbolizing Iurii's spiritual void and the destructive nature of his actions. Of course, this is exactly what makes the difference between Sanin and Dvoekurov: if the former "merely" functions as a catalyst confronting the other characters with the ultimate consequences of their worldview, then the latter's relentless pursuit of pleasure actually ruins other people's lives.

Although Iurii's violent death would seem to be the clearest possible indication that Hippius censors her hero's superficial lifestyle, some critics were unsure about the true intentions behind *A Devil's Doll*. In one of the first reviews, published when the novel was not fully serialized, A. Red'ko surmised that Iurii was intended as a positive figure, a man of "spiritual harmony."[74] When the novel was completed and had appeared in book form, neither the story's ending nor Hippius's own elucidatory introduction could convince the critic that she actually loathed her protagonist. In the novel, this loathing was blatantly absent, Red'ko maintained.[75] In an article entitled "Sanin's successors," Elena Koltonovskaia praised Hippius for her perceptive analysis of the new postrevolutionary mentality. The hero's sober worldview, his sincerity, his honesty (*spravedlivost'*) with himself and others, his "consciousness"—all these traits were indeed characteristic of the younger generation. At the same time, Koltonovskaia assumed that Hippius had attempted to unite these traits into a "new symbol of faith," that is, as a model for emulation. As such, Iurii Dvoekurov was not convincing, Koltonovskaia concluded.[76]

A more penetrating, though highly critical, reaction came from the prominent Socialist-Revolutionary Viktor Chernov, who also had his doubts about Hippius's attitude toward her hero. In a lengthy essay, he argued that she had failed to unmask Iurii Dvoekurov, as she had intended to, and had inadvertently begun to feel sympathy for him: "She simply wanted to be objective about him, but then this objectivism turned into an apology."[77] As a result, Hippius had created a character that was an enemy and an ally at the same time: a "devil's doll," whose vulgar materialism the author abhorred, but also an "example of spiritual completeness" (*tselostnost'*), a man who had managed to bridge the gap between theory and practice.[78] In that dual capacity, Iurii had come to play a productive role in the novel, Chernov pointed out, allowing Hippius to prove her case *ad contrarium*. Confronted with the inner harmony of this reactionary and nonbelieving bon vivant, doleful revolutionaries such as Mikhail and his sister Natasha were encouraged to understand the revolution like Hippius herself understood it: not merely as a sociopolitical event but also as a metaphysical and religious experience. Only by imparting a religious meaning to his actions would Mikhail be able to attain the true and pure "completeness" that Dvoekurov possessed in a distorted form.[79]

With his suggestion of an ambiguous alliance between Hippius and her protagonist, Chernov seems to have been one of the very few critics to anticipate that Dvoekurov's death marked the beginning of a new story—a story in which the "true" revolutionary Mikhail recovers his faith and acts in the name of God and Jesus Christ. His introduction to the "three-fraternity," a cohabiting trio of wise but ineffective men (a scarcely disguised reference to the collective of Merezhkovskii, Dmitrii Filosofov, and Hippius herself), marks the first step in his spiritual rejuvenation. This process is completed in *Roman Tsarevich* (*Roman-czarevich* [1912]), the sequel to *A Devil's Doll*. In this novel, the "contemporary hero of nonexistence" recurs once more as Roman Smentsev, the cynical and power-mad leader of a revolutionary-religious movement who comes to meet an equally nasty end as Iurii Dvoekurov. The future belongs to the truly God-fearing revolutionary Mikhail and his friends for whom there is "no more loneliness, no fear."[80] Probably because of this optimistic end, Hippius abandoned her original idea of writing a third novel that, Temira Pachmuss conjectures, "was to portray the perfect merging of love, faith, truth, revolution, and ecumenity [*sobornost'*] among the Russian revolutionaries."[81]

Given the initial scope of Hippius's undertaking, it would be naive to suggest that she was driven primarily by a desire to expose the banefulness of the "Saninist" mentality. Hippius herself certainly would have considered that to be too much honor for an author like Artsybashev. And yet, it is striking that what should have developed into a trilogy with an uplifting and religiously charged finale eventually became a diptych on the reactionary "hero of nonexistence." Not unlike Gogol, who would never finish his trilogy, *Dead Souls* (*Mertvye dushi* [1842]), Hippius found it easier to allude to her characters' spiritual perfection in the future than to depict it already fully realized. Even Litta Dvoekurova, Iurii's idealistic and high-minded younger sister who helps Mikhail to recover his faith, plays a secondary role, serving as a "foil for the hero," as Hippius pointed out in the introduction.[82] In view of the author's intentional focus on the "hero of nonexistence," then, the above comparison between *A Devil's Doll* and *Sanin* seems to me both legitimate and productive. Hippius's novel deconstructs Artsybashev's narrative of proud individualism and self-determination by showing the "real" destructive nature of a life bereft of higher moral principles.

A Trendy Novel?

Not everyone was so concerned over the Saninist type as Hippius. A handful of commentators dismissed Saninism as nothing more than a fleeting fashion and *Sanin* simply as a "trendy" novel: "The fashion will pass and *Sanin* will be assigned a modest place. People will forget about it."[83] Yet this emphasis on the novel's trendiness begged the question of why people proved so receptive to it and what its success signified. To answer this question, a reference to the "fleetingness" of modern life was often sufficient. Musing on modern man's inability to process the deluge of impressions and sensations that surround him, a character in Piotr Olenin's play *The Bacchante* (*Vakkhanka* [1912]) complains that "now everything is accepted without scrutiny.... Nietzsche, Kautsky, the decadents ... Nat Pinkerton, Sanin, ... and whatever else you have."[84] This seemingly random list of fashionable thinkers and literary heroes reduces Sanin from a "hero of his time" to a perishable pop icon who will be replaced by something equally shallow.

At the beginning of the second decade of the twentieth century, when the commotion surrounding *Sanin* had considerably subsided, this explanation became increasingly attractive. Saninism began to be perceived as "yesterday's hype," a mere example of the many short-lived infatuations that Russia had gone through since the turbulent events of 1905. Alarmed by the sudden and "abnormal" popularity of sport and outdoor recreation, one commentator wrote: "We have amused ourselves with Sanin and *saninstvo,* with mysticism, with Andrei Bely, even with Nat Pinkerton and Isadora Duncan, and with a lot of other things.... The newest trend ... is sport."[85] Looking back at the different stages through which the student community had passed, in 1917 student leader Boris Frommett remembered how, in the years 1907-8, one part of educated youth had been under the spell of "trendy Saninism."[86] Eventually, Saninism was reduced to one of the various forms in which the supposed shallowness of intellectual and political life during the postrevolutionary years found expression. Thus *Sanin* functioned as a framework for the intelligentsia so long as it sought to come to terms with its own disappointment with the revolution of 1905.

3

Counterliterature
The Search for Poetic Justice

Among the many reasons for which critics and readers found fault with Artsybashev, one of the most important was his decision to end the novel with the sudden departure of his hero. Sanin leaves his hometown as unexpectedly as he arrived, even deliberately avoiding a last encounter with his family. After two suicides and one rape, this denouement was perceived as highly unsatisfactory, for it implied, in the eyes of critics and readers alike, that Sanin's "immoral" behavior remained unpunished. Worse yet, the novel's very last sentence describing Sanin "striding forth to meet the sun" emphatically suggested that the author approved of his hero's conduct and had presented him as an example worthy of imitation.

Where was Sanin heading? What would his future look like? These were the questions with which many of Artsybashev's critics struggled in an attempt to establish his significance as a hero of his time. Judging by Sanin's self-confidence and insouciant mood in the closing scene, there seems little reason to assume that the events in his hometown have affected his views on life. Yet it is precisely this suggestion of ideological continuity that critics and readers deemed unacceptable and even implausible. One commentator maintained that the image of Sanin walking toward the sun was nothing but a pretentious symbol testifying to the author's inability to point the direction in which his hero was developing as both an individual and a social type.[1] The Marxist critic Vasilii L'vov-Rogachevskii attached great significance to the fact that Sanin boarded a train in the final chapter and "was on the move again." In his opinion, the journey metaphorically represented the birth of a new identity that would surely emerge in the near future.[2]

The symbolic potential of Sanin's sudden departure was so rich that it inspired a considerable amount of "counterliterature"—fictional works intended to serve as clear parallels to the original yet also seeking to debunk its ideas.[3] Though the number of texts seriously taking issue with *Sanin* is rather small, especially when compared to the number of parodies and slapdash adaptations for the stage, the total output of works that attacked, ridiculed, exploited, or otherwise referred to *Sanin* is impressive, specifically when considering that the texts I discuss here are, in all probability, merely the tip of the iceberg.

This chapter begins with a brief overview of a number of alternative endings that were proposed for the novel and other light-hearted material, some of which was never published. Subsequently, the discussion focuses on two "countertexts" that pretend to pursue a more serious agenda. Intended for entirely different audiences with different tastes, these texts also employ divergent narrative and rhetorical strategies to convey their messages. Whether or not we choose to regard *Sanin* as middlebrow or "boulevard" literature, these countertexts reveal that its resonance extended well beyond the boundaries of one particular class of readers. The final section centers on the reception of Artsybashev's second large novel, *At the Last Frontier*, particularly on the widely held view that it somehow "completed" the story of *Sanin* and marked the end of Artsybashev's career as a writer.

Adaptations, Satires, and Mock Sequels

As I stated, not all countertexts that *Sanin* provoked seriously attempted to convince the reader of its pernicious nature. Some authors simply made fun of the novel and its purported message of sexual freedom. Others may have sensed an opportunity to make a profit by exploiting Artsybashev's success. The archives of the St. Petersburg State Theater Library contain at least seven manuscripts of adaptations for the stage that do not betray a polemical or even satirical intent. Though the authors proved highly eclectic in selecting their material, some leaving out the rape scene with Karsavina, others ignoring Iurii Svarozhich's suicide, they never ventured beyond the closing scene in an attempt to show what happened (or *should* have happened) to Sanin after his departure from his native town. For the most part, these amateur playwrights appear to have been keen on preserving Sanin's heroic stature and suggesting that his actions are morally justified. The following stage direction from a play by an unknown author entitled *Sanin: Scenes from the Novel*, which is intended to render the infamous deflowering scene, clearly follows the novel, insisting that Karsavina consents to having sex with Sanin: "Powerfully Sanin lays her [Karsavina] down on the bench. The boat drifts behind a small island. A long silence. After a while the boat reappears. Karsavina sits on Sanin's lap, the boat drifts along with the stream."[4]

Unfortunately for the authors of these plays, the censorship reform of 1905, which gave such a boost to the country's publishing industry, did not apply to the theater. The authorities continued to view the stage with considerable suspicion and proved particularly strict in the provinces. Plays that had been approved for St. Petersburg or Moscow might be declared unfit for performance in Perm or Kherson.[5] In view of these unfavorable circumstances and the ban on the novel itself, it is hardly surprising that none of the adaptations of *Sanin* ever made it to the stage. Submitted mostly in 1908, they were all rejected by the censor the same year.[6]

Whereas the authors of these dramatizations took a neutral or even favorable stand toward the original, others did criticize Artsybashev, for example, for surrounding his hero with intellectual midgets incapable of exposing the immorality and inconsistency of his ideas. The impression of Sanin's superiority was misleading, these critics argued, and incompatible with realist aesthetics: "If a writer wants to be a realist, he cannot deviate from reality [*zhizni*] even for a single moment, yet in reality 'positive' people do not exist. . . . This is why Sanin is not convincing."[7] In order to deglamorize Sanin and reduce him to his true and "all-too-human" proportions, some readers wrote alternative endings featuring Sanin (or Artsybashev himself) in various embarrassing situations. Instead of his usual display of eloquence, we now see Sanin fumbling for words and being arrested by the police. Or he jumps off of a train again (as in the closing scene of the original), only this time he breaks his neck.[8] In a rather coarse comedy entitled *Sanin: A Farce in Three Acts with Quatrains*, which is replete with risqué jokes and salty songs, Karsavina's father forces Sanin to marry his daughter, thereby thwarting the hero's plans to run off with his own sister and live with her as "man and wife." Sanin's last words express the full irony of his own domestication: "What will Artsybashev say when he finds out

Counterliterature 79

> Изъ романа
> извѣстнаго писателя М. Арцыбашева
> „САНИНЪ"
> Эфектная пьеса
> **КАКЪ ЖИТЬ?!..**
> Пьеса въ 5 дѣйствіяхъ. Сюжетъ заимствов.
> изъ романа извѣстнаго писателя М. Арцыбашева "Санинъ"
> С. Трефиловъ и О. Ефимова.
> Дѣйствіе 1. Богатые люди. Два года люб...
> Въ паутинѣ жизни.
> Дѣйствіе 2. Роковое увлеченіе. Страсть не
> имѣетъ разсудка. Позоръ.
> Дѣйствіе 3. Самоубійство. Развязка романа.
> Спасеніе.
> Дѣйствіе 4. Паденіе. На пути къ счастью.
> Возрожденіе.
> Дѣйствіе 5. Кровавая расправа. Дуэль.
> Убійство.

Handwritten front page of theater adaptation of *Sanin* entitled *How to Live?* (St. Petersburg Library of Theatrical Art)

they forced me to marry—me, proud, free Sanin, who boldly grasped pleasure whenever he encountered it?"[9]

Another way of ridiculing the novel was to have its characters openly resent their own conduct and turn the tables on their creator. In one satire, for example, Lida comes rushing into Artsybashev's study, just as the author is undressing. The next moment, Sanin enters and complains that his actions in the story are not sufficiently motivated.[10] Aleksandr Amfiteatrov published a "letter to the editor," signed by Sanin, in which the latter points out a number of "inaccuracies" in the way in which he and his sister Lida are portrayed and then criticizes his creator for his notoriously poor style.[11]

Attempts to discredit Sanin's philosophy of life by poking fun at the author extended even beyond the boundaries of literature. In a sense,

Artsybashev's personal life, in particular his poor health, became a countertext in itself. Contemporaries often noted with a certain bewilderment (or relief) that the author of *Sanin* had little in common with his hero.[12] According to one correspondent, the surroundings of Artsybashev's residence in the Ukraine were exactly like the setting of the novel, and yet the author himself was the "most moral and ideal family man of all contemporary writers."[13] Another journalist reported that Artsybashev was constantly harassed by people who wanted to meet him in person, expecting to see some kind of living Sanin. "We can safely say, however, that every single one of these curious people would encounter a completely different person than he had expected."[14] Scrutinizing these observations, Beth Holmgren coins the phrase "second-glance redemption" to designate the tactics by which some critics sought to establish the "real" man behind the author of *Sanin* and thus to affirm their own authority as "discriminating critics." Not only did the "mad pornographer" Artsybashev turn out to be more sane and decent than most readers expected, but, despite the succès de scandale it was now enjoying, the novel possessed some undeniable virtues that would become apparent over the course of time.[15]

If these comments were not intended to ridicule Artsybashev but simply to note the "surprising" differences between him and his literary hero, then Vasilii Rozanov exploited this incongruity to expose Artsybashev's ideas as untenable. Startled to learn that Sanin's creator was not an "athlete, a centaur," but a "shy, quiet, and nondescript" figure, Rozanov was immediately reminded of Tolstoy's story "The Death of Ivan Il'ich" ("Smert' Ivana Il'icha" [1886]) in which the title character recognizes the rings under his son's eyes as the undeniable symptoms of onanism.[16] The herald of a "new" and supposedly more "natural" sexual morality, in reality Artsybashev turned out to be a tormented masturbator. An even more venomous interpretation of Artsybashev's "un-Saninistic" features came from the writer Skitalets, who would later recall that Artsybashev "had always wanted to look like Sanin but had never succeeded in doing so."[17] "His somewhat strange, democratic exterior with a perceptible physical deficiency presumably made little impression on the luxurious women of the Sanin-type, whom Artsybashev invariably paraded in his work and to whom he tried to reach out in life, but he was never successful and for this reason he revenged himself on them in his novels, stories, and plays."[18] In Skitalets's opinion, then, the sexual frustration that had prompted Artsybashev to write *Sanin* also took the edge off the novel's purported message.

What these reactions and the mock sequels have in common is that they focus on the lack of verisimilitude in the depiction of Sanin's behavior and thereby criticize the novel as a work of art. Other countertexts express genuine concern over the consequences of Sanin's philosophy when it is put into practice. Unlike the alternative endings, which simply make fun of the protagonist, these "serious" countertexts take the position that Artsybashev's novel does not tell the "whole" story and, consequently, needs substantial corrections. Not surprisingly, these texts are much longer than the mock sequels, because they clearly seek to instruct or even shock the reader by showing the full implications of Sanin's ideas.

Sanin, Mr. Artsybashev, and Woman: Ruin of a *Saninistka*

Presented in the introduction as the authentic diary of a female admirer, the anonymous story *Sanin, Mr. Artsybashev, and Woman* (*Sanin, g. Artsybashev i zhenshchina* [1908]) charts the process of a *kursistka*'s moral degeneration caused by her reading of Nietzsche and Artsybashev. The text totals twenty-two entries running from early spring until mid-August when the manuscript suddenly breaks off. Rumor has it that the author has poisoned herself, the editor explains, though some of her acquaintances maintain that she has died in a clinic for the treatment of venereal disease. Whatever the case, "Sanin's admirers die a terrible death," the editor concludes at the end of the introduction, thus lending the *kursistka*'s fragmented story a sense of closure.[19]

From the outset, the heroine appears endowed with all the characteristics that distinguish the potential *saninistka*. Coquettish and naive, she studies medicine without much dedication while detesting her politically correct classmates who keep harping about the revolution and the need for self-sacrifice. Such being her attitude to life, she is easy prey for the students Kornilov and Kruglov, who soon acquaint her with the works of Nietzsche and Artsybashev. Two weeks after Kornilov has started courting her, she loses her virginity; a few days later, she sleeps with Kruglov. She then deludes herself into believing that her licentious behavior is a sign of her growing consciousness, the ultimate confirmation of which she finds in *Sanin*—the "God to whom we all should bow."[20] Considering herself now fully enlightened, she surrounds herself with dissipated men and unashamedly takes part in their sprees.

This merry life abruptly ends when the *kursistka* returns to her parents for the summer break. To her alarm, she notices that her beauty is fading—a change she attributes to the absence of "strong sensations" in the provinces rather than to her bohemian lifestyle in the city. When it comes to light that she is pregnant, her father repudiates her, leaving her virtually penniless, and some of her former friends now pretend not to know her. As the last entry reveals, however, the *kursistka*'s desperate situation has not affected her views on Sanin. Living in a shabby hotel, she continues to consider herself a "true and faithful admirer."[21]

It is not difficult to identify the male students in this story as inveterate debauchers who rave about *Sanin* so as to seduce the heroine more successfully. To them, the novel is merely a means to an end. The *kursistka*, on the other hand, is the only true believer, as she sincerely adopts the principle of free love and affectionately calls her heroes Artsybashka and Saninek. Recalling Sanin's casual advice to his pregnant sister, Lida, she too stoically considers having an abortion. In short: the men are fully accountable but do not have to face the consequences of their deeds, whereas the heroine is victimized by the "voice of the animal instinct that calls woman into slavery to satisfy the whims of men."[22]

Elaborating on what he believes to be the reasons behind *Sanin*'s popularity, the author paints a similar picture of male "consciousness" and female "naïveté" in the introduction. In providing a portrait of the novel's audience, he intends merely to illustrate the massive interest in Artsybashev's novel, but the seemingly random fashion in which he lists readers of various ages and social groups is dictated by a distinct gender hierarchy: "Our entire youth reads this story and is captured by it, from the already fully formed *intelligent* to the working class girl or the second- or third-grade *gimnazistka*. In one library I happened to notice eleven- to twelve-year-old girls, their satchels in their hands, who instead of going to school came here to read *Sanin*."[23]

By positioning the "fully formed" male *intelligent* and twelve-year-old schoolgirls at opposite sides of Artsybashev's audience, the author implicitly characterizes the female reader as "naive" and "immature." As the diary is supposed to illustrate, such readers are particularly vulnerable to the delusions that Saninism encompasses.

Sanin, Mr. Artsybashev, and Woman suffered the same fate as the novel that it sought to debunk. Though the censor appreciated the author's noble intentions, he deemed the heroine's "cynical attitude toward her deflowering" and her "loose relations with students" an offense to public decency and therefore ordered the confiscation of the entire printing. Even the absence of "naturalistic" descriptions (the word "bosom" is never mentioned) and the heroine's tragic end, which imparts to the story some kind of poetic justice, could not mollify the censor. In spite of its edifying character, the story seemed to acknowledge the existence of sexual desire in women and, for this reason, was considered unacceptable.[24]

Count Amori's *Sanin's Return*

The mock sequels were based on the idea that Artsybashev's story was willfully one sided and incomplete. The authors either speculated on what *could* have happened to Sanin and his philosophy had he been surrounded by slightly less mediocre characters or they poked fun at the author by subjecting him to the same kind of voyeurism to which he subjected his female characters. The melodramatic sequel *Sanin's Return* (*Vozvrashchenie Sanina* [1914]) by Count Amori differs from these countertexts in that it seriously purports to show what *should* have happened to the hero in order to satisfy the reader's sense of poetic justice. Instead of suggesting alternative, more realistic plotlines that would reduce Sanin's Promethean stature and simultaneously undercut the premises of his teachings, Count Amori set out to describe the *only* outcome he deemed acceptable from a moral point of view. The following words, taken from the afterword to *The Finale* (*Final* [1914]), another of his infamous sequels to a scandalous work, also applies to *Sanin's Return*: "I have developed *my* idea, *my* answer to the question put forward by the author, and I feel the need to share *my* opinion with the Russian reader."[25]

Naive and pretentious as this may sound, Count Amori was by no means an uneducated man. Under his real name, Ippolit Rapgof, he enjoyed a considerable reputation as a music teacher and critic. He had even coheaded one of St. Petersburg's most prestigious piano courses in the 1880s. Following a disagreement with his brother and business associate in 1888, he embarked upon a new career, the course of which would be determined mainly by a number of technological and highly marketable novelties. Rapgof successfully promoted the gramophone in Russia, worked as an interviewer for the boulevard daily, *Peterburgskii listok* (*Petersburg Paper*), translated various popular books on sexuality, and eventually produced more than twenty screenplays for Russia's budding film industry.[26]

This remarkable ability to exploit anything new and fashionable strongly suggests that Rapgof's literary career, too, was sparked by the prospect of making a fast ruble. A closer look at the fictional works published under his pseudonym adds to the suspicion that his literary interest was almost exclusively commercial. Not unlike the tabloids for which he once worked, Count Amori's writings betray a clear predilection for the scandalous and the sensational and, in particular, a prurient interest in the alleged moral decline of the intelligentsia after 1905. His rambling and incoherent style, the inconsistent portrayal of his characters, the editions of ten thousand copies or more, and finally the price range of his novels (from five kopecks to a ruble or more) are further indications that he stood outside the literary establishment.[27]

And yet, this did not prevent Count Amori from writing highly moralistic novels that pretended to offer more than just entertainment. Just like the authors and critics of highbrow realism, he was anxious to enlighten his readers and to warn them about the new "hero of our time." This social engagement itself was not unique to Count Amori as an exponent of boulevard literature. Anastasiia Verbitskaia, for example, whose commercial success was symptomatic of the changing literary culture in fin-de-siècle Russia, took her social obligations as a writer very seriously. As Yuri Tsivian has pointed out, Russian mass culture distinguished itself from its Western counterpart by consciously seeking out appropriate themes and attitudes usually associated with "high" culture.[28] In *Sanin's Return*, this orientation to serious art has two dimensions: it manifests itself in the work's didactic pathos and, more specifically, in the hero's search for moral purification.

The moralistic intent of *Sanin's Return* is already clearly expressed in the introduction. According to Count Amori, Artsybashev himself was anxious to bring about some moral catharsis in his hero but did not succeed because of a certain duality in his psyche. On the one hand, Artsybashev is a "doctrinarian" (*doktriner*), Count Amori argues, who, like so many of his contemporaries, is obsessed with sexual issues.[29] He is also, however, a "talented author" whose descriptions of nature are a "delight to every reader." If Sanin's pernicious ideas reflect Artsybashev the "doctrinarian," then the story's peculiar open ending is an ethical correction of those ideas dictated by the author's artistic talent.[30] The reason that Sanin suddenly leaves his hometown is not because he is "bored" with his family and the revolutionaries (although he believes that himself) but because he can no longer face the consequences of his hideous deeds: "During his short stay in his parental house, after a sustained period of absence, Sanin has created such a mess, has ruined so many lives, that, having no desire to face the consequences, of course, he flees. There is a lot of truth in this. Sanin turns out to have a conscience after all. He becomes aware of his guilt, although he boasts of putting evil on the pedestal of the ideal."[31] Thus, Sanin cannot persevere in his ruthless hedonism, and so he begins to change toward the end of the novel. The artist in Artsybashev would have developed this idea, if his other half, the doctrinarian, had not prevented him from doing so. Torn between these two poles in him, Artsybashev could only allude to Sanin's spiritual crisis by having him abruptly leave his hometown and thereby end the story.[32] Artsybashev, then, was on the right track, but "had not finished his idea" (*ne zakonchil svoei mysli*). Count Amori was keen on doing that for him, merely "following the path already outlined by the author."[33]

In the beginning of *Sanin's Return*, the hero still appears to be the self-assured athlete from the original. He finds a job at the estate of an aristocratic family, where his strength soon attracts the attention of the local girls and, in particular, of Marusia, the daughter of the house. Sanin seduces her and, when she becomes pregnant, flees to Moscow, leaving her behind in despair. Later he reads in the newspaper that his victim has committed suicide.

In Moscow, Sanin is arrested on suspicion of revolutionary activities and sentenced to five years of forced labor in Siberia. So far, Sanin had been able to suppress a nagging feeling of guilt, caused by Marusia's suicide, but, in exile, with his health rapidly deteriorating, he begins to feel remorse over the role he has played in other people's lives. He also comes to understand that his hostility toward Zarudin did not spring from the laudable wish to protect his sister but from the fact that he was in love with her himself (Sanin dreams about Zarudin being *him*). This becomes clear when Lida arrives in Siberia and begins taking care of her brother. Not only are the two "inseparable" but their "relationship displays a tenderness that is rarely seen between siblings." In addition, the narrator stresses that, in the eyes of the local population, they are a "handsome couple" and that their intimacy engenders the "wildest rumors."[34] So, while refraining from any suggestive descriptions, Count Amori went further than Artsybashev, who only hinted at the possibility of an incestuous relationship between Sanin and his sister.

Sanin's happiness is short lived, however. Tormented by remorse over her relationship with her brother, Lida retires to a monastery, determined to do penance. A letter to her mother, in which she confesses her sins, produces a dramatic boomerang effect. Maria Ivanovna dies upon learning the horrible truth about her children, and the news about her death is too much for Lida. So, in addition to the two suicides in the original, Sanin is also responsible for Marusia's suicide and the deaths of his own mother and sister.

At the end of the story Sanin faces a bitter truth. Glancing through Lida's diary, he learns that although she did indulge her carnal passions with him, she never really loved her brother. In her heart, she always stayed true to Zarudin. Posthumously rejected by his own sister and deprived of any support from family or friends, Sanin reaches the end of his tether. The climax of the scene features Zarudin's ghost appearing to Sanin, who, nearly driven to insanity, prepares to hang himself. At the very last moment, the ghost of his mother intervenes, reaching out as though to stop him. Sanin falls on his knees, embraces the Christian faith, and eventually returns to the Ukraine.

Interrupted by completely irrelevant conversations, endless digressions on such topics as the degeneration of the European race and the glory of Russia, *Sanin's Return* often seems to forget its own claim to be a sequel to an existing novel. Its haphazard character abundantly testifies to the haste with which it must have been written and confirms the commercial nature of Count Amori's work. There is, however, some clumsy poetic justice in having Sanin repent and turn into a pious Christian. Though the story is too chaotic to discredit the hero's ideology successfully (at least to the taste of a more sophisticated reader), its specific moral logic makes such a discrediting somehow redundant. While claiming to respond to what is essentially a "tendentious" novel grounded in the tradition of social and didactic realism, the sequel is certainly not tendentious itself, at least not in the specific sense of the term. In my view, *Sanin's Return* should be read as a melodramatic adaptation of the original on the grounds that it relies on a completely different set of generic demands and ethical assumptions. That it does so can be seen, first and foremost, in its rejection of the device of the protagonist as a contemporary type, in the way it completely eliminates his "typicality."

In chapter 2, I showed how Sanin, as a historical personality, could be linked to a whole group of "types," each of which was believed to mark a specific stage in the ongoing conflict between society and the individual (that is, the Westernized intellectual). Sanin not only descended from Bazarov but, by implication, also from Rudin and from the romantic heroes Pechorin and Chatskii. Each historical period produced its own "hero of our time," and Sanin was the contemporary version of it.³⁵ In the introduction to *Sanin's Return*, Count Amori did not hesitate to repeat this whole argument, including the standard listing of Sanin's precursors, and concluded by saying that "unfortunately every intellectual is a bit like Sanin, and that is a fact."³⁶ Evidently, Count Amori was sufficiently well versed in realist aesthetics to reflect on Sanin as the embodiment of a specific mood in society. Yet, in an attempt to define Sanin's specific features, he singled out two shortcomings that appear to be of a generally human rather than a social-historical nature: "unlimited self-conceit" (*bezgranichnoe samomnenie*) and "injustice" (*nespravedlivost'*). Sanin did not only "think that he was much smarter than everybody else," but throughout the novel he also applies double standards. He grants himself the privilege of seducing women whenever he pleases but denies Zarudin the same right to take advantage of his sister. "Hypocrisy," Count Amori diagnoses, "is a fundamental characteristic of contemporary people."³⁷

In spite of the references to the modern intellectual and other "heroes of our time," Count Amori emphatically ignored the category of "typicality." Sanin's ideas on free love are not presented as part of a coherent (albeit immoral) worldview, typical of a particular social group in a particular historical situation, but as devices, tricks, and ad hoc strategies with which he seeks to fulfill his own petty desires. Whereas Artsybashev portrayed his hero as the bearer of a "new" morality, Count Amori transforms him into a villain whose entire raison d'être is to violate all norms but without revolting against society as such. Count Amori's assurances to the contrary notwithstanding, in the sequel Sanin has lost his social typicality, representing nobody but himself.

This lack of social typicality is characteristic of a number of genres in popular fiction, notably the picaresque novel and its modern form, the boulevard novel. Viewed in even more general terms, one can say that it is a definite feature of all melodramatic literature, ranging from Dostoevsky's novels to modern soap operas.³⁸ Characters appearing in melodramas do have a degree of social identity, of course (after all, in *Sanin's Return*, Sanin is explicitly said to belong to the Russian intelligentsia), but the dramatic situations in which they find themselves have a universal significance that goes beyond class distinctions. Critics immediately connected Sanin's hedonistic philosophy of life to his social background, pointing out that he was an intellectual and a former revolutionary. Count Amori repeated this argument in the introduction, as we have seen. Yet Sanin's actions in the sequel are not shown to be rooted in any class-bound ideology but are rather governed by pure selfishness.

Sanin's overt villainy in the sequel is perhaps the clearest indication that Count Amori is consistently melodramatizing the subject matter of Artsybashev's novel. In keeping with the demand for "poetic justice" typical of melodramatic fiction, *Sanin's Return* refracts the questions raised in the original through a narrowly moralistic prism.[39] In addition to promoting a straightforward ethical message, it also presents a highly personalized vision of evil that locates it in the hero rather than in society.[40] Predictably, Sanin's "friendly smile" (*laskovaia ulybka*)—his hallmark in the original—has suddenly acquired an unmistakably diabolic character. Observations such as "his smile had something Mephisto-like about it" and "a nasty smile disfigured his face" clearly establish him as purely evil.[41] Therefore, instead of debunking Sanin's ideology, as the authors of other countertexts attempted to do, Count Amori does away with Sanin himself by having him spiritually reborn in Siberia.

Poetic justice, then, is of vital importance in *Sanin's Return*. The evildoer is punished and repents the sins he committed in the original. Yet the demand for it is more than the need for a happy ending, a simple "all's well that ends well." As Peter Brooks has shown, melodramatic morality has a distinctively metaphysical dimension.[42] Ethics is felt to be not a matter of convention or rational decision making (a morality based on a "social contract") but one of absolute and eternal truth, the "moral occult." This view of ethics is particularly evident in melodrama's predilection for dreams and similar states of being, a preference it shares, of course, with the gothic novel.[43] Besides adding to the suspense required to enthrall the reader, nightmares and visitations from beyond function as the ultimate medium through which the moral occult reveals itself. Asleep or delirious, the villain is confronted with his terrible past, which he normally is able to suppress.

Dreams and terrifying visions play a significant role in *Sanin's Return*. Not only do they reveal the "genuine" immoral nature of Sanin's actions, both to himself and to the reader, but they also help Lida to return to the straight and narrow after she has committed incest with her brother. Her decision to leave Sanin and to do penance in a monastery immediately follows a dream in which she sees her late father reproachfully pointing to a church in which she herself appears as a nun. Sanin's nightmares, as we have seen, center mostly on Zarudin, for whose death—in Count Amori's vision—he is directly responsible. In addition to enhancing his sense of guilt, the dreams about Zarudin also reveal that, in many respects, the two men are of a kind. When he approaches Zarudin's coffin and glances over the rim, Sanin discovers *himself* lying in state, as Lida stands by in tears.[44]

The dreams set in motion a process of moral purification, but it is not until the dead begin to visit Sanin that his spiritual resurrection takes place. The horror scene featuring the ghosts of Zarudin and Sanin's mother fighting for his soul marks the final crisis from which Sanin eventually emerges as a new man. In this connection, it is interesting to note that *Sanin's Return* follows the same mythic pattern that stands out in far more distinguished novels such as Dostoevsky's *Crime and Punishment* (*Prestuplenie i nakazanie* [1866]) or Tolstoy's *Resurrection* (*Voskresenie* [1899]). Here the hero's moral regeneration also occurs in Siberia, which serves as the functional equivalent of a temporary death.[45]

All in all, Count Amori's sequel voices an optimism that is typical of melodramatic literature. Sanin repents and becomes a new man. Lida atones for her sins in a manner so convincing that she wins the hearts of all the nuns in the monastery. The overall impression is one of justice and moral satisfaction confirming the social and political status quo that the original seemed to challenge. This "reactionary" strand in *Sanin's Return* is another defining feature of melodrama, which does not tolerate the moral ambiguity of realist literature. The sequel thus refurnishes the amoral universe of Artsybashev's novel with the "traditional imperatives of truth and ethics."[46]

And yet in the final analysis, *Sanin's Return* is more than a "timeless" tale of good and evil in which the hero is propelled by universal passions. Considering the novel's lack of social typicality, it is all the more striking that Count Amori stubbornly keeps reminding us that his hero is a representative of the intelligentsia. A comment such as "every intellectual is a bit like Sanin," for example, clearly suggests that the sequel does not purport to tell everybody's story, and this ambition is precisely what makes it such an intriguing text. Its story is specifically about the intelligentsia, but the overwhelming majority of its intended audience must have consisted of nonintellectual readers. In effect, in pirating Artsybashev's plot, Count Amori not only shifts the genre from the "sophisticated" tendentious novel to the "un-sophisticated" form of melodrama but also transforms the rhetoric of the story by introducing a particular social antagonism that is absent in the original. Count Amori certainly did not promise his readers "more pornography" (and if there is any in Sanin, there is absolutely none in the sequel), but he offered them the possibility of freely indulging their moral outrage and feeling good about it because it would be directed at a different social class.[47]

Despite its undeniably commercial character, then, *Sanin's Return* is also a political statement about the Russian intelligentsia and its revolutionary aspirations. By having his hero cast off his old identity and convert to the Christian faith, Count Amori passed judgment on the radical intelligentsia. "Following the path already outlined by the author," Count Amori was able to complete the story, which the doctrinarian in Artsybashev had prevented him from telling, namely that the revolution was a dead end and that Sanin's personal faith proved it.

Beyond Sanin

Contrary to what the authors of countertexts were trying to prove, in Artsybashev's novel, Sanin is, of course, a static character. Whatever discussions he engages in and whatever situations he encounters, they only confirm the soundness of his philosophy. Unlike the other characters, who are forced to revise their views on life, Sanin remains the same throughout the story. And yet, in his conversation with the suicidal Soloveichik, Sanin refers to a period in his life in which he was different and certainly less assertive. When he was still at the university, he considered himself a pupil of the meek Ivan Lande, a math student under whose influence he tried to live by Tolstoy's principle of nonresistance to evil. After having been beaten up by a fellow student, however, Sanin came to understand the "falsity" of the Tolstoyan idea of nonviolence and immediately broke with his teacher.

It was not only this episode in Sanin's life but also Artsybashev's earlier story "The Death of Lande" ("Smert' Lande" [1904]) that critics kept adducing in order to argue that Sanin's spiritual stability was only illusionary. Although Sanin himself does not figure in the story, it can easily be read as a prehistory to Artsybashev's most notorious novel (some characters make an appearance or are referred to in both texts).[48] Moreover, the story contains a gripping scene that is rather similar to the defining moment in Sanin's personal development featuring two characters who, in retrospect, can be regarded as representing the "old" Sanin as Tolstoyan and the "new" Sanin as we know him from the novel.

"The Death of Lande" describes the downfall of the title character, a student whose ascetic lifestyle and extraordinary meekness initially command the respect of his friends but, in the end, evoke only confusion and even contempt. For all his genuine willingness to help his fellow men, Lande remains extremely ineffective. When he is assaulted by Tkachev, a frustrated former disciple of his (like Sanin), he does not resist but immediately complies with Tkachev's demands, including the most humiliating one: to take off his clothes and hand them over. In doing so, Lande acts literally in accordance with the Gospel of Matthew: "But I say unto you, that ye resist not evil: but whosoever shall smite thee on thy right cheek, turn to him the other also. And if any man will sue thee at the law, and take away thy coat, let him have *thy* cloak also."[49] The robbery does not succeed, however, thanks to the interference of muscleman Molochaev (a prefiguration of Sanin), who knocks Tkachev to the ground and thereby "proves" the inferiority of a philosophy based on weakness. To the bystanders, this incident ultimately discredits Lande's ideas about reacting with nonresistance to violence. He remains true to his ideals and, consequently, is not exposed as a fake, but his followers come to reject his doctrine as contradicting the very demands of life.[50]

"The Death of Lande" is an important work in Artsybashev's oeuvre. Although some critics construed Lande as a positive character, it also seems plausible to view the story as an early expression of Artsybashev's life-long fascination with physically and mentally strong heroes.[51] More important, the story marks the beginning of what critics would later recognize as a major narrative that chronicled the hopes and disappointments of the Russian intelligentsia during the first decade of the twentieth century. Within this chronicle, *Sanin* represented only a particular stage; it was a symbol of the many wanderings of "our roaming intelligentsia," as L'vov-Rogachevskii put it. Like many of Chekhov's characters, Artsybashev's hero was constantly "on the road": "The voluntarily poor dreamer and Tolstoyan Lande was only an episode in Sanin's life.... From the Christian ideal of forgiveness and nonresistance he then switched to revolutionary activism.... [In the novel] we engage him for the first time when he returns to his family and dedicates himself to women, changing them even more frequently than his religious and political sympathies. On the last pages of the novel one senses beforehand a change. It is not accidental that Sanin quickly packs his things ... and moves on. He is on the road again—this is a significant fact."[52]

Thus Sanin's personal biography merged with the most recent history of the Russian intelligentsia into a narrative that encompassed the stages of Tolstoyanism (nonviolent resistance), militant activism (the revolution of 1905), "Saninism," and "post-Saninism." But what would this new "post-Saninist" stage in the development of the intelligentsia look like? And did Artsybashev himself give any clues?

Artsybashev published his next and bulkiest novel *At the Last Frontier* (*U poslednei cherty*) in his own almanac, *Zemlia* (*Earth*), between 1910 and 1912.[53] Although it does not feature any characters from *Sanin* and can therefore hardly be considered a sequel to it, the general feeling was that *At the Last Frontier* certainly dovetailed with Artsybashev's scandalous novel and even took things a step further. Moreover, the excruciatingly pessimistic tone of this novel and its almost apocalyptic title left the impression that the author's gloomy spiritual journey had come to an end. Artsybashev himself was the first to suggest that his latest novel was a sort of closing act to *Sanin,* if not to his entire oeuvre. In an interview, he stated that *Sanin* represented the process of life and *At the Last Frontier* the conclusion to that process. "I therefore assume that if Sanin and Naumov [a character in *At the Last Frontier*] met, they would understand each other perfectly well."[54] In a 1912 letter to his friend Evsei Aspiz, Artsybashev used remarkably similar language in describing *At the Last Frontier* as his swan song: "The thing is that my novel *At the Last Frontier* has a specific character: by writing it I have burned my bridges. After its final statements, beyond that very last border, I think it would be strange to write anything else. In this novel I have drawn the conclusions to my outlook on life. Every step in my life convinced me that I was right."[55]

What did Artsybashev's "conclusions" amount to and how do they relate to *Sanin*? It is tempting to speculate that Artsybashev was merely trying somehow to top the *Sanin* scandal or to capitalize on the widely reported "suicide epidemic" that had allegedly struck Russia after the events of 1905–7.[56] Artsybashev certainly had a reputation for being very resourceful in causing public scandals so as to generate free publicity for his work. The writer Sergei Sergeev-Tsenskii describes a meeting with Artsybashev in 1913 at which the latter proudly showed a pile of newspaper clippings detailing his own outrageous behavior upon learning that the theater performance he had wanted to attend in the Crimean town of Balaklava was sold out.[57] According to Evsei Aspiz, around the same time, Artsybashev publicly toyed with the idea of suicide, wondering how this news would be received in the press.[58] There are reasons to assume, however, that, in writing *At the Last Frontier*, Artsybashev was driven by motives other than purely commercial ones and that he did intend it as a further elaboration of the ideas he advanced in *Sanin*. To substantiate this point, let me quote from another letter to Aspiz in which Artsybashev recounts an extraordinary experience he had in 1909. In that year, he received a hysterical letter from a mutual acquaintance, a certain Stoianovskii, who had just been told that he was deadly ill. According to Artsybashev: "This was not a letter but a sheer cry of grief and horror blending into despair. I did not do what the majority of people would have done in my place. I did not try to persuade or comfort him. I wrote him a long, gloomy letter, which I concluded by stating that the only possible attitude toward death is a noncowardly one. I received an unexpectedly quiet and courageous reply that more or less foretold his death, . . . and after this such explosions of despair did not repeat themselves in Stoianovskii's letters. This provoked a paradoxical idea in me: fear of death does not diminish through faith or optimism but through firmly acknowledging the horror and the inevitability of the end."[59]

Leaving aside how successful this experiment on Stoianovskii really was, the letter to Aspiz suggests that Artsybashev became convinced of the therapeutic effect of letting someone "at the last frontier" face the full horror of being mortal. Only by being confronted with this reality, could man overcome, or at least manage, his fear of death.[60]

At the Last Frontier seems to apply similar shock therapy to the reader. The novel features no less than eight suicides, five nonsuicidal deaths, and a number of gripping death scenes with extremely plastic details. Even the characters who stay alive appear to be obsessed with death and decay, such as, for example, the indifferent Dr. Arnol'di, who considers himself a dead man already, or the aforementioned Naumov who sees life as an "absurd comedy" that can only be stopped through the destruction of the entire human race. Whereas in *Sanin*, fear of death is presented as a weakness that can be warded off, at least temporarily, by embracing life and indulging the pleasures that it offers, no such solution is given in *At the Last Frontier*. One can appreciate why the novel was rumored to be called "The Suicide Club" when work on the manuscript was still in progress.

The main character in the novel, the handsome and successful painter Sergei Mikhailov, is much more involved emotionally in the action than Sanin. He too is an avid seeker of sexual pleasure who scoffs at the traditional ideal of matrimonial fidelity and blames society's outmoded conventions rather than his own lasciviousness for the impossible situation in which a "fallen" woman is bound to end up. And yet, the differences between him and Sanin are immediately obvious. Defending himself against the charge that he has mistreated one of his female admirers, Mikhailov cannot avoid displaying a "spasm of pain" and a "distorted grin." In the same scene, the narrator describes his face as changing "suddenly and sharply"; one can even read the expression of "grief and pain" in his eyes.[61] Mikhailov is not only a weaker personality, then; without yet acknowledging it, he also seems to question the very premises on which his attitude toward life is based. This becomes increasingly clear toward the end of the novel when, in a conversation with Dr. Arnol'di, he describes the dreariness of his love life and the sensual saturation that he has come to experience. After the first great love of his life—an affair that broke down when it started becoming routine and jealousy crept in—Mikhailov engaged in a sort of serial "monogamy in overdrive," hoping to escape life's ever-lurking boredom: "Then I started to drift from one woman to another, looking only for a quick change and strong striking sensations. This was a vivid time. I lived like this for a couple of years, and I thought I had found what I wanted. But I was deceived! I suddenly noticed that the same vague but unbearable desire emerged in me, the same feeling of emptiness and superfluity! . . . I know everything down to the smallest details, I know in advance how it will start and end with each and every woman: I have heard the same words from dozens of them, I have seen the same caresses over and over again. . . . And apart from boredom, longing, and revulsion there is nothing left. I have emptied my soul, exchanged feelings for trifles."[62]

In this almost Pechorin-like confession, Mikhailov finally raises an even more dramatic question than the one that tormented Soloveichik. Instead of asking *how* to live, he asks Dr. Arnol'di why one should live at all ("Dlia chego zhit'?"). Acknowledging that he has "only loved himself" and that it is impossible to "fill your soul with pleasure only," Mikhailov sees no other option than to take his own life.[63]

Because *At the Last Frontier* contains so many motifs and stock images of Artsybashev's earlier work and the author himself stressed its "concluding" character on more than one occasion, critics found it impossible not to read it as a sort of closing statement on *Sanin* or, rather, as a description of the death-throes of Saninism. Mikhailov was, in the words of Aleksandr Izmailov, the "second, revised, and expanded edition of Sanin."[64] In depicting this new type, Artsybashev apparently did not want to distance himself too much from his old hero, who had brought him such enormous success. According to L'vov-Rogachevskii,

Sanin had not reached the sun, as Artsybashev had predicted in 1907, but the last frontier, the open grave: "If the novel *Sanin* was Sanin's apotheosis, then Artsybashev's last work is a prayer for the dying Sanin."[65]

By reducing *At the Last Frontier* almost to an epilogue to *Sanin*, critics such as Izmailov and L'vov-Rogachevskii contributed to the widespread idea that Artsybashev's talent was declining at the beginning of the 1910s. Once a fashionable writer who had raised serious questions about sexual morality and the revolutionary movement, he now began to lose touch with reality, confining himself to describing the last convulsions of a historical mentality that was rapidly disappearing: "With the glowing eyes of the maniac Naumov, he [Artsybashev] keeps repeating his dead, misanthropic words. He does not see, does not notice that a new life is being created, that this new life stands not at the last but at a *new* frontier."[66] *Sanin* was ultimately remembered as an "interesting" novel, as the "brightest" but also as the "last flash" of Artsybashev's talent, whereas *At the Last Frontier* was utterly forgotten.[67] Depicting life as utterly meaningless in the face of death and having his characters draw the ensuing conclusions, Artsybashev not only showed what had happened to Sanin after his sudden departure from his hometown but also had declared the bankruptcy of his own pen.[68]

Three Narratives

At the Last Frontier was not Artsybashev's swan song. Though he felt increasingly misunderstood and marginalized by the "crazy success" of writers such as Amfiteatrov and Verbitskaia, he remained rather productive until the end of his life, writing, among other things, several plays, a film screenplay, and a novel.[69] However, after the publication of *At the Last Frontier*, it became commonplace to refer to Artsybashev as a writer who had fully exhausted his talent and drawn the final conclusion to his seemingly life-affirming, but essentially pessimistic, philosophy of life. As a result, Sanin was no more, and neither was Artsybashev the writer.

No less than three narratives, then, converged in the debate on the meaning of *Sanin*'s open ending. The first narrative concerned the plot proper that, with its many loose ends and lack of "poetic justice," provoked a stream of countertexts in the narrow sense of the word: texts that sought to debunk the novel's perceived message by ridiculing the hero and, especially, by showing the devastating consequences of his conduct (venereal disease, suicide). With the exception of Count Amori's sequel, *Sanin's Return*, these texts came to light immediately after the novel was published, expressing the moral outrage of many an anonymous reader.

The second narrative was about the Russian intelligentsia (or, rather about its "aristocratic" and "bourgeois" elements), which, after 1905, was believed to have exchanged its revolutionary ideals for Sanin's cynical "live-by-the-day" mentality. Always "on the road," Sanin would eventually develop into yet another contemporary type and abandon his views once more. The suicidal Mikhailov, the central character in *At the Last Frontier*, can be said to represent that next stage (though most critics preferred to view him as the last or ultimate Saninist rather than as a new "hero of our time"). Because his fate showed Saninism in its most extreme manifestation, *At the Last Frontier* was believed to correct or even discredit the ideas put forward in *Sanin*. Thus critics read Artsybashev's most voluminous novel in a way that was rather similar to the intentions of the anti-Saninist countertexts discussed at the beginning of this chapter.

Finally, we can discern a narrative about Artsybashev the writer, whose "undeniable talent" had extinguished after writing his most controversial and yet arguably most "interesting" novel. According to this view, after *Sanin*, the author went under in a well of pitch-black pessimism and thus reached his own "last frontier."

4

The Pornographic *Roman à Thèse*
Publication, Censorship, Ban

As I mentioned briefly in the introduction, *Sanin* has always enjoyed the dubious reputation of being one of the quintessentially pornographic works of Russian literature. It was not only labeled as such by many of Artsybashev's embarrassed contemporaries, but less than a year after its serialization, it was banned for violating, among other things, the 1001st statute, popularly known as the "statute on pornography."

Literary histories and encyclopedias published during the Soviet years were extremely reticent in dealing with this aspect of the novel. The *Literary Encyclopedia* of 1929 singled out the "bright colors of the impressionistic landscape descriptions" as the work's only merit but added, on a more critical and somewhat confusing note, that "these are pervaded with eroticism" (*proniknutyi, odnako, erotikoi*).[1] Two histories of Russian literature (1954 and 1964) emphasized the novel's "antisocial" and "antihumanistic" (*antigumanisticheskie*) tendencies, as well as its overall "reactionary" character, but did not mention the sexual issue at all.[2] The *Short Literary Encyclopedia* (1962) went a bit further, stating that Artsybashev had "preached immorality [*amoralizm*] and sexual dissipation."[3] In the most extensive discussion devoted to *Sanin*, the author pointed out that the idea of egocentrism in the novel was indissolubly connected with the "sexual problem," but he shied away from elaborating on this issue.[4] Preferring to avoid the term "pornography," these publications considered the novel almost exclusively in terms of its perceived political message.

That the memory of *Sanin* as a sensational and pornographic novel remained nonetheless intact became clear when a rudimentary commercial book market emerged at the end of the 1980s and an array of forgotten and suppressed masterpieces was returned to the Russian reader. *Sanin* reappeared for the first time in 1990 in an untidy reprint of a Western reprint of a prerevolutionary edition, suggesting that the publishers were in a hurry to capitalize on its scandalous reputation.[5] In 1991 a more sophisticated volume was published containing eleven short stories and a decent introduction in addition to *Sanin*.[6] This was followed by a collected works of three volumes in 1994, which remains the most comprehensive post-Soviet edition of Artsybashev's work to date.[7]

The initial republication of *Sanin* and its subsequent inclusion in a multivolume collection of Artsybashev's work reflect a general trend in the publishing business of the early 1990s. After the first overly hasty publication of once forbidden texts, more sophisticated editions appeared, which have by now contributed to lending the authors in question a certain respectability (another case in point is the republication of Ivan Barkov's obscene poetry in a collected works). At the same time, it seems likely that the marketing strategy to promote *Sanin* as a prerevolutionary pornographic potboiler quickly exhausted itself simply because, by late twentieth-century standards, it could not live up to its reputation.[8] Indeed, if we define pornography as "the explicit depiction of sexual organs and sexual practices with the aim of arousing sexual feelings," then *Sanin*'s notoriety appears exaggerated, if not outright deceptive.[9] Its erotic vocabulary is limited and lacks the marked explicitness that we usually associate with pornographic writing. Furthermore, the verbose monologues in which the hero expounds his views on unlimited sexual freedom seem to annul all erotic tension beforehand.

The indignant reviews and comments that appeared in 1907 and 1908 give the impression that most of Artsybashev's critics were largely overreacting. This fervor should not blind us to the fact that not everybody considered *Sanin* to be pornographic, however, and those who did view it in this way sometimes disagreed as to what that meant. The well-known critic Kornei Chukovskii, for example, discerned certain conspicuously "Russian" pornographic qualities in *Sanin*, which he juxtaposed to the more "straightforward" pornography of Germany and France.[10] In short, the reception of *Sanin* as a highly licentious text is less homogeneous than its undeserved reputation suggests.

This chapter discusses the arguments that have been put forward both in support of and against the notion that *Sanin* is a pornographic work. It also examines how critics assessed its popularity as a licentious text and how they situated the novel within the tradition of Russian literature. The confusion over *Sanin* as an alleged work of pornography, I suggest, largely grew out of the demand for "objectivity," which had always occupied a central place in realist aesthetics, especially in connection with the "tendentious" novel. I then turn to a number of reviews that scrutinize more specifically Vladimir Sanin's ideal of free love. My analysis indicates that the novel caused a stir, not just because it dealt openly with sex (although that *did* play a considerable role, of course) but also because of the ultimate consequences that its philosophy was believed to entail. Peculiarly enough, it is here that we encounter certain criteria that come closest to a contemporary definition of pornography. Not the novel itself, but the world that—in the vision of some critics—it seemed to adumbrate, a world of emotional aloofness and anonymous sex, can indeed be regarded as pornographic. This chapter concludes with a discussion of *Sanin*'s publication and reception history in Germany; Germany also banned the novel (if only for a short period) yet approached the issue of its allegedly pornographic status in a very different and nonpoliticized way.

Publication and Confiscation

In the previous chapter, we saw how critic Piotr Pil'skii refuted as irrelevant Artsybashev's claim that *Sanin* had been written before the revolution of 1905. The novel was published in 1907, Pil'skii insisted, and that in itself was significant. Although he was referring to the novel's "reactionary" orientation, in a way Pil'skii was certainly right. Without the abolition of preliminary censorship in 1905, *Sanin* would probably never have appeared in print. Before that, the censorship committees could prevent the publication of politically or morally suspect texts simply by rejecting the manuscript. The decision of the censors thus had an immediate effect on the availability of texts. After 1905 the censorship committees (which were then renamed "press affairs committees") could only *re*act by ordering the confiscation of material already published and by having the author, the publisher, or the printer prosecuted.[11] Even if the Ministry of Interior retained its authority and the level of censorship was not necessarily less than it was before 1905, the newly established press affairs committees were always lagging behind. Assured of a relatively quick return of investment, publishers could make a considerable profit before they were fined and their publications confiscated. Obviously, this situation worked in favor of a novel like *Sanin,* of which twenty thousand copies were sold before it was effectively banned.

The trouble over *Sanin* started as early as May 1907, when Artsybashev's apartment was searched by the Yalta police and his personal papers were confiscated, including the manuscript of *Sanin.* It is unclear whether the police acted on the personal initiative of the head of police, General Dumbadze, as Artsybashev himself was inclined to think, or at the instigation of the St. Petersburg Committee on Press Affairs (see below).[12] Apparently, the authorities could not find anything objectionable in *Sanin,* because the manuscript was returned to the author. During the seven months following the publication of the final episode in September 1907, Russian readers had the opportunity to read the novel as a perfectly legal text either in its serialized or book form.

Alarmed by critical reactions in the media, the St. Petersburg Committee on Press Affairs renewed its investigations in April 1908. On April 17 it asked the prosecutor to press charges against Artsybashev and to confiscate the entire print runs of both editions of *Sanin* on the grounds that it violated the 73rd statute (on blasphemy) and the 1001st statute (on the corruption of morals, the "statute on pornography").[13] In elaborating its request for prosecution, the committee named no less than three offenses, one of which, technically speaking, was not covered by either article. Apart from being a blasphemer (a charge probably referring to Sanin's comment that "Christ was magnificent but Christians are ineffectual"[14]), Artsybashev had also proven himself an enemy of good morals by describing his hero's amorous adventures in language so explicit that it offended anyone's sense of common decency. Even more worrying than the obscenity of the novel, however, was the hero's revolutionary background. This made him not only reject commonly accepted morality but also scoff at "incommensurably more important questions." Here again, the censor referred to Sanin's assumed atheism ("for example, Sanin hates Christianity") and repeated that he considered Artsybashev's hero the sorry product of the revolutionary movement.[15] Using the laws against blasphemy and pornography, the St. Petersburg Committee on Press Affairs was primarily concerned with warding off the political danger that Artsybashev's novel was believed to represent.[16]

Despite the euphoria that the initiative of the committee evoked in the boulevard press, it accomplished little more than prevent the publisher from printing a third edition. The first two editions were sold out before the police could confiscate any copies. According to German translator André Villard, readers had been so anxious for the second edition that they had been prepared to pay thirty to forty rubles for a secondhand copy. Moreover, *Sanin* remained available in serialized form for a considerable period of time.[17] The Central Board on Press Affairs didn't ask the local committee of St. Petersburg whether the relevant issues of *Sovremennyi mir* had been confiscated until November 27, 1909, at the earliest.[18] Privy Councillor Vorshev replied that no such action had been undertaken at the time of the novel's serialization, claiming that an accurate assessment of the novel's message from a legal point of view was possible only after the last episode was published: "For it very often happens that a novel's final message compensates for certain awkward places in a text" (*iskupaet otdel'nye neudobnye mesta*).[19] It is unclear whether the St. Petersburg committee had really investigated the matter in 1907 (thereby causing the delay in the serialization) or was now pretending to have been extremely circumspect only to cover up its initial sloppiness. In any case, it had not followed up on the matter after the last episode was published, as a result of which *Sanin* remained available in serialized form. Moreover, the final order to destroy any remaining copies was not given until November 24, 1910.[20] On June 23, 1911, the mayor of St. Petersburg informed the Central Board on Press Affairs that the command could not be carried out, as no copies were found in the bookstores or in the print shop.[21]

The police had thus been unsuccessful in retrieving and destroying any copies of *Sanin*. They had not been able to prevent readers from familiarizing themselves with the novel, even if it took time for them to lay their hands on a copy (the practical issue of reading a controversial text in demand is dealt with in chapter 5). In that sense, the committee's handling of the case is a good example of its ineffectiveness after the reforms of 1905. What is more important, though, is that the authorities appear to have been primarily concerned with the novel's political message rather than with its supposed obscenity. Branding *Sanin* a "pornographic" and a "blasphemous" work, the St. Petersburg Committee on Press Affairs was anxious, above all, to stop its "revolutionary" message from being disseminated.[22]

The 1001st Statute and the Question of Authorial Intent

Even if the authorities considered *Sanin*'s political message more harmful than its obscenity, the decision to have the novel banned for violating the 1001st statute confirmed its budding reputation as a work of pornography. Some critics argued that the all-pervasiveness of sex in the story was "unrealistic" and incompatible with the demands of the "social novel" (*bytovoi roman*).[23] An article in the provincial daily *Minskoe slovo* (*Minsk Word*) even referred to *Sanin* as "Artsybashev's famous, pornographic novel" and applauded the decision to press charges.[24] Yet not everyone considered *Sanin* to be pornographic, and even those who did sometimes adduced very different arguments in support of its alleged status as a work of unprecedented obscenity. To some of the most outspoken critics, pornography was synonymous with any kind of literature exploring erotic love, including the poetry of Konstantin Bal'mont and Valerii Briusov. To others, like Kornei Chukovskii, pornography presupposed sexual arousal but not necessarily through the explicit depiction of sexual organs (the "contemporary" definition supplied in the opening to this chapter). All in all, it would be difficult to give a straightforward definition of what pornography meant in early twentieth-century Russia, and this is not surprising if we consider that even the "law on pornography" was notoriously vague.

According to Paul Goldschmidt, the ambiguity of the 1001st statute was one of the law's charms, enabling the court to define pornography as it wished.[25] The statute spoke of "works that aim at corrupting morals or that are clearly offensive to morality and decency or contain seductive images tending in that direction."[26] The phrase "works that *aim* at corrupting morals" (*sochineniia, imeiushchie tsel'iu razvrashchenie nravov*) was highly problematic in itself, for it raised the question of authorial intent. Who was to determine what goal a writer had pursued in describing or even simply hinting at loose morals? The matter was further complicated by the fact that *Sanin* was written, and certainly received, in the tradition of the tendentious novel, which was believed to offer, with almost scientific exactness, an accurate but ideologically colored view of contemporary social life.[27] Once *Sanin* was labeled "pornographic," readers faced the difficult task of determining its real intent.

On the one hand, the common feeling was that the novel gave an accurate picture of contemporary Russian society. Many critics agreed that Vladimir Sanin embodied the mood of the Russian intelligentsia after the revolution of 1905 and could therefore even be regarded as a contemporary Bazarov. On the other hand, since the tendencies in question were considered harmful, radical critics expected Artsybashev to do more than simply reveal them. Aleksei Achkasov—one of the reviewers who maintained that the importance of sex in *Sanin* was not realistic— reproached him for having only "passively depicted" the sexual craze among the intelligentsia instead of also "unmask[ing]" it.[28] In effect, Achkasov insisted, Artsybashev seemed to endorse and even encourage what ought to be condemned outright.

The ambiguity of the 1001st statute was not the only problematic issue, then. The notion of the tendentious novel's "objectivity" proved to be a significant source of confusion as well. This became abundantly clear at a "literary test trial" organized by students of the University of St. Petersburg in February 1909, at which Artsybashev, Mikhail Kuzmin, and Fiodor Sologub were tried on charges of "pornography." Characteristically, the trial centered on Artsybashev's responsibilities as an author and his novel's supposed message rather than on any tantalizing scenes in particular. The prosecutor argued that Artsybashev had not depicted life's "filth" objectively because in depicting it he had tried to prove that it was a pure well. Moreover, in order to prove that his hero was morally "right" in pursuing sensual pleasure, Artsybashev had not recoiled from "cynical depictions of sexual acts with the aim of arousing the reader." The defense objected to this on the grounds that Artsybashev could only be charged with pornography if it could be established that his intention was *exclusively* to arouse the reader's sexual appetite. This had not been proven, however. Artsybashev belonged to a certain class of writers that had emerged from the revolution of 1905, and had used his novel to profess "new ethical principles." These principles might be morally wrong, the defense conceded, but Artsybashev deserved credit for having preserved the "chisel of the realist writer."[29]

As this peculiar blend of juridical discourse and literary criticism already suggests, this test trial was not about pornography. The questions under dispute were whether or not *Sanin* qualified as a realist work of art and what exactly it meant to depict deplorable tendencies in a realistic and supposedly objective manner. The concept of the tendentious novel, as formulated by the critic Piotr Tkachev, assumed that an objective and accurate depiction of negative phenomena would elicit their negative nature. Yet *Sanin* seemed to undermine this assumption in that it *idealized* negative tendencies while, from a stylistic and epistemological perspective, it displayed all the characteristics of a realist novel.

In summary, we can say that the authorities decided to confiscate *Sanin,* claiming that it violated the 1001st statute. This decision, which stained the novel with the label "pornography," provoked a discussion about that notorious article of law and also raised the question of whether it really applied to Artsybashev's novel or not. Yet to answer this question, it had to be decided if Artsybashev had objectively depicted reality. Since there was general disagreement on this point, *Sanin*'s status as a pornographic text was unclear: those who disputed the objectivity of Artsybashev's method regarded the novel as pornographic and incompatible with the venerable tradition of Russian literature to act as an agent for social change. Those who believed Artsybashev *had* objectively described contemporary society argued that precisely in reflecting the mood of a particular social group and offering a philosophical program *Sanin* was a contemporary manifestation of the aforementioned tradition. That program might be immoral, but the specific accusation of pornography should be dismissed as groundless.

Pornography and "Principled" Literature

Critics who decried *Sanin* as pornography did not do so solely on the basis of its lack of objectivity, however. They adduced additional "evidence" to support the claim that Artsybashev's novel was licentious and harmful. A point often made—which again, like the objectivity argument, referred to something outside the text—was that political reaction following a period of social unrest always triggered a proliferation of pornographic writings. From this perspective, the publication of *Sanin* appeared to some observers as very nearly historically inevitable. As one critic put it, Sanin "didn't fall out of the sky. He couldn't but be born and could only be born as Sanin."[30] Radical critics eagerly drew parallels between their time (the aftermath of 1905) and the beginning of the 1880s, when Alexander III's reactionary politics had caused exactly the same reaction. It was believed that in those days, too, hedonism had triumphed over the traditional demand for political commitment and that pornography had been preferred over "principled literature" (*ideinaia literatura*).³¹ Some critics even drew parallels between Russia's revolution and those of other countries. The Marxist G. S. Novopolin, for example, had no qualms about comparing the situation in postrevolutionary Russia with the state of France during the Directory and just after the revolt of 1848.³² Furthermore, there were critics who considered the pornographic output to be an old trick to which the authorities had resorted in the hope of distracting the masses from more pertinent political issues.³³

But the tables could also be turned against the liberation movement. In an interview with the boulevard daily, *Peterburgskii listok*, a spokesman for the Ministry of Enlightenment argued that social unrest always went hand in glove with a decline of morals. The newspaper quoted him as saying that, without a doubt, the liquidation of the revolutionary movement would also put a stop to the revolution in sexual morality.³⁴ Thus, depending on the observer's political views, pornography and hedonism could be construed as "typically revolutionary" phenomena or as the auxiliary devices of an overall strategy designed to subdue the revolutionary spirit.

Central to these historical parallels, in the vision of left-wing radicals, was the dichotomy between pornography and "principled literature," fiction that was supposed to heighten the reader's political consciousness by expressing a particular, preferably socialist, worldview. Although the demand for an ideological message or a "tendency" had become something of a precondition for realist literature in general, the very term *ideinost'* itself carried connotations of political activism and social service. For example, Novopolin in effect identified pornography with the reactionary forces in Russian society, especially with the highest circles, and "principled literature" with its more progressive minds by his very juxtaposition of the terms, neither of which he cared to define.

Having defined pornography as an essentially social phenomenon, Novopolin could easily make the stunning assertion that the "pornographic element" had nearly always been present in Russian literature. Just like the gases of a swamp signaled decay, pornography revealed the steady disintegration of a rotten society. Since Russian society had always been rotten, it followed that the pornographic element in literature had always been operative in some way. Yet in drawing a parallel between his own time and the 1880s, Novopolin stayed true to the teleological vision of human history as proposed by Marxism. The unprecedented outburst of sexual literature after the revolution of 1905 not only illustrated the immediate link between pornography and political reaction but also served as an indication that the end of the present, fully corrupt political order was near.[35] The founding of a new society, which, as Novopolin assured the reader, could not be far away, would also mean the disappearance of pornography from the literary scene.[36]

Surprisingly, Novopolin's extensive discussion of *Sanin* focuses primarily on the hero's philosophy and on Nietzsche's possible influence on Artsybashev. It remains unclear why the novel is "pornographic" and not "principled," those being the only two tendencies in literature that Novopolin acknowledges. Indeed, a number of critics arrived at exactly the opposite conclusion, stressing that the novel purported to deliver a message and was therefore *not* pornographic. Elena Koltonovskaia, for example, writing for the liberal journal *Obrazovanie* (*Education*), argued that *Sanin* attracted so many readers, not because of the sex in it but because it offered a manual for living.[37] She asserted, moreover, that this manual very accurately reflected a new tendency in society, which she termed "hedonistic realism." Vladimir Sanin represented a new type of the "ideological hero" (*ideinyi geroi*), Koltonovskaia maintained, which made him a hero of his time, just like Pechorin and Bazarov before him.[38] In a combined review of Artsybashev and Anatolii Kamenskii—another alleged "pornographer" enjoying massive popularity—Maksimilian Voloshin went so far as to assert that *Sanin* had been written in the best traditions of the Russian *roman à thèse* (*ideinyi roman*).[39] Thus the consideration of *ideinost'* as a critical criterion led the majority of the critics to one of two conclusions: (1) *Sanin is* pornography, and consequently, it breaks with the respected tradition of *ideinost'* and the use of literature as a vehicle for the expression of political ideas; or 2) *Sanin* is *not* pornographic, precisely because it continues that tradition and offers the reader a so-called manual for living.

Kornei Chukovskii, one of Artsybashev's more eloquent critics, did not subscribe to either point of view. Instead, he combined these opinions and defined *Sanin* paradoxically as "pornography with ideas." This, he argued, was a specifically Russian branch of pornography because, unlike the unambiguous pornography produced by the French and the Germans, this one also purported to instruct the reader: "Artsybashev does not simply describe Sanin's lascivious actions but calls on everyone to follow his example: 'People should enjoy love without fear or inhibition', he says. The word 'should' is a vestige of the habits of the old intelligentsia, a remnant of the old moral code that is disappearing before our eyes."[40]

Although Chukovskii's comment is very much to the point, there is little reason to believe that the novel was actually read as a *roman à thèse* or that it inspired its readers to emulate Sanin's behavior. Of course, the boulevard press did not miss a single opportunity to suggest that the novel had a direct and corrupting influence on educated youth and reported on the so-called free love leagues, underground organizations in which would-be Sanins supposedly indulged in group sex (see chapter 6). One newspaper even produced a list of porn classics, which the members of these free love leagues were reported to read (the list included Artsybashev, Lermontov, Barkov, and Paul de Coque).[41] But there is little evidence that Sanin's philosophy was ever adopted as a strategy for living. That the novel actually functioned as the "Bible" of an entire generation, as has been suggested, seems highly unlikely. I return to this issue in chapter 5.

Pornography, Hyperrealism, and the Annulment of Man

Contrary to what one would expect, perhaps, few critics concerned themselves directly with the immediate effect that *Sanin* had on the individual reader. The question of whether or not the novel did sexually arouse or was intended to arouse—which in our perception is indissolubly linked with the notion of pornography—was largely overshadowed by the debate over the lack of "objectivity" and *ideinost'*. The issue of the novel's immediate effect on the reader did receive some attention in a query among students of the University of Tomsk (only 12 percent of whom admitted to having read *Sanin*). Comparing Leonid Andreev's well-known stories "The Abyss" ("Bezdna" [1902]) and "In the Fog" ("V tumane" [1902]) to *Sanin,* one student responded that, whereas Andreev's work shed light on the "psychology of sexual arousal without enhancing this feeling," Artsybashev's novel did not. Reading such literature left "something filthily voluptuous in one's soul."[42] Yet it should be stressed that we seldom encounter reactions like these in critical articles devoted specifically to the novel.

Perhaps the only critic to make a serious attempt to put his finger on *Sanin*'s pornographic features was Arkadii Gornfel'd, a distinguished reviewer from the prestigious journal *Russkoe bogatstvo.* Although we may smile at his prudishness and reject his conclusions, Gornfel'd implicitly applies very specific criteria, some of which could be deemed valid even today. In other words, we may disagree with his diagnosis, but his conception of pornography—which he does not directly define but nevertheless can be inferred from his discussion of *Sanin*—is refreshingly narrow in scope and free of historical argument.

Gornfel'd initially dwells on what he perceives to be the all-pervasiveness of sex in the novel and the constant state of sexual arousal in which the characters appear to be.[43] Read in this manner—and Gornfel'd was certainly not the only one to do so—*Sanin* seems to contain two essentially pornographic ingredients: "unrealistic" foregrounding of sex as the only thing in life that matters and the equally "unrealistic" suggestion of relentless sexual excitement. Gornfel'd finds more proof of *Sanin*'s pornographic status where the modern reader would least expect it: in its erotic vocabulary, specifically in the frequent use of the word "bosom" (*grud'*). A common feature of hard-core pornography is its explicitness, which, in its written form, manifests itself primarily in the use of obscene language. According to Lucienne Frappier-Mazur, the obscene word has a fetishlike quality that exceeds ordinary language. Owing to its perceived "directness," the obscene word does not merely represent the object to which it refers, as a euphemism does, but, in a way, *is* the object itself: "The obscene word, just like the insult, harks back to the time when the child does not distinguish very well between the representation of words and the representation of things." In effect, "the child treats words as things."[44] Commenting on Frappier-Mazur's article, Lynn Hunt remarks that the explicit language of pornography constitutes a kind of "hyperrealism."[45]

Admittedly, it is difficult to define the word "bosom" in *Sanin* as obscene, but perhaps its repetitive use could create an effect very similar to the one described by Frappier-Mazur.[46] Gornfel'd was not only disturbed by Artsybashev's "detailed" descriptions of people's love life, both in *Sanin* and in other works, but he also literally found it difficult to quote the various qualities that the author discovered in a woman's bosom:

> With surprising obtrusiveness Mister Artsybashev keeps referring to so-called "secondary sexual characteristics." You may never find out what color the heroine's eyes are, but you will always be informed what kind of bosom she has, how the men surrounding her sniff at her, etc. It is rather embarrassing to bring out these details here [*nemnozhko korobit vydvigat' eti detali*], but I have to in order to prove my point. A woman's bosom is "solid and firm," "small, resilient," "rounded, low" ["Morning Shades"], "soft, resilient, velvety," "protrusive, tight,

daringly rocking, alluring men" ["Human Life"], "high, resilient," "voluminous," "white, elusively tender": this thirst for telling epithets reveals something persistently nightmarish, like the sadistic dreams of an ascetic, struggling with the flesh.[47]

Gornfel'd's embarrassment seems to have been caused by the fetishizing of a word that, although not obscene in itself, refers to a sexual part of the female body that becomes somehow "present" through the word's repetition. It is remarkable that almost ninety years before Lynn Hunt, Gornfel'd used the term "hyperrealism" (*sverkhrealism*) to capture the immediacy that he perceived as the effect of sexually explicit language.[48]

In his attempt to lay bare the allegedly pernicious nature of *Sanin*, Gornfel'd did not resort to the oppositions pornography vs. realist literature or pornography vs. principled literature (both of which overlapped considerably, of course). Instead, he introduced a classical and equally unconvincing opposition by contrasting pornography to "genuine Art," which he defined as "contemplation" (*myshlenie*).[49] Since Artsybashev's writings emphatically appealed to "dark sexual instincts," they could not at the same time provoke deep thoughts, which was the main task of genuine literature, Gornfel'd believed. In inducing sexual excitement, a work like *Sanin* ceased to be art.[50]

Having denied it a place in the lofty realm of literature, Gornfel'd nonetheless shied away from calling *Sanin* "pornography." Writers such as Artsybashev and Anatolii Kamenskii should not be ignored, he insisted, if only because they published in respected and widely read journals. Their "sexual realism" (*polovoi realizm*) might be a bad thing, but it registered a certain mood in society and therefore deserved critical attention. While defending them against the accusation of pornography, however, Gornfel'd criticized the "shallow" way in which these young writers treated the matter of sex. What they were concerned with, he believed, was not love but sensuality, not Eros but eroticism. Here, Gornfel'd objected to what many critics seem to have abhorred: Artsybashev's supposedly impersonal, less-than-human conception of erotic love. Referring to Vladimir Solov'ev's platonic ideal of male and female as two parts of a larger whole, Elena Koltonovskaia dismissed *Sanin*'s understanding of love as "primitive" and "one-sided."[51] Evgenii Trubetskoi was appalled at the notion that *Sanin*'s understanding of love denied the uniqueness of the partner, which, in his view, was exactly what distinguished love between humans from the sexual urges of animals: "For someone in love the object [of love] is the *only* creature in the whole world; and this longing for the one and only undermines man's capacity to be infatuated with other objects, subdues in him flashes of passion toward other people. Love between humans allows one to behold the infinite value of the beloved person, to behold his or her undying, *unconditional* significance. Love between humans therefore goes far beyond a single moment and resists the destructive force of time. It is *this* sort of love that makes man want to be united with his beloved *forever*, to engage with him or her in an indissoluble union. Every other sexual love is not a human, but an animal-like emotion."[52]

All the connotations that Koltonovskaia and Trubetskoi attribute to *Sanin*'s conception of sexual love (rude, shallow, one sided, primitive, animal-like) are premised on the assumption that unlimited sexual freedom meant indifference as to the identity of the partner and would eventually result in the annulment of man's individuality (Trubetskoi speaks of the *uprazdnenie cheloveka*). "Genuine" love, on the other hand, not only affirms the partner's uniqueness; it is also a lifelong affair and a matter of destiny.[53] It may be argued that the "annulment of man," as Trubetskoi put it, is indeed what critics had in mind when they characterized, or came close to characterizing, *Sanin* as pornography. In his portrayal, they saw a world in which people continually swapped partners without making any emotional commitment to them. This vision, which Trubetskoi took to be the novel's message, *does* seem to border on pornography in that man, in Susan Sontag's words, is seen "only from the outside, behavioristically." Hence, the tendency in pornography "to make one person interchangeable with another and all people interchangeable with things."[54] This fear of "interchangeability" may also have contributed to the myth of the free love leagues, which I discuss in chapter 6. The novel does not even allude to the possibility of group sex, but the press suggested that the leagues practiced sexual acts according to Vladimir Sanin's preaching. Significantly, the "yellow" newspapers made much of the fact that these orgies took place in a dark room: young people reportedly indulged in sex in the dim light of candles or waited until darkness had set in completely. In one way or another, anonymity was guaranteed.

Trubetskoi missed the point, then, when he interpreted *Sanin*'s advocacy of free love as a gospel of anonymous sex. Rather, the novel seems to follow up on a crucial question that is put forward by Pozdnyshev, the main character in Tolstoy's *The Kreutzer Sonata* (*Kreitserova sonata* [1890]): if we understand "real love" to be a person's preference for one particular human being above all others, then how long does it have to last to be considered real? Isn't two hours as sufficient as two months or two years? Sanin's erotic encounter with Zinaida Karsavina may have been a one-night stand, but their preference for one another at that particular moment (no matter how clumsily suggested) is beyond doubt. Considering that the novel does not offer an impersonal vision of erotic love, one is forced to conclude that Artsybashev should be acquitted of the charge of pornography.

Sanin in Germany

In view of the ineffectiveness of the Russian authorities, it may be worthwhile to turn to Germany, which also banned the novel, if only for a relatively short time. A German translation of *Sanin* became available as early as mid-September 1908. Initially, sales figures were far from impressive, publisher Georg Müller later recalled, as Artsybashev was virtually unknown to the German reader.[55] Gradually, however, the novel received more exposure in the press, partly as a corollary of the sensational reports on "Saninists" and secret sex clubs, which German translator André Villard had eagerly exploited in his introduction. One may surmise that *Sanin* would never have been banned if Villard had introduced the novel and its author in a more restrained manner.

The first edition of *Sanin* was banned less than three months after its publication because of its "lewd [*unzüchtig*] character."[56] Following police inquiries about the storage and distribution of the novel, the police court of Munich ordered its confiscation on November 23, 1908, arguing that a "normally perceiving reader" (*einer normal empfindende Leser*) was likely to be offended by the novel's overt eroticism.[57] The judge based his decision on the report of only one expert, a Dr. Karl Boll, who considered the novel nothing less than "poison for the youth" because of its explicitly erotic and sometimes even sadistic descriptions. It was precisely the novel's sadism that made it difficult to decide, Dr. Boll admitted, whether Artsybashev had acted in good faith ("bona fide") or, on the contrary, with the intention of arousing the reader's sexual appetite. Although Artsybashev's nationality could be construed as an argument for the former, in the end, Dr. Boll came down on the side of the latter: "It may be that we should treat him [Artsybashev] according to the saying: scratch the Russian and you will see a barbarian. In that case it would be possible that in the country of the knout such a sadistic view would not be considered a sign of pornographic eroticism. But the opposite is also possible and personally I am inclined to assume that the novel's titillating (*aufreizend*) effect was intended not to put honestly forward a social program but to tickle the senses."[58]

It is conceivable that the debate in the press and the prospect of a trial gave a belated boost to the sales figures of *Sanin*; when the police proceeded to execute the court's decision, they managed to confiscate twelve hundred copies in the Leipzig branch of Müller's publishing house but no copies in Munich, as the novel had already sold out.[59]

Publisher Georg Müller appealed the decision to the county court but initially to no avail. On December 1, 1908, it confirmed the verdict of the police court of Munich that *Sanin* was an obscene and harmful text. However, it also asked six other experts to review the novel, five of whom concluded that it could not be considered licentious and that consequently its confiscation had been unjustified. The only dissenting voice came from senior teacher (*Oberstudienrat*) Nicklas, who maintained that the novel and Villard's introduction in particular were a major threat to the moral purity of German youth. Yet Nicklas was not the only reviewer to take offense at the role of the translator. University professor Karl Brunner found nothing objectionable in Artsybashev's novel but concluded that Villard's introduction referred far too eagerly to the "wild sexual intoxication" that *Sanin* had supposedly caused among Russia's youth. By emphasizing the sensational effect the novel was supposed to have had, the introduction undermined its objective, cultural-historical value.[60] Apparently, Villard had to yield to this criticism, because the introduction to the second edition does not contain any references to free love societies or Saninists engaging in wild sex.

In order to decide whether or not the ban on *Sanin* should be lifted, the court asked the experts to comment on the nature of the sexually explicit scenes and to give their opinion on the novel's literary merits. If it could be proven that the erotic descriptions served some kind of "scientific" purpose and were not intended to arouse sexual excitement, then the charge of licentiousness would prove to be unfounded. Another potential extenuating circumstance was the novel's artistic and historical significance. Did *Sanin* qualify as "high" literature providing aesthetic gratification and raising serious questions, or did it merely appeal to the lower instincts? The six German experts were far from unanimous in their judgment but, on the whole, they were considerably more positive about the novel's literary qualities than the Russian critics.

Even if some reviewers criticized the novel's "sloppy" construction, all of them (with the exception of senior teacher Nicklas) praised *Sanin* as a highly significant document on contemporary Russia. Writer Ludwig Ganghofer even called it a "poetically high-minded creation" that would doubtless occupy its legitimate position alongside the masterpieces of Gogol, Turgenev, Dostoevsky, and Goncharov.[61] Wilhelm Weigand (profession not specified) thought the novel to be flawed, among other things by the fact that the hero was very much a "constructed figure" (*konstruierte Gestalt*) who instead of acting himself was designed to incite the other characters to act (a characteristic that the reviewer deemed "very Russian").[62] Weigand, however, was also convinced of the historical significance of *Sanin*, which he claimed had helped him personally to understand the intellectual life of contemporary Russia. In that respect, the novel could well be compared to Turgenev's *Fathers and Children*.[63]

Having familiarized itself with the reviews of the six experts, the county court lifted the ban on *Sanin* on March 26, 1909.[64] A clever marketer, Georg Müller not only resumed printing again immediately but also published a special edition of *Sanin* containing the six reviews, all the official documents (decisions of the courts), and a preface of his own. Should readers still have doubts about the supposedly lecherous character of the novel, the "extras" in this special edition would doubtless convince them otherwise.[65]

Despite, or perhaps thanks to, the temporary ban, *Sanin* became a commercial success in Germany. During the remaining eight months of 1909, Müller contrived to publish at least fifteen consecutive editions.[66] Commercially, the novel was apparently quite attractive, as two other publishers jumped on the bandwagon and quickly published their own translations.[67] All three translations were republished several times in the 1920s and 1930s, and Villard's translation was reissued even as late as 1971.[68]

Sanin's reception in the German-speaking world was not a purely literary phenomenon, however. In the early 1920s, two directors succeeded in doing what Russian cinematographers had found impossible before the revolution: to adapt the novel for the screen.[69] *Lydia Sanin* (1923), as the title already suggests, presents Sanin's sister not simply as one of the main characters but as the film's one and only protagonist.[70] Though the story ends like a simple feel-good movie with Lydia [Lida] finding true happiness in her marriage with Dr. Novikov (a marriage of convenience at best in the novel), she appears much stronger

Ad for Friedrich Fehér's 1924 screen version of *Sanin*. (*Der Kinematograph* 869, April 20, 1924. Stadt- und Landesbibliothek Dortmund)

and independent than in the original. Talked out of her suicide plans by her brother, she settles accounts with Zarudin herself by shooting him. Thus Lida appears to become the master of her own fate, whereas in the original she is not capable of such firm action. Whether because of her seduction or the violent denouement, the German censors declared the film inappropriate for secondary school students.

Released a year later, the second adaptation (*Ssanin*) stays much closer to the original. Again the story's central events are Lida's thwarted suicide plans and Sanin's ensuing scuffle with Zarudin, but the focus is very much on aloof Sanin himself.[71] Interestingly, though, the film ends with Sanin resuming his revolutionary activities and being convicted and sentenced to one year of forced labor, "a year that will pass very quickly," the synopsis concludes optimistically. Ultimately, the film appears to have been a story about the trials and tribulations of a Russian revolutionary rather than a eulogy of the new man, let alone a blue movie. The ad called Artsybashev's novel "world famous" and proudly announced the author's own involvement in the film but did not even allude to *Sanin*'s pornographic reputation.[72] In all likelihood, eroticism did not play a significant role in the film, as the censors left it alone.[73]

In Germany, then, *Sanin*'s pornographic aura quickly evaporated. The novel was primarily received as a philosophical and fascinating, though artistically far from impeccable, document on the Russian revolution that was read by new generations of readers again and again at least until World War II. Perhaps the pinnacle of this tendency to "de-pornographize" *Sanin* is Maximilian Barck's 1993 *Iurii's Dream*, an experimental prose piece that completely ignores the novel's erotic scenes and deliberately chooses a scrambled, "dreamlike" style that is incompatible with the uncomplicated and straightforward discourse of pornographic literature.[74] In short, if *Sanin* was banned as pornography for political reasons in Russia, then the ban was quickly lifted in Germany because the novel qualified as genuine literature.

5

Sanin and Its Readers
A Bible for an Entire Generation?

So far, I have restricted myself to discussing the reactions of the literary establishment and the intelligentsia at large. With the exception of a few dissenting voices, an overwhelming majority of critics were appalled by the novel and vilified Artsybashev for lionizing an immoral hero or simply expressed their apprehension over the intelligentsia's "escapist" mood, which *Sanin* seemed to embody. We have also caught glimpses of a more enthusiastic response in the anonymous plays based on *Sanin*, but the reception of the novel by the "ordinary" reader has not yet been properly addressed. No matter how problematic this category of readership is, without the notion of some "average" reader devouring Artsybashev's bestseller, the myth of Saninism never would have emerged.

At issue, then, is the question of how representative Dokshitskii's elated reaction, quoted at the beginning of this book, really was. Did other "ordinary" readers respond in a similar way, or did they agree with the majority of professional critics who rejected the novel or, at best, considered it an unnerving diagnosis of Russian society? This chapter attempts to provide the beginning of an answer to that question by examining statistical data, comments by contemporary critics, and reports in daily newspapers that attempt to portray the "typical" *Sanin* reader. Although an exhaustive and accurate reconstruction of such a reader is not possible, important insights can be gained from the different reader profiles that critics involuntarily designed when they ventured to explain *Sanin*'s incredible success. Mutually exclusive or partly overlapping, these profiles may help to create an understanding of how the reputation of *Sanin*, as a cult book, emerged.[1]

After some practical considerations on the availability of *Sanin* to ordinary readers, I examine the deeply ingrained notion that *Sanin* served as a Bible for an entire generation By juxtaposing the critical literature on this topic with the few concrete and reliable reader reactions that we possess, I show that the response of "ordinary" readers was far more diverse and subtle than has often been assumed. Subsequently, I turn to the aforementioned reader profiles in order to excavate their underlying political agendas, again in the hope of providing more arguments for a critical reassessment of *Sanin*'s reputation. Finally, I dwell on the debate over Vladimir Sanin as a possible role model for the radical student movement and the anti-Saninist mood that this provoked. Although the paucity of statistical data and explicit comments by ordinary readers makes it difficult to draw any far-reaching conclusions as to how *Sanin* was actually read, let alone what effect it had on individual lives, hopefully the following discussion will generate a more balanced and less sensational picture of *Sanin*'s audience than the one we find in many handbooks and other scholarly writing.

Some Practical Considerations

Let us start with a practical question: who had access to *Sanin* and how did they get access to it? Was it readily available to every schoolgirl as Mirsky seems to have assumed when he claimed that *Sanin* "became for a few years the Bible of every schoolboy and schoolgirl"?[2] Even if this statement was not meant to be taken literally, we still may want to know how easy or difficult it was for an early twentieth-century Russian adolescent to get hold of a novel that everyone wanted to read.

As noted in chapter 2, *Sanin* was serialized in *Sovremennyi mir*, a fashionable "thick" monthly with a substantial circulation of fifteen thousand copies. In 1907 and 1908 the novel was published in book form as the third volume of Artsybashev's collected work in two separate editions of ten thousand copies each. Consequently, the total number of copies of *Sanin* available to Russian readers in the spring of 1908 (just before the novel was banned) was thirty-five thousand. This figure tells us little about the number of readers, however. According to a survey conducted in 1901, a copy of *Sovremennyi mir* belonging to an individual subscriber passed through the hands of eight different readers (family members, friends), whereas library copies were usually read by no less than thirty patrons.[3] Moreover, since the novel was spread out over several issues, a complete "copy" of *Sanin* in serialized form could—at least in theory—be read simultaneously by six readers, each having a separate episode at his disposal. Although there are no data on how many people read *Sanin* in book form, here too we may safely assume that each copy was read by far more people than merely its owner. Finally, the practice of joint reading sessions is another factor to consider when speculating on the size of Artsybashev's readership. One way of acquainting oneself with the latest political and fictional literature was to join an (illegal) study circle, where the texts would be read aloud.[4] Thus, although it is impossible to give a precise figure for the total number of *Sanin* readers, it must have been an impressive multiple of thirty-five thousand.

That being said, it should not be overlooked that Russian readers and school-going youth in particular often faced considerable difficulties in quenching their curiosity not only about contemporary but also classical literature. With the exception of well-to-do adult readers in the capitals, most provincial readers were restricted to public libraries or libraries of educational institutions, the holdings of which were under strict control of the Ministry of Enlightenment or the Holy Synod. Keen on protecting ordinary people and juvenile readers from inappropriate literature, these departments were extremely cautious in selecting material for the libraries under their jurisdiction. According to Nikolai Rubakin, a prerevolutionary authority on Russia's reading habits, the officially approved list of literary works for pupils of parish schools featured Turgenev's *Sportsman's Sketches* but none of his novels or love stories. Of the other great nineteenth-century novelists, Dostoevsky and Tolstoy were represented only with shorter works such as *Poor Folk* and *Childhood*. A writer such as Ivan Goncharov was absent altogether.[5]

If familiarizing oneself with the classics of Russian literature was problematic, keeping up with the latest developments using only school libraries was simply impossible. Schools usually did not subscribe to the monthly literary journals in which the most recent literature was published. The following quotations were taken from an article presenting the results of an opinion poll conducted among students of a parochial school in Vologda during the fall of 1910. It constitutes a sample of comments by students expressing their disappointment with the school library's holdings:

> I haven't read Tolstoy's *Confession*, because it is difficult to get hold of it (sixth grade).
>
> It would be interesting to read Tolstoy's Gospel, but I have to admit that I was not able to find a copy (fifth grade).
>
> I would like to read Andreev's work. In the newspapers you read about it all the time; you hear about different reviews, and you don't know what that work is really like (second grade).
>
> I am amazed that the library of the seminary does not possess the works of contemporary authors (second grade).
>
> I would very much like [it if] . . . among the journals to which the seminary subscribes were also journals like *Russkoe bogatstvo* and *Sovremennyi mir*. It would be a good thing to have all current literature within reach so that you could keep up with it.[6]

With school libraries offering only a limited choice of mostly classical works, pupils of secondary educational institutions curious about contemporary literature often had to rely on public libraries, which received at least some of the most sought-after periodicals. The school administration usually did not encourage this practice and could issue additional rules of comportment that restricted students' use of the public library. If it did not put forth such regulations, however (or if the students found a way of dodging them), the enormous demand made it difficult to keep abreast of the latest novels.[7] Interviewed in 1912, pupils of three provincial gymnasia complained that the works most frequently discussed in the press were simply beyond their reach, the few copies available in the local library being always checked out.[8]

Though it seems beyond doubt that most (adolescent) readers who were interested eventually did get hold of a copy of *Sanin*, for a considerable time many of them, especially those in the provinces, may have known about the novel only from hearsay. The ban on *Sanin* in the spring of 1908 exacerbated this situation in that it unwittingly heightened the novel's scandalous aura while it simultaneously prevented the publication of subsequent editions that could have satisfied the increased demand.

More importantly, the enormous interest in *Sanin*, which was partly fueled by spectacular reports in the newspapers, tells us little about its reception by "ordinary" readers. Were they infatuated with Vladimir Sanin, just like Moisei Dokshitskii, or did they interpret the novel as a depressing but accurate representation of Russian society after the events of 1905? Were some of them perhaps disappointed with the novel from a purely literary point of view? Even if some critics noticed a "healthy" dismissive reaction among young readers, as we will see, other critics found the notion that *Sanin* functioned as a Bible for an entire generation considerably more attractive.

"They Have One Gospel"

In order to understand how this reputation could have emerged and how it could have been perpetuated, I think that at least two factors should be taken into account. First, we must consider the didactic intent of most nineteenth-century literature and, specifically, its use as a vehicle for the conveyance of revolutionary propaganda and social change. The reverential, almost religious attitude toward the written word ensuing from this specific use—unwittingly enhanced, of course, by the pressure of the authorities—is commonly seen as a given of Russia's literary tradition.[9] Hero-centered, as most Russian novels were (see chapter 1), and heavily indebted to the aesthetics and didacticism of nineteenth-century realism, *Sanin* was believed to be capable of making the reader adopt the hero's ideology. As I hope to prove in the course of this and the next chapter, there is little evidence that readers did in fact become Saninists. In my opinion, the novel's infamous reputation is partly the result of certain deeply entrenched notions about "how Russians read" rather than the product of genuine enthusiasm among Artsybashev's audience.

The second factor accounting for *Sanin*'s supposed status as a manual for living is the mythology of the 1860s, which continued to serve as a powerful paradigm for defining youth identity during the first years following the revolution of 1905. As is well known, the very notion of a novel serving as a Bible for an entire generation dates back to the reception of Chernyshevsky's classic *What Is to Be Done?*, which was often referred to as a new Gospel. Abounding in biblical imagery, the novel enjoyed the status of a sacrosanct text among radical students. Memoirs and autobiographical writings testify that the novel inspired several generations of Russian radicals to transform their personal lives, supplying them with a clearly defined behavioral code. As Olga Matich has shown, the novel exerted considerable influence, even on circles usually not associated with political activism, the never consummated marriage of Zinaida Hippius and Dmitrii Merezhkovskii providing a striking example.[10]

Though the analogy with Chernyshevsky's classic was hardly ever evoked at the time, the idea of *Sanin* as a new Gospel proved to be highly significant for its reception history. As we saw in chapter 2, one of the things that worried the censor was precisely Sanin's supposed kinship with other nihilist heroes, such as Mark Volokhov, Bazarov, and Rakhmetov. Even the popular images of the "new nihilists" could be strikingly similar to those employed in the 1860s. In *The Free Love League* (*Liga svobodnoi liubvi* [1910]), for example, a dilettante play by D. A. Funkendorf that depicts the moral downfall of some naive *Sanin* readers, one of the female debauchers is described as an "old spinster, a *kursistka*, . . . ugly, with manly manners [*s muzhkimi manerami*], hair cut short, wearing glasses, smoking."[11] This caricature seems to be directly transposed from the antinihilist novels of the 1860s and 1870s.[12]

Instances where *Sanin* is directly referred to as the "Gospel" can be found, among other places, in the boulevard press, which, in the spring of 1908, published a number of sensationalist reports on juvenile debauchery supposedly propelled by the reading of "pornographic" literature, particularly *Sanin*. According to one reporter who covered the juicy story of a free love league in Kiev, the local profligates recognized only Sanin as their primary ideologist. Grouping very disparate authors with whose work he probably was not familiar himself, this journalist evoked the image of a religious sect engaging in erotically charged rituals: "They have one Gospel: *Sanin* and his four evangelists in the person of Artsybashev, Kamenskii, Potiomkin, and Kuzmin. It is reported that the rooms where the league members hold their dances [*radeniia*], are entirely covered with texts by these authors."[13] It appears that readers often shared this idiom, referring to Artsybashev's and Kamenskii's work as a "Gospel" and a "manual."[14] The spectacular rumors about the free love leagues are examined in more detail in the next chapter.

These examples show how eagerly commentators (and especially the yellow press) posited a causal relationship between reading *Sanin* and the behavior of its audience. This in itself does not make the novel's reception history unique, of course, the influence of literature (or television) on its recipients being a perennial concern of those claiming authority in matters of education and moral upbringing. What *is* revealing, though, is the fact that in defining this influence, many observers unconsciously drew on the mythologies and literary practices of the 1860s, thereby constructing a caricature of *Sanin* readers as uncompromising zealots determined to implement the novel's ideas in their personal lives.

Undeniably, some of this has trickled down into the work of modern scholars. Echoing the anxiety of Artsybashev's contemporaries, Richard Stites, for example, believes that the "Saninist phenomenon . . . became a style of behavior among the young," resulting even in "Saninist sex clubs springing up in Russian cities."[15] Writing on vulgarized Nietzscheanism in Russian turn-of-the-century literature, Edith Clowes simply reiterates D. S. Mirsky, stating that "the novel soon became the Bible for a whole generation of young people disillusioned with social and political activism."[16] More recently, Laura Engelstein has proven more cautious, analyzing the preoccupations and ideological biases of those condemning *Sanin* rather than the novel's alleged influence.[17] Eric Naiman, on the other hand, argues that *Sanin* was "influential" because it purported to offer a "unified world view that blended changes in contemporary attitudes about morality into a new sexual ethos." Instead of introducing a completely new behavioral model, Naiman seems to imply, *Sanin* helped to articulate certain ideas already in the air.[18] Marina Mogil'ner's 1999 study *The Mythology of the "Underground Man"* marks a definite return to the myth of *Sanin* as the new Gospel. Devoting an entire chapter to it, Mogil'ner asserts that imitation of Artsybashev's hero was rampant.[19] Finally, an even more recent history of turn-of-the-century literature claims that "groups of 'sanintsy' proliferated among the educated youth."[20]

Whether they regard *Sanin* either as a mirror or a model or both at the same time, most scholars seem to agree that it enjoyed enormous popularity. The question they have failed to ask, however, is why the novel elicited so few positive reactions if it did strike a sympathetic chord with the interrevolutionary generation. Why, if it really was that popular, did virtually no one speak out in favor of its purported message? Why did the "Saninists" keep still? The next section is an attempt to restore the rare and feeble voices of those anonymous readers who may have felt genuinely attracted to *Sanin* and its perceived message. Yet again we will see that, in most cases, these voices are embedded in the speech of a critic or a memoirist who deeply deplores the Saninist phenomenon or dismisses it as a short-lived rage among school-going youth.

Voices from the Readers

Inevitably, very few personal accounts of ordinary readers have been preserved. Nearly all comments on *Sanin*'s alleged cult status were made by people who either rejected its message, belittled its literary merits, or simply were skeptical about the originality of Artsybashev's ideas. If we turn to those rare instances where anonymous readers were given a chance to make themselves heard, we discover that the general attitude toward *Sanin* appears to have been less reverential than is usually assumed. Let us briefly examine a few reactions of adolescents who, like Moisei Dokshitskii, saw no option other than to consult the oracle at the estate of Iasnaia Poliana, Lev Tolstoy. Even if most of these comments have reached us through the writing of Tolstoy's personal doctor and chronicler, Dushan Makovitskii, Makovitskii's "fly-on-the-wall" approach makes it possible to establish fairly accurately what these *Sanin* readers were trying to say (or, at least, what they were *not* trying to say).

In his well-known *Notes of Iasnaia Poliana* (*Iasnopolianskie zapiski* [repr. 1979]), Dushan Makovitskii briefly relays a conversation between Tolstoy and a young visitor who seemed quite impressed with *Sanin*. In Makovitskii's words: "Young Iunge spoke about Artsybashev's *Sanin*, saying that it contains a good, truthful description of what is going on; that Artsybashev is done an injustice by those who condemn him, as well as by those who feel nothing but admiration for him."[21] In accordance with his function as a chronicler, Makovitskii reports this conversation in an impartial manner letting the characters of his narrative speak for themselves. "Young Iunge" is clearly very positive about Artsybashev, but he is not depicted as being infatuated with him. In fact, the very choice of words suggests that Iunge appreciated Artsybashev's novel as an accurate analysis of Russian society ("a good, truthful description of what is going on") but did not necessarily admire its protagonist or its program.

Two months later, Tolstoy was visited by a gymnasium student who, according to Makovitskii, "defined the central message of *Sanin* as follows: 'Enjoy yourself completely, live just as you wish, there is no morality'" (*veselis' vovsiu, zhivi kak vzdumaetsia, nikakoi nravstvennosti net*).[22] Makovitskii gives Tolstoy ample opportunity to condemn such a carefree attitude toward life, and it seems as though the student is condoning Sanin's behavior and Tolstoy is "correcting" him. Yet it is feasible that this student was merely summarizing the novel's message as he understood it and wanted Tolstoy to pronounce his verdict.

An even more ambivalent reaction to *Sanin* can be found in a letter to Tolstoy written by a certain Gol'berg on behalf of the educated youth of the town of Cherkassy in the Ukraine. The author claims to know for a fact that the novel has made a "strong impression" on Russia's youth, but apparently the response of Cherkassy was not exactly ebullient: "We also belong to the educated youth and having read this work, we don't know what to think of it." Clearly, Gol'berg and his fellow students were at a loss as to how their own response to Artsybashev's novel could differ so much from that of their peers elsewhere in the country.[23] Written on November 20, 1909, this letter illustrates how readers' expectations were shaped by the novel's spectacular reputation, which then turned out to be unfounded.

Confusion, doubt, and disbelief—these, and not so much genuine enthusiasm and admiration, were the feelings that *Sanin* readers experienced, according to Zinaida Hippius. Writing from Paris, where she emigrated to in the 1920s, she remembers how students and other young people would visit her and ask for her advice: "To live or not to live according to Sanin?"[24] The Hamletesque ring of this question suggests that the students did not expect she would have an answer.

But what about Dokshitskii, who claimed to have found in *Sanin* the answer to all his questions, even if this feeling did not last very long? Was he an exception? Not quite. One finds, for example, the following elated reaction jotted down in the margins on an old edition of *Sanin*: "What a wonderful book! After reading it one wants to live even more!"[25] But it is impossible to tell whether this view is representative of the thousands of anonymous readers who did not record their impressions or whether the author of this comment took anything from the novel except a general life-affirming message. Disappointingly, perhaps, even the few uninhibited reactions of ordinary readers that we possess leave the impression that the general response to *Sanin* was critical or lukewarm at best and that even a more positive judgment does not necessarily imply endorsement of the perceived message.

Another way to establish some of the effect of *Sanin* on its readers is to look for statistical data. At the end of the nineteenth century, statistics were held in high esteem as an exact discipline that would enable scientists to acquire reliable quantitative information on such perennially mysterious phenomena as suicide, sexual behavior, and literary preferences. Unfortunately, statistical data on Artsybashev's readers and their response to his work are extremely scant. Unlike Lidiia Charskaia's public, for example, which was clearly defined and frequently queried by her publisher for commercial reasons, Artsybashev's more heterogeneous readership was never the object of polling specifically about him and his work.[26] His name does appear in surveys of a more general nature, however, though not as frequently and persistently as his reputation would suggest.

In 1910 the journal *Vestnik znaniia* (*Herald of Knowledge*) published the results of an opinion poll conducted among primary school teachers, civil servants, priests, workers, and students from various parts of the country (including Siberia). Respondents were asked to name the six most important writers of Russian literature. A total of 3,068 votes were cast, only 16 of which went to Artsybashev. The competition was formidable (respondents could include dead authors as well), but, still, the votes in favor of Artsybashev constituted less than 0.5 percent.[27] A similar survey conducted among the pupils of a provincial gymnasium in the Moscow district in May 1914 brought to light that Tolstoy, Dostoevsky, and Lermontov were Russia's most popular authors, followed at some distance by Andreev and Charskaia. Of the 183 pupils who bothered to give their opinion, only one named Artsybashev.[28]

Sanin also figured in queries about lifestyle and sexual behavior among the youth, especially when the respondents were asked about their reading habits and attitude toward pornography.[29] Yet these polls tell us little more than that *Sanin* was widely read by students (that is, in the big cities), not necessarily that readers all over the country stylized themselves in the hero's image, as many disdainful critics maintained. Some respondents contrasted Tolstoy (*The Kreutzer Sonata*) and Andreev ("In the Fog" and "The Abyss") favorably with Artsybashev, whose work they considered "corrupting" and "titillating."[30] One student, queried in 1912, went so far as to admit that he had been a "Saninist" in principle for some time but added that he had rapidly lost interest and had never even considered putting his ideas into practice.[31] This student's comment suggests that *Sanin* functioned primarily as a convenient narrative for framing (one's own) moral dissolution rather than as a behavioral model to be adopted at all costs. The paucity of more or less spontaneous and accurately recorded reactions, as well as the crudeness of opinion polls with their often highly leading questions, makes it impossible to determine what influence, if any, *Sanin* had on the behavior of individual readers. And yet, even on the basis of this flimsy material, we can conclude that readers responded with considerably less zeal than popular belief has it. Of course, one could object that only readers tormented by feelings of doubt and confusion felt the need to consult Tolstoy, whereas a hard-core Saninist would not even consider doing so. In other words, the reactions examined in this section could reflect only one part of a wider range of possible responses. But even if this were so, the absence of any real enthusiasm for Sanin's ideas in the opinion polls and the letters to Tolstoy undermine the popular conviction that *Sanin* functioned as a second *What Is to Be Done?* The first documented case of a historical personality taking his inspiration from Artsybashev's novel and copying the protagonist's behavior has not yet been delivered.

Sanin and the Female Reader

Sanin's exaltation of sensual pleasure was widely considered immoral or at least immorally one sided, but critics, especially on the left, believed his attitude to be particularly degrading to women. The revolutionary code of honor, founded on the principle of equality between the sexes, dictated that men regard their female colleagues as comrades rather than as potential sexual partners—a behavioral paradigm exemplified by the celibate marriage. Sanin's aggressive erotic individualism challenges this model, for although his relationship with Karsavina eventually acquires a sense of comradeship, it is clearly the physical attraction that comes first. Artsybashev goes even further: if the behavioral code of the 1860s "de-eroticized" the relationship between husband and wife, making it resemble the asexual relationship between siblings, then Sanin does exactly the opposite by repeatedly casting a lustful gaze at his own sister.[32]

What did female readers think of Vladimir Sanin's behavior? Were there any women who modeled themselves on the female characters or, perhaps, on Sanin himself? Eric Naiman, the first modern scholar to pay attention to the misogynistic overtones in the novel, finds it "hard to imagine that any woman reading *Sanin* would adopt its professed ideology." While pretending to attack sexual hypocrisy, Naiman argues, the novel actually delights in depicting female humiliation. Even its seemingly neutral motto acquires a thoroughly misogynistic ring when read in the context of the original passage of Ecclesiastes, which deals with the difference of women and the role they are expected to play.[33] Though Naiman does not discuss the novel's reception by ordinary readers, his remarks seem to imply that *Sanin*'s popularity among female readers must have been limited.[34]

From a modern point of view, Naiman's comments may seem entirely plausible, but some of Artsybashev's contemporaries were convinced of the opposite: that *Sanin* seemed to be considered required reading particularly among girls and young women. Reports on the scandalous behavior of Artsybashev devotees often stressed that women's involvement was equal to that of men. An article on the secret sex club that went by the name of Darefa, published in the generally highly regarded daily *Birzhevye vedomosti* (*Stock Exchange News*) in 1908, reads: "The most horrible and shocking thing about the despicable activities of 'Darefa' is that its members do not contend themselves with their own ruin but make propaganda on a broad scale among their fellow students and intensively recruit new followers. Girls too are involved in carrying on propaganda and recruitment."[35] One lecturer speaking at a gymnasium for boys was perplexed to find that female readers were *especially* fond of Sanin given his deprecatory treatment of women.[36] Like Naiman, this commentator acknowledges the novel's male chauvinist slant, but, unlike Naiman, he was nonetheless convinced of its popularity with female readers.

The recurring image of the *kursistka* captured by the virile figure of Vladimir Sanin doubtless reflected a general anxiety about the degeneration of the educated classes as well as more traditional notions about the intellectual inaptitude of women. Yet the novel itself probably conduced to the idea of a predominantly female response as well. What appears to have disturbed many of Artsybashev's critics, apart from Sanin's own behavior, is the novel's presumption to offer a new sexual ethic to both men *and* women. Though to the twenty-first-century reader, as Naiman suggests, this is one of the least convincing aspects of it, *Sanin* does seem to extend to women the traditional male privilege of sexual liberty. Even if this professed female empowerment is only the product of male fantasy, the novel clearly challenges late nineteenth-century notions of female sexuality by portraying young ladies as capable of experiencing and even exploring sensual pleasure.

In the opinion of such renowned psychiatrists as Cesare Lombroso and Veniamin Tarnovskii, healthy women would submit to intercourse only for the sake of motherhood. Any female sexual activity not directed at procreation was therefore deemed pathological.[37] In addition, Artsybashev's contemporary, the Austrian philosopher Otto Weininger, whose *Sex and Character* (*Geschlecht und Karakter* [1903]) created a sensation in Europe and Russia, asserted that female pursuit of sexual gratification was only observed among prostitutes. Against this background, Artsybashev's valorization of woman's sex life as something meaningful in itself was a shocking novelty in Russian literature—one that unwittingly helped define the female *Sanin* reader as a sexually aggressive deviant: the *saninistka*. Anastasia Verbitskaia, creator of the "Sanin in a skirt," acknowledges her debt to Artsybashev by having her promiscuous heroine Mania El'tsova read and debate the novel.[38]

Cultural mythology provided another explanation for why *Sanin* was supposedly so popular among girls. Behind the image of the *saninistka* often lurked the stereotype of the "provincial young lady" (*provintsial'naia baryshnia*) who naively reads her own spiritual history into the lives of her literary heroes (of course, the paradigmatic example is young Tatyana in *Evgenii Onegin*). Female readers, and girls in particular, were vulnerable to Sanin's philosophy, it was assumed, precisely because they were too gullible and frivolous to understand its true nature. Not surprisingly, popular depictions of female *Sanin* followers that tapped into this tradition invariably cast them in the role of victim while assigning to male readers the traditional role of seducer. Men appear as distorting women's natural logic—which manifests itself in the latter's supposed aversion to sex—by infusing them with the "unfeminine" feeling of lust. A virulent column by the brilliant polemicist Vasilii Rozanov illustrates this point in more detail.

As we have seen, the author of the anonymous countertext *Sanin, Mr. Artsybashev, and Woman* interpreted *Sanin* as an unabashed legitimization of male vice. In so doing, he reflected received wisdom, which held that sexual pleasure (let alone prowess) was unknown to "healthy" women. Ideally speaking, woman's natural "logic" simply resisted the hedonistic pursuits in which men like Vladimir Sanin engaged.

The publicist and literary critic Vasilii Rozanov expressed this idea more explicitly in his column in the right-wing daily *Novoe vremia* (*New Times*). Published in the same year as *Sanin, Mr. Artsybashev, and Woman*, it relays a conversation between a narrator (clearly a mouthpiece for Rozanov) and a reluctant female follower of Sanin. Typically, the girl is characterized as a provincial *kursistka*, "somewhere from the Urals," whose "rural looks" and common sense are said to contrast sharply with the "unnatural" ideas she is trying to defend. Rozanov's point is that this pure and healthy girl from the Russian heartland abhors Sanin's gospel of free love, but she is pressured by a few male students to move in with them and "live just like Sanin."[39] After an indecisive attempt by the girl to justify Sanin's philosophy, Rozanov takes over and eloquently exposes Sanin's ideas as myopic and unnatural. By professing sensual pleasure without giving much thought to the consequences, the *artsybashevtsy* do not simply "give heed to nature," Rozanov explains; on the contrary, they act *un*naturally, because they shirk the responsibilities that come with parenthood.[40]

Given the importance of the notion of "naturalness" (*natura veshchei*) in this conversation, Rozanov's choice to have Sanin represented by a backsliding female disciple speaks volumes, of course. The daughter of a Russian priest, she is firmly rooted in the "time-honored Russian way of life" and destined to follow the example of her two older sisters, who are already married.[41] The girl's lukewarm reaction to the students' proposal, Rozanov intimates, is nature itself revolting against such irresponsible hedonism. By helping to silence the *artsybashevets* in her ("She fell silent. I helped her"),[42] Rozanov simultaneously allows her to retrieve her true natural self.

As these examples indicate, female *Sanin* readers were viewed as too naive to recognize its genuine destructive message or, on the contrary, as standing too close to nature to internalize it. In either case, they appeared ill-equipped to deal with the perils of Saninism independently, that is, without the interference of "nature" and the moral guidance of some (male) mentor figure. The *saninistka* was thereby defined primarily as an "unnatural" creature, in contrast to her male counterpart whose licentiousness might be immoral or irresponsible but not necessarily "abnormal."

Absent in these portraits of female *Sanin* readers is the political explanation so frequently used in connection with male interest in Saninism. Contemporaries never singled out disappointment with the revolutionary ideals of 1905 as the cause of sexual corruption. This is in keeping with Laura Engelstein's observation that the revolution failed "to provoke images of disruptive female passion."[43] What prevailed was the figure of the provincial *baryshnia* who desperately tries to keep pace with the latest trends but is ignorant of the real social issues. This also accounts for the ambiguity with which the image of the female *Sanin* reader was invested. Commentators often tried to downplay the significance of Saninism by claiming that it was just a trend among schoolgirls and *kursistki*. Yet, accustomed to viewing woman as a measure of society's moral standards, they simultaneously singled out the *saninistka* as the most unsettling proof of the nation's moral decline.

The Provincial Reader

As we saw in chapter 2, liberal and leftist critics trying to come to grips with Saninism faced the difficult task of incorporating a "reactionary" phenomenon into a teleological model of historical progress. One way of solving this problem was to suggest that Russia was merely witnessing the last convulsions of a regime doomed to disappear in the near future. In keeping with this view, the author of *Sanin, Mr. Artsybashev, and Woman* characterized Artsybashev's hero as individualism's last shimmer (*posledniaia vspyshka individualizma*) before the final triumph of communal ideals.[44]

Other critics, however, focused their attention on the provinces, hoping to find evidence that the sexual vogue in Russian literature was a purely urban phenomenon and that, consequently, revolutionary momentum in the country as a whole had not subsided. In so doing, they drew on a long-standing tradition of presenting the supposedly less enlightened parts of Russia as a reservoir of the true national spirit—a tradition that dated back at least to Aleksandr Radishchev's travelogue *Journey from St. Petersburg to Moscow* (*Puteshestvie iz Peterburga v Moskvu* [1790]). Yet even for those who did not share this propensity to idealize the Russian heartland, the provinces could serve as an indicator of the nation's political mood. In this light, the reception of *Sanin* by the "average" provincial reader appeared as a litmus test of the people's political consciousness.

Of all the commentators who tried to assess the provincial response to sexually explicit literature, no one painted as paradoxical a picture as Piotr Pil'skii, one of the most outspoken opponents of Artsybashev.[45] Like many highbrow critics, Pil'skii rejected *Sanin* because of its "vulgarized" Nietzscheanism—a feature he contemptuously labeled "provincial": "The novel *Sanin* is superficial, it is completely shallow with its shallow-naive purport, its uncomplicated little idea, its provincialism."[46] However, though Pil'skii may initially have used the term metaphorically to expose the author's "distorted" understanding of Nietzsche, in his account of his lecturing tour through southern Russia and Ukraine in the spring of 1908, *Sanin* emerges as a best seller among provincial *readers*. Thus, the term "provincial" suddenly took on a social-geographic immediacy.

Pil'skii's account of his tour reads almost like a nineteenth-century travelogue in which a narrator (a bewildered and amused resident of St. Petersburg) is typically confronted with Russia as it "really" is. Pil'skii's real Russia is a realm of naive, provincial readers who imbibe the latest literature—pornographic literature in particular—with almost endearing seriousness. Not only are *Sanin* and Kamenskii's "Leda" constantly checked out of the local libraries of Kiev and Kherson, Pil'skii observes condescendingly, but Artsybashev's provincial readers appear to identify with the protagonists to the extent that "every town now has its own Sanins and Karsavinas." In contrast to the Petersburger, for whom a "book by a *belletrist* can never become a Koran," the provincial reader has little interest in literary analysis; he merely wants to be told "how to live."[47] This explains, according to Pil'skii, why even a "book on sexual freedom," such as *Sanin*, could very easily become a kind of Bible.[48] Pil'skii then gives a patronizing description of the "confused poor young ladies of Kherson," who desperately try to lay their hands on a copy of *Sanin* but are prepared to settle for Turgenev's *On the Eve*.[49]

Given the significance that he attached to the provincial reader, one would expect Pil'skii to be dismayed with the success of *Sanin*—a novel he thoroughly disliked, as we have just seen.[50] Yet, in a peculiar twist of revolutionary optimism, he interpreted its popularity as evidence of the nation's general discontentment. The form in which this discontent manifested itself might be "reactionary," he conceded, but it was still a protest against the existing order. Under the present circumstances, the reading of sexually explicit literature was to be understood as an act of resistance, a promising sign that the "children" still rejected the bourgeois morality of their "fathers." By and large, Pil'skii concluded, Russian youth was "healthy." Thus, by turning the provincial reader into a bearer of political virtue, Pil'skii contrived to accommodate the perceived spread of Saninism to his belief in the revolution.

Pil'skii's description of the provincial reader devouring *Sanin* suggests that its reception might have been somewhat different in the Russian heartland than in St. Petersburg or Moscow. Indeed it is tempting to assume that provincial (and, perhaps, inexperienced) readers responded to *Sanin* in a more spontaneous manner, whether or not they accepted its message. The most uninhibited reactions to the spectacular rumors that *Sanin* helped to create came, as we have seen, from readers in the provinces. Still, there is too little reliable information on the "provincial" response to *Sanin* to substantiate Pil'skii's highly subjective picture. What we can infer from it is that those who attended his lectures were very interested in the novel, not that they endorsed its ideology. Like the authors who claimed *Sanin* was just a fad among schoolgirls, Pil'skii eagerly exploited the cliché of the provincial young lady in order to make the commotion around *Sanin* look more innocent. While repeatedly poking fun at the "poor young ladies of Kherson," he upgraded provincial readers, promoting them as a barometer of political sentiments.

It is interesting to note that the populist critic Iakov Danilin arrived at similar conclusions as Piotr Pil'skii on the basis of entirely different observations. *Sanin* might be popular with the corrupted elite of St. Petersburg, Danilin intimated, but a cursory look at the provincial newspapers was sufficient to ascertain that the nation as a whole condemned it. Unlike the critics in the capital, Danilin argued, the provincial critics still shared the tastes and opinions of their audience. In effect, their diatribes against *Sanin* could be said to "reflect the mood of the average gray reader."[51]

Danilin found additional evidence of the nation's healthy response in *Sanin, Mr. Artsybashev, and Woman*. In this artistically clumsy attempt to debunk Artsybashev's ideas, Danilin again discerned the voice of the "average gray reader." In keeping with the intelligentsia's traditional prerogative to speak on behalf of the common people, Danilin articulated the "true" intention behind *Sanin, Mr. Artsybashev, and Woman* in typically populist fashion: "This little book, which does not state the author, or the publisher, is a profound symbol of that nameless Russia that, with tens of thousands, has silently [*molcha*] read Artsybashev's masterpiece and has silently [*molcha*], yet wisely and correctly, rejected it."[52] Danilin, like so many Marxist and populist critics, saw Saninism primarily as a class-bound phenomenon. Convinced of the moral superiority of the common folk, he disposed of it by dismissing it as yet another manifestation of modern city life that, by its very nature, was "alien" to the Russian people.

Educated Youth: The *Sanin* Reader in the Popular Press

Characterized either as silent and critical, on the one hand, or as fanatical and naive, on the other, the provincial *Sanin* reader was a product mainly of the intelligentsia's preoccupations: the vulgarization of highbrow culture and the moral purity of the common people. The commercial press, catering to a different audience, presented a somewhat different reader. In its sensationalist reporting on the inroads of Saninism, it concentrated almost exclusively on students of secondary schools and institutions for higher education, in short, on what was generally referred to as "educated youth" (*uchashchaiasia molodezh'*).

This preference did not mean that the press entirely abandoned issues of class or political orientation, for it focused in its reports of juvenile depravity mostly on the children of the intelligentsia and white-collar workers. It simply redefined the question of Saninism in less abstract terms by attributing it to a loss of moral discipline among the youth caused by the latter's increased disregard for both state and parental authority. In effect, in the perception of the mass-circulation press, Saninism could manifest itself both in the public and private domains. It could be understood as an outgrowth of political activism among pupils of secondary schools during the years 1905-6 and at the same time could be linked to the perceived deficiencies of the modern family and its apparent neglect of children's moral education. The media thus furnished the reader with conflicting images, reporting sometimes on students' rowdy behavior, sometimes on schoolchildren reading *Sanin* on the sly and signing up for a Saninist sex club. As I discuss in chapter 6 in more detail, the uniting signifier connecting these images was the topos of "fathers and children," understood both traditionally as an ideological conflict between generations and more topically as a crisis of modern family life.

Although newspapers occasionally published shortened versions of public lectures on *Sanin,* journalists were not concerned with literature as such. They begrudged the "dissipation" of the young in more general terms remarking, by way of illustration, on the increased interest in "pornographic literature" and listing Artsybashev indiscriminately with Anatolii Kamenskii, Kuzmin, Sologub, and even Bal'mont. However, reports on massive imitation of literary heroes focused almost completely on *Sanin*—its hero being readily stigmatized as a dangerous role model for youth. Some newspapers went so far as to portray the Saninists as publicly proclaiming their source of inspiration.

In March 1908, for example, the *Moskovskii golos* (*The Moscow Voice*) reported that a crowd of over three hundred youngsters had broken up a literary evening dedicated to *Sanin* by loudly declaring, "We are Saninists! We no longer recognize old-fashioned conventions!"[53] When the speaker suggested that the lecture be canceled because of the increased fire hazard with such a large crowd, the Saninists climbed up on the stage and started smoking. In its report on the same event, the widely read newspaper *Russkoe slovo* (*The Russian Word*) asserted that the crowd had consisted not of three hundred but of three thousand hooligans, "all of them students, the majority female!"[54] Iakov Danilin, however, who claimed to have been an eyewitness, emphatically denied that anything untoward had happened that night. The speaker's condemnation of Sanin's worldview was applauded by almost the entire audience, he insisted, so that the "general mood at that evening was far from Sanin-like."[55]

A few days after the alleged incident, *Moskovskii golos* published a comical poem titled "Song of the *Sanintsy*," in which the Saninists challenge the "yoke of morality" by glorifying their own behavior. Though the author seems to mock the coverage by the media rather than trying to expose the unsavory intentions of Artsybashev's followers, the very choice of the subject suggests that the original reports had aroused considerable public anxiety. The song is a typical example of the "city newspaper feuilleton"—a flourishing poetic genre in local turn-of-the-century newspapers that treated topical issues and rumors in a light-hearted manner.[56]

SONG OF THE "SANINTSY"

We Saninists are the heroes
Of suggestive novels
And we're twice, even three times, as shameless
As hooligans on the boulevard.

. . . .

That's right! The truth can only
Be found in Artsybashev's novel.
For the sake of our education
We wander around like a herd.

. . . .

We're children of the yellow press,
We're just as shameless,
We're eternal but different,
We're Saninists! We're demons!![57]

Evidently, this picture of the Saninist as a noisy troublemaker is grafted onto that of the hooligan who consciously violated the boundaries of the respectable and assaulted street life. Yet even in this "song," which invokes hooliganism as a measure of boisterous and provocative behavior, the Saninists are identified as young and educated people determined to realize a specific program. This clearly sets them apart from the "real" hooligans, who were from the lower strata of society and were not driven by any kind of ideology. Moreover, as *Russkoe slovo* did not fail to point out, Saninism supposedly enjoyed the support of both men and women—another crucial difference with the exclusively male character of hooliganism.[58]

Sanin and Its Readers

On other occasions, boulevard newspapers would stress the youthfulness of Artsybashev's audience, sometimes even presenting them as mere schoolchildren. In fact, so convincing was the caricature of the dissolute *Sanin*-reading gymnasium student that it became a saleable commodity ensuring the expedient author instant success. A good example of this is Roman Dobryi's *Why Do Young People End in Suicide?* (*Pochemu molodezh' konchaet samoubiistvom*), a purely market-driven collection of stories published in 1911. Though thinly disguised as "social-literary sketches" that probe into the moral crisis of the younger generation, they are in fact nothing but quick rehashes of sensationalist newspaper reports on juvenile "dissipation."[59] In the first chapter, characteristically called "The Influence of Contemporary Literature on Our Youth," Dobryi's narrator reproduces a conversation he has had with a fourteen-year-old "brat" (*balbes*) and his younger sister. Much to his dismay, the narrator discovers that the popular authors of his own childhood, such as Jules Verne and James Fenimore Cooper, are no longer in demand. Nowadays, the youth prefer detective and other crime fiction, but they also keep up with contemporary Russian literature:

—And what else do you read besides detectives?
Brother and sister exchanged a quick, almost imperceptible glance.
—Well . . . various contemporary authors.
—Like whom, for example?
—Artsybashev, Andreev, Kamenskii, Sollogub [*sic*].
—Who gives you these authors?
They looked at me in surprise.
—What do you mean, "Who gives us these authors"? We get them ourselves.
—Where?
—Partly from our parents, partly from friends, from the library, or we just buy them.
—And do you like, say, Artsybashev?
—O yeah, very much! Especially *Sanin*.
I didn't continue the conversation. Why? What was the point? When even a young girl reads and imbibes such psychopathological pornography, the product of an author who aims at the basest of tastes, what else is there to say or to be surprised about?
Would you be crushed or bewildered, if such a *saninistka* killed herself one beautiful day?[60]

Dobryi's use of clichés and stock images clearly betrays his indebtedness to the penny press. The indignant and simultaneously resigned rhetoric, the portrayal of *Sanin* readers as young gymnasium students, and the inevitable listing of the "canonical" authors of Russian pornography—all this belongs to the repertoire of the commercial press. The fact that Dobryi relied so heavily on it not only indicates the marketability of juvenile vice in Russian turn-of-the-century popular fiction but also shows how familiar and self-evident the image of the sexually corrupted gymnasium student had become. The names of Artsybashev and other "pornographic" authors in this context merely served as indices of moral dissolution intended to trigger preconceived notions about educated youth.

Sanin Read by Students

As we have just seen, critics believed Artsybashev's hero to be a role model either for readers in the provinces, for women readers, or for the school-going youth. These profiles of the "average" *Sanin* reader were informed by nineteenth-century cultural stereotypes and by popular imagery employed in the mass media (the "corrupted youth"), but they were certainly not what we would now call the novel's target group. *Sanin*, as I argued in my discussion of Count Amori's commercial sequel, *Sanin's Return*, is a novel about and intended for the Russian intelligentsia. That its intended audience was the intelligentsia did not necessarily exclude the aforementioned groups from its readership, of course, but it was the intellectual and, more specifically, the university student who could have been expected to read his own life into the novel and identify with the hero. Moreover, the two main characters (Sanin and Svarozhich) are former students and political activists who still visit study circles and engage in philosophical debates, even if their enthusiasm for such things has disappeared. What response, then, did *Sanin* generate among the members of its target group? Was it perceived as a novel about "us" and, if so, how did this affect its evaluation?

Sanin's potential status as a role model was particularly acute for the radical student movement, which had grown uncertain of its course and identity after 1905.[61] Its traditional self-image as a unified revolutionary vanguard proved no longer viable because the social and political diversity of the student population rapidly increased and because the newly acquired freedom of expression encouraged students to discuss nonpolitical topics, such as sexual morality and economic hardship. Even money matters were not without relevance for the debate on

Saninism. It is not accidental that Artsybashev portrayed his hero as a hardy and self-sufficient *ex*-student who "often had to go hungry and roam around."[62]

Still, in many ways, the notion of a crisis within the student community was as misleading as the idea of a homogenous movement that had existed before 1905. As Susan Morrissey has aptly noted, what had changed was less students' actual behavior than the interpretative framework with which they constructed a collective self. The large number of journals and study circles springing up in these years testifies to the community's vibrancy rather than its demise. Yet, "what was missing was a myth of unity, a symbol of cohesion, and a feeling of coherence," as Morrissey puts it. "Students mourned the absence of a meaningful new story."[63] The stereotype of the self-denying young activist was replaced by new clichés expressing the supposedly escapist mentality of the postrevolutionary era: the student as careerist, drunkard, or syphilitic.

It is in this context that we should situate the debate on Vladimir Sanin among students of higher education. Although he was widely considered a defeatist who had betrayed the ideals of the radical intelligentsia, some students took the line that Artsybashev's hero possessed the willpower and the boldness needed to recapture revolutionary momentum. One polytechnic student, for example, who approvingly noted the similarity between Sanin's vision of future happiness and Nietzsche's, argued that critics had missed the most valuable aspects of the novel. Instead of concentrating on its supposedly pornographic content, they should have highlighted the author's call for strength and courage, his appeal to fight dauntlessly for whatever goal one pursued: "I don't subscribe to the conclusions at which Sanin arrives. I'm appalled at the principles in accordance with which he tries to reach his goal; they arouse a strong aversion in me. Yet his straightforward pursuit of an ideal, his brave denial and struggle against prejudices and conventions, which Gorky stigmatized as slavishly bourgeois—*that* we should adopt and implement in life, sweeping away all obstacles on our road."[64]

Sanin's plea for a conscious and daring way of life not only appealed to him personally, this student maintained, but to youth in general, which explained, in his eyes, why the novel was so successful with them: "Social life has come to a standstill and to revitalize it is not in the power of such feeble wimps as Soloveichik and Svarozhich but only of people who go straight toward their goal without fear."[65] Distancing himself from Sanin's ideology, this student nonetheless valued him as a cleansing force whose ruthlessness might serve as an example to the younger generation.

How representative were these positive assessments of the views of the student community at large? And what did such assessments mean in terms of practical behavior? The sources available to us suggest that the majority of students were appalled by Sanin's program or, at best, skeptical of its practicability. Susan Morrissey describes a public discussion of the novel at St. Petersburg University, where *Sanin* was criticized for offering only a vague promise of future happiness instead of a broad and more detailed program. Whereas some considered the novel's preoccupation with sexual issues to be merely unsavory, others maintained that Sanin's hedonism was incompatible with the general development of culture and human society. As Morrissey concludes, "For [these students], the cult of pleasure seemed more an inversion of the traditional value of social service than a viable alternative to it."[66]

It is important to note, however, that the literary evening described by Morrissey was held in the fall of 1907, when the last installment of *Sanin* had just appeared and the tremendous public outcry was still ahead. Hence, the relatively moderate tone with which the St. Petersburg students condemned the novel. When the general indignation finally set in during the spring of 1908, attacks on Saninism as a philosophy of life acquired a more vigorous character. If in the first months after the publication of the novel, interest in it had been largely theoretical, now, tens of articles on *Sanin* later, it seemed that Saninism had made considerable headway. Despite the overwhelmingly critical attitude toward the figure of Vladimir Sanin throughout the press, many students became convinced that his ideas enjoyed wide support, particularly within their own ranks. The anxiety over this moral fall led to a further proliferation of articles on *Sanin*, many of which were expressly designed to unmask the hero and expose the "reactionary" nature of his ideology. Rapidly gaining discursive momentum, Saninism increasingly seemed to be a very real phenomenon that called for decisive action.

Readers Fighting Saninism: The Case of *Molodye Poryvy*

Founded in Rostov-na-Donu in the fall of 1908, the literary journal *Molodye poryvy* (*Youthful Impulses*) proved to be a particularly hospitable platform for anti-Saninists. Though the majority of contributors were probably students of some institution for higher education (university or polytechnic), the journal was open to "young literary talents" in general, provided they shared the editors' predilection for "strictly didactic literature and serious creative work." In accordance with this mission, Molodye poryvy published a series of indignant articles condemning the dissemination of pornography among young readers and the inroads of Saninism in particular.[67] Significantly, in their eagerness to strip Sanin of what they perceived as his "treacherous" charm, the authors of these articles often employed a pedantically argumentative tone as though they assumed their audience was inclined to disagree with them and side with Artsybashev's hero.

A certain A. Makeev, for example, began his lecture before an audience of gymnasium students with a quasi-philosophical remark on deceptive appearances in life. Only after this general statement did he proceed to his actual topic: "Sometimes ugly things seem beautiful when you look at them from their advantageous side. I'm talking about Sanin, the hero of Artsybashev's well-known novel." What followed was a philippic on Sanin's idleness, his contemptuous treatment of women, and his callousness toward the suicidal Soloveichik. The rhetorical end of the lecture—"What is so beautiful about this? Are we really going to follow his example?"—suggests the author feared that a considerable part of his audience might be receptive to Sanin's ideology.[68]

A similar endeavor to show Sanin's "true" nature by one B. Kaplan resulted in the conclusion that Artsybashev's hero was not a revolutionary but a fully developed bourgeois. His petty selfishness, his indifference to the weak, and his belief in sexual freedom for men and "total, almost oriental *enslavement of women*" (italics in original) clearly established him as such. At the same time, Kaplan maintained, in the political context of modern Russia these very traits—his being "a major, unabashed, strong capitalist who reckons with bourgeois morality . . . and crushes the weak and women"—did make Sanin the "new man" that would lead the nation out of the present crisis. According to Kaplan, the popularity of *Sanin* was not only indicative of the political climate in Russia but more specifically signaled the embourgeoisement of the Russian intelligentsia, which had "found its ideal in the strong and selfish type of man."[69]

Placed next to each other, these two venomous reactions clearly reflect the traditional heuristic paradox of radical criticism discussed in chapter 1. Whereas Makeev saw *Sanin* "didactically," that is, as a novel of ideas, Kaplan considered it a chronicle of contemporary life, a text that, so to say, "could not help" showing what went on in society. Both authors seemed to agree, however, that Saninism was not a purely literary phenomenon but also manifested itself in everyday life. Either inspired by the novel or simply portrayed in it, educated young people behaved like Vladimir Sanin.

To radical students, the most unsettling aspect of it was that the Saninist was basically one of their own. In contrast to the populists and the conservatives, who were quick to turn Vladimir Sanin into the social and political Other, members of the educated youth, though condemning his ideology in the strongest possible terms, could not really exclude the Saninist from their ranks. In the group's collective self-image, he was distinctly present.

Consider, for example, the following protest in *Molodye poryvy* directed against the advertising of erotic literature in the media. Signed by a group of over fifty young people, it attacked, first and foremost, the "sly entrepreneur," who tried to lure young readers into buying pornography by cunningly tagging his goods "for adults only." Yet, in describing the consequences of this unashamed pursuit of profit, the petitioners represented youth as a divided community consisting of a group of sexually depraved "victims" and another group of pure young martyrs resisting the erotic temptations of contemporary literature. Although we may assume that the protest was signed solely by people who considered themselves members of the "martyrs," it is noteworthy that they did not fully marginalize their corrupted peers. A victim of failing sex education and entrepreneurial greed, the Saninist was still seen as a member (albeit a sick one) of the collective body of students: "One weak part of youth, which is keen on such things ["pornographic" literature] and was raised in a sort of obscurity about the sexual question, has reached out for the alluring Sanin and continues to amuse itself with him. Everybody is accustomed to that and it seems nobody really minds. But the other part, the pure part of youth . . .—these young people look with sadness at their comrades, they feel offended, they are indignant when they see and read that for their friends who are weak in spirit and in the flesh the cobweb spreads out of a growing number of squalid entrepreneurs that are selling their goods and their publications right under the very nose of parents and society."[70]

The reference to the parents' leniency suggests that some of the petitioners may have been secondary school students or, in any case, that the group pretended to speak on behalf of youth in general. Yet, whatever the exact composition of the group of protesters, it is noteworthy that they referred to their dissolute peers as "comrades" and "friends," blaming the latter's fall on their parents for not giving them proper sex education and on society for allowing the entrepreneur to conduct his smutty business. While locating the responsibility for the youth's moral corruption outside the group, the antipornography lobby of *Molodye poryvy* created a collective self-image that was, by implication, "Saninist." Though the speakers condemned the pornographic vogue, they acknowledged its pernicious influence on their group as a whole.

The perceived ubiquity of sexual dissolution also raised the question of personal responsibility. How were those who had remained pure supposed to react when confronted with the unhealthy tastes of their corrupted comrades? Four members of a circle for self-education were divided over the question of whether or not it was morally right to sell pornography to "depraved people"—a dilemma that had actually assailed one of the members when someone had expressed an interest in buying the "well-known pornographic collection *Zhizn'*" (*Life*) from him.[71] Without explaining what this particular member was doing with a copy of an almanac edited by Artsybashev, the circle posed the question to the readers of *Molodye poryvy*. Was it possible to cure a depraved person without meeting at least some of his abnormal wishes, or was it a decent person's duty to simply destroy pornography at all times?[72] In the next issue, one of the editors responded by answering the latter question in the affirmative. Under all circumstances, it was wrong to sell pornography, but especially to perverted people as this would only accelerate their moral corruption: "Destroy pornography! Fight with all the means you have against the corrupting influence that pornography exerts, especially on the young."[73]

What had initially been a rather narrow debate on *Sanin* as a potential ideological platform developed within a year into a much broader discussion on students' behavior in general. Attempts to debunk Vladimir Sanin's philosophy as deceptive and indeed harmful automatically shifted the attention from the novel to its audience, thus enhancing the impression that students were either actively supporting Artsybashev's hero or unconsciously behaving like him. Saninism, most students agreed, was manifest in everyday life. At the same time, the specter of the sly entrepreneur mercilessly exploiting young people's naïveté by publishing "pornography" presented students with a more straightforward enemy than the Saninist, whom many considered a morally disoriented fellow student, a comrade led astray. Admitting that Saninism was a given of contemporary life, students were actively looking for practical ways of fighting it. Destroying literature deemed pornographic was one of them.

The *Sanin* Reader: Fact or Fiction?

What, then, can we say with certainty about *Sanin*'s audience other than that most people of the educated classes had probably read it? Was the "typical *Sanin* reader" merely an invention of the commercial press and the critics to boost print runs and tarnish the political enemy? Not entirely, for no matter how grotesque the caricatures handed down to us by Roman Dobryi and D. S. Mirsky, there is no reason to doubt that *Sanin* enjoyed the status of "required reading" among educated young people roughly between the ages of fifteen and twenty-five. Featuring almost exclusively young characters in search of self-fulfillment and a charismatic hero with a life-affirming ideology, the novel may have struck a sympathetic chord among searching adolescents and young adults. Though most youthful readers seem to have rejected Saninism as a philosophical program, it did not stop at least some of them from admiring Artsybashev's hero for his vigor and boldness. The very notion of a "hero of our time" who possessed the rigor to overcome the doldrums of revolution induced certain members of the student movement to view Vladimir Sanin in a more positive light.

More important still, without ever enjoying the status that contemporary observers attributed to it, *Sanin* occupied an important place in the expression of youth identity, in particular, in the collective self-image of students of higher education. To them, the committed *Sanin* reader was not necessarily some social or political other but an errant member of one's own group: the student community. The next chapter shows how this Saninist collective self-image also imposed itself on pupils of secondary schools and what traumatic dimensions this imposition could achieve.

6

Hard-core Saninism
The Case of the Free Love Leagues

In the summer of 1909 the town of Novokhopiorsk was up in arms. Gymnasium director Shostenko had declared the city's only park a no-go area for his pupils. In his opinion, the presence of a booth selling alcoholic beverages and the sometimes obnoxious behavior of its clientele made the park an inappropriate location for adolescents. A group of fathers was so outraged by this decision that they sent a denunciation directly to Aleksandr Shvarts, the minister of enlightenment, in which they argued that the director's "remedy" was much worse than the "disease" he sought to cure. In the park, at least, the children were under constant surveillance by the gymnasium's superintendents and their own parents, who were themselves regular visitors; now, with the children being banned from the park, nobody knew what they were up to: "Because the director has denied them access to the park, where everything is illuminated, where everything is visible, boys and girls gather in small groups and make their way to the river or to the forest, and what are they doing there? We dare to inform you that they organize all sorts of orgies by organizing some sort of free love leagues. Since we mean well by the youth and by our own sons in particular, of course, we beg and ask your excellency most humbly to cancel the decision of the debauched director and to allow . . . our children to visit the park."[1]

We do not know if the director's decision was the only cause for indignation; the fact that the fathers appealed directly to the minister and, in passing, accused the director of fornication, suggests that they had been at loggerheads with him before. But whatever the reasons behind the denunciation, the fathers considered the situation sufficiently alarming to lay it on thick and paint the darkest scenario imaginable: parents and teachers could no longer keep a check on the children, who, as a result, had organized a "free love league" at which they engaged in uninhibited sexual activity.

It is precisely this disproportionate argument that demonstrates the cunning rhetoric of the otherwise rather illiterate denunciation. The letter conjures up the specter of massive moral corruption among school-going youth by referring to the mysterious free love leagues, which had caused a national stir a year before. Although an official investigation into the veracity of the rumors about the leagues never produced any material evidence, contemporaries did not stop discovering symptoms testifying to the existence of such organizations in which schoolchildren read "pornographic literature" and turned to debauchery. Whether or not the fathers of Novokhopiorsk themselves believed the leagues to exist is impossible to ascertain, but they clearly hoped to strike a raw nerve with the minister by exploiting the spectacular rumors, which had recently caused his department so much concern.[2]

These preliminary remarks on a minor scandal in the Russian provinces serve to introduce a topic that pertains directly to the reception history of *Sanin*: the alleged moral corruption of secondary school students, in particular their rumored membership in secret sex clubs popularly known as the free love leagues or "school *ogarki* (*shkol'nye ogarki*, the exact meaning of which is discussed below). This is not to argue that the rumors about the free love leagues were *caused* by the novel or that the more profound issues behind the rumors did not exist before. The estrangement between parents and children, the hostility between family and school, the secret life of the adolescent, the police regime of the gymnasium—all these issues, which also figure in the denunciation of the fathers of Novokhopiorsk, had been openly discussed in pedagogical and medical journals well before *Sanin* was published. There was also no shortage of fictional accounts dealing with these and similar topics. And yet, the frequency with which the novel is mentioned in the context of the free love leagues indicates that the two were perceived as being indissolubly connected.[3]

Inevitably, as I turn to examining the establishment and development of the myth of the free love leagues, as I intend to do in this chapter, Artsybashev's novel itself will temporarily recede into the background. The focus will be on newspaper articles and archival materials as well as literary texts written by amateurs responding to salacious reports in the press about the immorality of young people in the schools. In the first place, I am interested in the relationship between traditional ideas concerning the social meaning of literature—literature that supplied stereotypes of young students—and the sensational discourse of the gutter press that followed the latest news. The role of the latter is extremely important, as the slackening of censorship in 1905 led to a real blossoming of periodicals.[4] This directly affected the fate of rumors, such as those circulating around the free love leagues. The intensive discussion of these rumors in newspapers made them even more plausible in particular to the grassroots audience of readers, the number of which sharply increased during the period twenty years before the revolution. It is altogether possible that without greater openness among the lower classes, the myth of the free love leagues might never have arisen.[5]

The second task of this chapter is to show that the popular discourse about the free love leagues and the depiction of the adolescents' way of life in fiction exerted a definite influence on the collective consciousness of school-age young people that is expressed in letters to the editor and in various protests against proposed actions by league members. The caricature of the dissolute gymnasium student not only became a salable commodity ensuring the expedient author high print runs; more importantly, it contributed to the creation of a collective, though ambivalent, self-image of secondary school students who, to use Foucault's terminology, developed from an "object of information" into a "subject in communication."[6] By holding the youth up to mockery or, on the contrary, by expressing pity for them and "making them the emblem of the post-revolutionary crisis," as Susan Morrissey has put it, journalists and authors of popular fiction unwittingly forced students to reflect on their identity as a group.[7] It may even be argued that—at least to a certain extent—they appropriated the clichés developed in the boulevard press, thus turning them into a refashioned group stereotype. The enigmatic history of the free love leagues was an important episode in the self-definition of school-age young people in search of their identity.

The Free Love Leagues in the Boulevard Press

At the beginning of April 1908 the local press of Minsk reported with indignation that a secret organization called the "free love league" had recently arisen in town. A manuscript copy of the league's rules, which a journalist of the daily *Okraina* (*The Outskirts*) claimed to possess, stated that the members of the league were guided by a desire to restore the "old ideal of physical beauty" by introducing a "fresh and salutary stream into the abnormal atmosphere" of society. Aspiring toward this "love of pleasure," the league recruited its disciples exclusively from among graduates of secondary schools with "good recommendations."[8] The article in *Okraina* concluded with a request that readers in possession of more accurate information about the league make it available to the editors of the newspaper.

The details that reached the right-wing newspaper *Minskoe slovo* were of a more practical nature. The newspaper claimed to have discovered that the league had "three assembly points" in various sections of town and that its members referred to each other by their first names only. The author of the article also did not fail to imply what actually happened at these meetings, although, apparently, it needed no additional explanation: "At the sound of the bell they extinguish all lamps and one hour is devoted to 'unconstrained' activities of those in attendance, after which they all disperse!"[9] Three days later, the same newspaper published a long article with a detailed description of the initiation ritual that each person wishing to enter the league would have to undergo. The solemn ritual consisted of a medical examination "in the dim light of a candle end" and the reading of excerpts from *Sanin* and from the works of Mikhail Kuzmin.[10]

Okraina's request to readers to "share more detailed information" on the free love leagues did not fall on deaf ears. In the course of one week, the editors claimed to have received several anonymous letters that shed light on the internal organization of the league and on the number of its members. It turned out that there were about seventy people who had joined and that the league was continuing with all "necessary caution" to register new members from grammar schools (*realshulen*) "as well as a dental school."[11] The existence of a special fund for the support of women who joined the league and then got pregnant testified to its foresight. Its income was derived from the three-ruble fee paid by all neophytes, entitling them to membership cards issued upon entrance to the league. Finally, according to testimony supplied by anonymous correspondents, information about the semimystical setting of these gatherings proved to be entirely true: the league's "rites" took place "exclusively in the dim light of candle ends."[12]

In publishing such secret information, newspapers did not stint on reports regarding various manifestations of social life that, directly or indirectly, testified to the presence of the league in town. Thus skeptical readers could convince themselves that the league "really" did exist and was even encroaching on the lives of nonleague members. In its editorial correspondence, *Okraina* published one letter from the mother of a schoolgirl detailing how her daughter was lured to the league's premises where she was a witness to the "most horrible orgies." Managing somehow to get home, the young woman became seriously ill and subsequently received a threatening letter from her persecutors.[13]

Even if the debauchers behaved with extreme caution, an attentive observer could certainly pick them out of crowd in the town. In no way resembling normal people, these league members bore, as one reporter for *Minskoe slovo* pointed out, "the seal of dim-witted idiocy with a dose of repulsive animal egoism mixed in." "To spend time in the company of such beings—even if only a few moments—is very difficult and painful: one feels terrified."[14] Further, the fact that the rumors did not vanish immediately could be regarded as proof. The league simply had to exist, as one journalist affirmed, his own sympathies supporting the idea of "free love" (i.e., love not based on any economic considerations), "because there are so many detailed accounts of the functions of this society, including even the names of several members."[15]

The workers in the local periodical press often mentioned other towns in their reports in which rumors of the free love leagues had also been circulating "for some time," insisting that these reports were wholly factual. Whether readers in Kiev had heard details of such leagues in Moscow or Oriol, the existence of a "precedent" conveyed ever greater plausibility to the reports of the existence of a Kievan league. This method allowed the local newspapers to create a gripping narrative in which they presented their own town as the last in a long series of places to have fallen victim to the epidemic of debauchery. For example, the first article about the leagues in *Poltavskii golos* (*Voice of Poltava*), which appeared on April 18, 1908, reported that such organizations could be encountered in Kiev, Viatka, Oriol, and even Ekaterinoslav, but it did not allude to the existence of a similar group in Poltava.[16] However, on April 26 a brief follow-up mentioned the formation of the "Poltava division of the Saratov league"; this information had been received from a "fairly reliable source."[17] A more detailed account in the next issue confirmed the worst fears; the plague of leagues "apparently had not passed our Poltava by." The information on which the newspaper relied provided "sufficient foundation so as not to have any doubts."[18]

In order to enhance the impression of complete authenticity, reporters often suggested that they appreciated all the delicacy of the theme of the leagues and therefore treated it in a rather restrained manner. Supposedly, their professional honor did not allow them to disseminate unsubstantiated information. For example, in the first account of the league in Poltava, the author claimed to be in possession of more information about its composition, but he noted that he considered it "premature for the time being."[19] The contributor to *Kievskie vesti* (*Kievan News*) manifested similar caution. He "simply refused to believe" rumors concerning the existence of a free love league in Kiev until such time as a group of young people paid a visit to the editorial office of his newspaper and managed to convince him that the opposite was true.[20] Once engaged in serious research on the matter, this reporter soon established that the league had existed for "a year and a half"; that it had been known about "for a long time and by very many people"; that its members "numbered around eighty, even up to a hundred"; and that it had at its disposal "as many as five apartments."[21] Thus the reader could conclude that a conscientious correspondent had, far from chasing after some sensational story, underestimated the dimensions of the revolting phenomenon from the very beginning, and so since he was writing about it openly now, his information had to be accurate.

Of course, some restraint was appropriate in connection with the censorship that, in the case of particularly blatant exposure, could result in seizure of the newspaper in accordance with the 1001st statute "on pornography." For this reason, it was essential to maintain the disgusted tone of a guardian of morality, one moved by sympathy for young students who were abandoned by their parents to the whims of fate. Even so, expressive declarations in the newspapers of a sincere desire to assist the younger generation did not always preserve them from the censor's interference. When *Minskii kur'er* (*Minsk Courier*) published a feuilleton under the title "House of Love," supposedly based on the results of an investigation into the local league, the vice governor went to court and the newspaper had to cease publication for several months.[22] A similar description of a gathering of league members, containing insistent hints about group sex, incurred the public prosecutor's disapprobation. It is conceivable that it was precisely the criminal case against the *Minskii kur'er* that compelled the editors of *Okraina* to block publication of a feuilleton on a similar theme, based on a "handwritten confession" of a repentant young woman, a former league member.[23]

Other attempts to exploit rumors about the leagues with more candid descriptions of orgies were also suppressed by the threat of censorship. Sketches by Roman Dobryi under the title *Secret Societies of Young*

People (Tainye obshchestva molodezhi [1908]) were seized despite the fact that the author, as the press affairs committee put it, "appeared to be issuing a warning to keep young people away from evil."[24] Of the numerous plays that touched upon the theme of the free love leagues in one way or another, only an extremely small number received permission to be produced.[25] It is characteristic that, among those admitted to the stage, we find a comedy in which one of the main characters is a frivolous writer and author of a play entitled *The Free Love League*. Having learned that such a society really exists and that his own daughter is frequenting it, the writer immediately comes to his senses and burns the manuscript of his play.[26]

The Book as a Guide to Life

In contrast to pedagogical periodicals and "thick" journals, newspapers discussed only indirectly the question of the reasons for the supposed decline of morality among youth. Analysis of the situation did not usually exceed the bounds of thunderous tirades concerning the neglect of "liberal" parents and the necessity of reestablishing discipline in schools. The mental state of students, which was described at length in the medical and pedagogical literature of the period, was rarely discussed in the popular press. On the other hand, it eagerly took up arms against contemporary literature, the influence of which it readily connected to the emergence of the free love leagues. In a commentary written in typical style, the editor of *Okraina* explained their appearance by the fact that young people, "having read the likes of Artsybashev, Kamenskii, and other contemporary pornographers," appropriated their works as reference manuals (for an extensive and highly characteristic description of a free love league, see the appendix).[27] As we have seen , the notion that *Sanin* was read as a manual for life was informed by the reception history of Chernyshevsky's novel *What Is to Be Done?*, which did enjoy the status of a sacrosanct text.

The newspaper *Novoe vremia*, which particularly relished the rumors of a Minsk league, reported on the adventures of a certain Aleksei, who had imagined himself to be Vladimir Sanin. The young man not only led an extremely wild life but also corrupted others; as a result, an entire "gang of Saninists" was established in Minsk.[28] It is characteristic that the author of this report derived his information about Aleksei of Minsk in part from the "The House of Love," but he himself added that, in this story, *Sanin* played a "decisive role" (whereas the novel is never mentioned in the feuilleton). Presenting the events described in the feuilleton as entirely indisputable facts, the author supposed a direct causal link between Artsybashev's novel and the dissolute behavior of youth.

The repeated mention of "rites" in descriptions of the leagues shows that they were considered the same as secret societies of sectarians, in particular, the flagellants. This connection is comprehensible if one recalls that the sect rejected traditional marriage, a position that gave rise to its dubious reputation. One can therefore say that, to a considerable extent, the model for interpreting rumors about "collective depravity" already existed. In addition, rumors about the free love leagues coincided with a high point in the Russian investigation of sects, at the foundation of which lay, as is well-known, not merely ethnographic interest.[29] It is altogether possible that the "flagellant aspect" of the myth of the leagues was conditioned by the broadening of discourse concerning sectarianism in the period that interests us.

Yet there were other aspects that contributed to the formation of the quasi-mystical aura of the leagues. The writers of feuilletons often mentioned the use of "candle ends" (*ogarki*) in the light of which these league meetings were reputed to take place. According to several versions, these candle ends burned down or were extinguished, and that signaled the beginning of "free sexual relations." Here is a description of a certain "faction" in Perm that includes almost all the characteristic elements: "Participants of both sexes gather at a location rented by the 'faction,' each person contributing a candle end of a certain size. While these *ogarki* are still burning, the young people engage in conversation, read, and drink beer. When darkness reigns, the realization of 'freedom of sexual relations' begins, that is, an orgy of open debauchery."[30]

The paradoxical nature of this picture—the league members wait for the onset of darkness to engage in *open* debauchery—is an indication of its deeply rhetorical nature: it is not so much the activity itself but rather the circumstance that it takes place in "darkness" that arouses suspicion (although, if one were to reason logically, this circumstance would make the debauchery less open). In general, we are dealing with a denunciatory text, the roots of which go back at least to the time of the Schism. In his book entitled *Khlyst (Flagellant)*, Aleksandr Etkind quotes a denunciation (from 1672) against the heretical-*kapitony* that is structured according to a scheme strikingly similar to that in the reports from the *Permskie vedomosti* (*Perm News*): "And in the evenings, when

Hard-core Saninism 151

they put out the lights, they engage in fornication. And they say about that fornication: even though it's fornication, there's nothing sinful about it."[31] It is clear that the detail of extinguishing the light reflects the moral-evaluative system of the denouncer for whom "fornication" is a shadowy affair that can only be carried out in darkness.

And so, despite the fact that the popular press stubbornly insisted on trying to create the impression of unprecedented moral catastrophe, the figurative language used consisted of an assortment of stereotypes that derived from the cultural mythology of the 1860s and from even older representations of the sexual depravity practiced by mystical sects. From these two sources, the first proved to be the most important. The very word "league" conveys more educational than mystical connotations, which, in general, was more fitting with the conception of league members as intelligent young people engaged in reading recent literature in common.[32] The task of the free love league—in the opinion of the press and of those writers who made use of rumors in one way or another—was "conscious" struggle with obsolete forms of sexual morality. As the principal debauchee and ideologist of the league in the amateur melodrama *Children of the Twentieth Century* (*Ogarki*) (1908) declares: "The fundamental and most important doctrine of our religion is—liberated from all conventions and absurd prejudices—free love!"[33] In the final analysis, the popular press considered the reason for the emergence of the free love league not mysticism but political radicalism and moral nihilism.

Ogarki, Failures, and Candle Ends

The activation of the "sectarian" subtext in the myth of the free love leagues very likely arose by virtue of the somewhat enigmatic semantics of the word *ogarki*. At first sight, its interpretation as a "source of light" corresponds to the idea of a secret gathering and therefore seems entirely convincing. However, one can well pose the question: why, precisely, did the newspapers glom on to the word *ogarok* (candle end) when they could easily have made do with the word *svecha* (candle)? The functional difference is not substantial; nevertheless, the more specific word *ogarok* was much preferred.

The repeated use of the word *ogarki* in reports about the free love leagues, in all likelihood, was conditioned by the appearance in 1906 of a tale by the same title by the writer Skitalets. *Ogarki* is the derogatory sobriquet for a group of drunkards who reside together in an underground location nicknamed the Den of Funereal Venus. Their wild merriment causes the irritation of the local population living in fear of a cholera epidemic. But even the rowdy lack of concern of the *ogarki* themselves has its opposite side. In the depths of their souls, they are ashamed of their absence of "genuine activity and real life, worthy of them."[34] Imbued with awareness of their own uselessness, they have broken with the intelligentsia (a "culturally isolated race") and have created an "independent faction of *ogarki*" that will arise and "someday utter its *ogarki*-like pronouncements."[35]

Skitalets's *ogarki* are unified more by their lack of success than by their common social origin. Among them, one finds a dismissed student and a former seminarian but also workers. Defending himself from the critics accusing him of depicting Gorky-like tramps, Skitalets subsequently considered it necessary to emphasize that his heroes were relegated to the role of *ogarki* by their own "inherent talents."[36] As a whole, they were all capable people, possessing gifts of enormous spiritual strength but, given the current state of affairs, they were unable to advance, to take up the position they deserved.[37] If one believes the author, then *ogarki* were a kind of bohemian proletariat who could be encountered throughout the country: "One can assume that there were many *ogarki* in Rus', that this 'faction' existed in all of Russia's climatic zones."[38]

In Skitalets's tale, it is easy to identify those elements that we regularly meet when investigating rumors of school *ogarki* and the free love leagues. In the first place, there is the idea that the faction of the *ogarki*, which happens to live in Samara, is only part of a larger movement that unites the unfortunate throughout the country. As we have seen, the discovery of the wide distribution of *ogarki*—a common element in conspiracy myths—is one of the principal components in reports concerning organizations of young people devoted to debauchery. In the second place, there is the idea of wasted talent and broken lives. Skitalets's heroes are people who are "consumed" prematurely, that is, they are people who are wasting their life forces in drunkenness and depravity. Hence, the word *ogarok*, which, in this context, must be understood metaphorically. The literal meaning ("candle end") was actualized only afterward, in part as a result of its erotic associations. It was precisely the contamination of literal and figurative definitions that allowed *ogarki* to be interpreted as simultaneously meaning both "candle ends" and "unsuccessful person."[39]

Skitalets's story is particularly interesting inasmuch as, for some time, it did in fact serve as an object of self-identification for secondary school students. For them, the image of the *ogarok* was significant in the figurative sense as a symbol of unrealized talent and oppressed youth identity. Although, once again, we do not have any testimony supporting the direct imitation of Skitalets's heroes, one can say with conviction that his tale provided a designation for a definite type of "desperate" behavior directed, in theory, against the educational function of secondary school.[40] But how exactly did this linkage of story and "reality" come about?

The first rumors of school *ogarki* arose in Oriol at the beginning of March 1907 and immediately provoked an entire avalanche of letters to the editor from pupils. The majority of these appeared in the liberal newspaper *Orlovskii vestnik* (*Oriol News*) that willingly took on the role of young people's tribune. The young correspondents, well acquainted with Skitalets's tale, apparently understood the term *ogarki* only in the figurative sense and never broached the question concerning the sexual depravity of the Oriol "faction." The conservative newspaper *Orlovskaia rech'* (*Oriol Speech*), however, preferred to publish the acerbic commentaries of its own employees, one of whom did not refrain from including a detailed description of the ritual around extinguishing the candles.[41]

The pressing provocation for the discussion of Skitalets's tale in the Oriol press was a letter from a young woman signed with the pseudonym Zanoza (literally "splinter"; figuratively "thorn in one's side"). According to her observations, students of secondary schools in Oriol were willingly and openly imitating Skitalets's alcoholic heroes; worst of all was the fact that they had appropriated only the external characteristics of the phenomenon of the *ogarki*, ignoring the main idea of the tale. If the literary prototypes had been granted "powerful and proud souls" and drank because they did not want to reconcile themselves to their situation, then intoxication itself was sufficient for the school *ogarki*: "Our *ogarki* are not great people; rather, they are great . . . drinkers. They spend all their time in orgies; they have not understood the idea of [Skitalets's] *ogarki*; they have distorted it." An incident in the town of V. showed how all this could end; the *ogarki* got a young woman inebriated and then aroused "filthy animal passion" in her: "She began cursing foully, throwing her arms around the necks of those schoolmates who got her drunk. . . . Her fall would have been inevitable, if chance had not interfered."[42]

Zanoza's criticism of the one-sided and superficial imitation of Skitalets's *ogarki* was denied by a student of the First Oriol Gymnasium, who viewed attraction to the phenomenon of *ogarki* as a desperate but totally conscious gesture of "ideological" youth suffocating under the burden of the political-bureaucratic regime in secondary school. Although most young people, in this pupil's opinion, had already lost all hope that the events of 1905 would bring about a transformation, they still could not submit to the old order once again. Therefore, youth "was poisoning itself gradually, horribly, consciously." It was not the external imitation of some literary heroes but a genuine disenchantment with the absence of reform that explained, in the author's eyes, the unprecedented hard drinking of these young people. He evaded the question of sexual depravity with silence.[43]

Excessively extenuatory at first glance, perhaps, this pupil's reaction was far from unique. It fitted in with a more general tendency among left-wing observers to liken the gymnasium to a prison and to construe almost any kind of self-destructive behavior of youth, including taking one's own life, as a political protest against the bureaucratic school regime. As Susan Morrissey has recently shown, after 1905 young people eagerly borrowed the model of the heroic suicide, originally cultivated among political prisoners, thus emphasizing the revolutionary status of their actions.[44] Although the pupil of the First Oriol Gymnasium does not explicitly mention suicide, his very choice of words (*"poisoning itself gradually, horribly, consciously"*) leaves little room for doubt that he believed *ogarchestvo* to be functionally and ideologically equivalent to it. In this student's eyes, the analogy between tormented adolescents and Skitalets's protesting *ogarki* was a valid one.

The reaction resulted in a new round of letters from readers (including a second letter from Zanoza). The idea of "ideological and conscious" intoxication was either rejected or insisted on in these letters. A few readers went further than Zanoza, proposing that these *ogarki* were "simply drunkards" who had always existed in the past and of whom "there would never be a lack in the future."[45] However, judging by the majority of the letters to the editor published in the *Orlovskii vestnik* and by the commentaries in *Orlovskaia rech'*, these explanations reassured very few people. The general opinion was that the phenomenon of *ogarki* bore witness to something else that, like drunkenness, had also existed "from well before yesterday."[46] In the opinion of one seminarian, the usual inebriation and depravity of secondary school students had, in fact, ceased during the revolutionary euphoria of 1905; these behaviors were immediately resumed after the onset of the political reaction. It was the old school that formed the breeding ground of drunkenness and of the *ogarki*.[47]

The picture presented on the pages of *Orlovskaia rech'* was in direct contradiction. This newspaper posited a causal connection between the decline of school discipline and the dissolute behavior of the students. It not only insisted on the restoration of the practice of extramural surveillance by staff members but also made every effort to discredit parents' committees on the grounds that parents took a "casual" approach to the moral upbringing of their children.[48] Parents' "extreme laxity" was the central topic of numerous articles by a certain V. Brianskii, who described the activities organized by parents' committees as drinking bouts for the youth during which parents themselves "imbibed champagne and flirted with each other."[49] Thus, if for the majority of those writing to the editor of *Orlovskii vestnik*, the *ogarki* was testimony to the actualization of the "old" problem—the police regime in the secondary schools and its detrimental effect on students—for *Orlovskaia rech'* it was as a relatively new phenomenon, resulting directly from weakened student supervision and the establishment of parents' committees.

Beneath the argument concerning the underlying cause of the phenomenon of the *ogarki* lay the question of the division of responsibility for upbringing between family and school. This question had arisen before the school reforms undertaken by Dmitrii Tolstoi, minister of the people's enlightenment from 1866 to 1880, who, in order to combat "nihilism," paid particular attention to the moral education of young people.[50] Published in 1874, the *Compilation of Instructions and Regulations Regarding Gymnasia and Progymnasia*, describing in detail the required conduct of secondary school students both while at school and outside its walls, left no doubt whatsoever that responsibility for the moral upbringing of students fell, first of all, on educational institutions and not on parents.[51] The school was supposed to maintain their moral purity and, at the same time, insure the formation of a politically reliable elite by subjecting students to constant observation.

Russian literature and memoirs at the beginning of the twentieth century contain an abundance of descriptions of everyday life at schools, an overwhelming majority of which bear witness to the complete *absence* of any moral authority. It is not surprising that an essential element in the "myth" of the Russian gymnasium, as John McNair has shown in an article on this subject, is the presence of the student's "secret life," in which he or she seeks deliverance from the dispiriting school routine.[52] Gray ordinariness drives them to drinking and depravity from which they can be rescued only by alternative education in the form of independent reading of radical critics and recent Russian literature. Even Aleksandr Izgoev, who in general had a negative relationship with underground education, considered that "if it were not for that, the number of children who would sink into inebriation and depravity, stupefied both morally and mentally, would be far greater than it is now."[53] One can consider the history of the phenomenon of the *ogarki*, which arose in the aftermath of the 1905 revolution, as the culmination of this myth, precisely the realization of its tragic potential.

Fathers and Children Revisited

For the further development of rumors concerning the *ogarki* and the free love leagues, the opposing point of view on the educational incompetence of parents turned out to be no less important. It found expression in pedagogical journals and in the right-wing periodical press, which insisted on the abolition of parents' committees. More importantly, this counterpoint of view exerted a significant influence on the self-awareness of the students themselves. The bugaboo of the languishing adolescent in need of parental moral supervision—but finding it neither in school nor in the family—was adopted, to a large degree, by young people who tuned it into their own autonarrative.

The wave of moral panic that the *ogarki* provoked reignited the "old" question of the alienation of children from their parents. On the very threshold of the twentieth century, the "family crisis" was one of the most pressing themes in the pedagogical periodical press. Although the participants in this debate reached different conclusions about the nature of contemporary upbringing, reproaching the parents either for their overly negligent or, on the contrary, excessively demanding relationship with their children, everyone was in agreement that the traditional rift between "fathers and children" had not decreased but had grown practically to the size of an abyss.[54] As one employee in *Vestnik vospitaniia* (*Herald of Education*) wrote in 1903: "Chilly, distant relations between our two generations have become a phenomenon that increases, rather than decreases with each passing year."[55]

A symbol of the family crisis on the eve of 1905 was the well-known drama by Sergei Naidenov titled *Vaniushin's Children* (*Deti Vaniushina* [1901]), which enjoyed exceptional success both in the capital and the provinces. The conventional relationship in this play, as well as its exposure of the stifling nature of the "bourgeois" family, explains why it continued to be produced during Soviet times; it enters into the repertoire of the more traditional theaters to this day.[56] The climax of its uncomplicated plot is the scene in which an inebriated adolescent who has already lost his innocence is discussing with his father his expulsion from the gymnasium, reproaching those who live "down below," that is, adults, for their ignorance of the spiritual world of those who live "up above," that is, children. The spatial formulation of this opposition became a popular metaphor conveying the message, in the eyes of Naidenov's contemporaries, that it was not only in school that the boundary between the adolescent's official life and his secret life manifested itself but also within his parents' house.[57]

Naturally, one must examine these inclinations in the context of a wider interest in the lives of adolescents that emerged on the brink of the twentieth century throughout Europe.[58] However, if we restrict ourselves to the situation in Russia, it is impossible not to see that, in the liberal and populist press after 1905, it was precisely this idea of the collective guilt of the older generation, having allowed the "premature" corruption of its children, that assumed foremost significance. Hence, the multitude of plays on the theme of the *ogarki*, the model for which was, in the last analysis, *Vaniushin's Children* with its accusatory tendency.

For example, in *Children of the Twentieth Century*, the lonely hero Grigorii stands up for school reforms and, at the same time, struggles against depravity among youth. Only Vera (Faith) shares his lofty ideals: she is his chaste, clever classmate, who supports him in his conflict with Edward von Bach, the founder of the local free love league. It is the same von Bach who carries the day, however. He not only manages to seduce Grigorii's younger sister Liubov' (Love) and her friend Sof'ia (Wisdom), but he also succeeds in recruiting Vera into his camp: she turns out to be powerless when confronted with his diabolical charisma. The painful final scene (in which the father, usually busy, suddenly realizes his own guilt with respect to his ravaged children) forces us to accept the conclusion that parents are no less guilty than the school for the emergence of von Bach's organization.[59]

The "fathers'" guilt is not limited merely to the educational negligence that hastens their children's early fall. Living in filth, the fathers literally doom their children to ruin. In *The Free Love League* (*School Ogarki* [1908]), by one S. R. Cherniavskii, a sixteen-year-old gymnasium student named Petia learns, to his horror and disgust, that his father frequents brothels and is infected with syphilis. At the same time, after announcing a war against pornography in the gymnasium, Petia's class monitor casually escorts his older classmates to dubious institutions. Exhausted by the daily routine of the gymnasium and surrounded by Nietzschean *ogarki*-classmates, Petia sees no option other than to take his own life.[60]

Judging from the indignant tone and general amateurishness of these works that never saw the light of day on stage, one can assume that the authors were adolescents or, at least, closely tied to the school environment. Stigmatizing the vices of the "fathers," they openly sympathized with young people and claimed the right to speak on their behalf. However, the students' most immediate response to the rumors concerning the *ogarki* and the leagues can be found in numerous letters to the editor and in verse published in the press (especially the provincial press) during the spring of 1908. From these, it is clear that the generally accepted view held by the ruling powers of the catastrophic decline in morals among students was acknowledged to a significant degree by young people themselves, serving as a principal component of their identity after the 1905 revolution. Despite the fact that almost everyone who wrote to the editor condemned the activity of these league members (which, it would seem, indicates the moral attitude of the younger generation), the very idea of a moral crisis was seldom if ever questioned.

Take, for example, the following poem published in the newspaper *Poltavskii golos* on April 30, about the time the commotion about the free love leagues was reaching a climax.[61] Hackneyed and clumsy, the poem nonetheless warrants closer analysis, as it pretends to speak on behalf of the young in general:

VIDEANT CONSULES!

As (our) brothers and sisters are drowning in the mire
(Our) fathers and mothers are sleeping soundly,
And their children in their ignorance regard
Rotten and vulgar debauchery as love.

People, learning, books are forgotten
The sanctuary is defiled—while conscience is asleep . . .
Everything is forgotten—and the hand of the disgraceful "league"
Reigns over the merry young people

> You keep silent? Hasn't the mob of priests
> Of printed vulgarity slain enough victims already?
> Or are you waiting for a common grave
> To cover the young sons of the fatherland?
> ....
>
> When a frail boat is sinking at sea,
> From the shore people hurry to the rescue...
> Why are you taking so long? Or has grief blinded you
> So that you don't see your ruin?
>
> Fewer words, don't be embarrassed by your weakness,
> Or else society, the family will perish.
> Hurry to rescue those perishing,
> Before the boat has sunk entirely.
>
> Evgenii, a gymnasium student

At first sight, this poem displays the characteristic features of the social elegy, a genre that became immensely popular through the writings of the spokesmen of two generations: Mikhail Lermontov (1830s) and Semion Nadson (1880s).[62] A social elegy usually begins as an act of self-pity or self-accusation in which the poet bemoans the geriatric impotence of his own generation, a condition he believes to have occurred "prematurely," not in accordance with its youthful age. The elegy may end on an optimistic note, especially in the case of Nadson, with the poet appealing to his fellow sufferers to cast off their torpor and renew the political struggle, but many poems in this class lack such a positive conclusion.

"Videant Consules" is clearly grafted on the Nadson pattern. The poem begins with a sobering diagnosis of youth's moral crisis, then poses a number of rhetorical questions intended to convey the speaker's indignation, and ends with an ardent call for action. There is also a substantial difference, however. Traditionally, in the social elegy, speaker and addressee belong to the same social or ideological group. Being a member of the collective himself, the speaker is entitled to call it to account. In this case, the youthful speaker (youthful, because we feel inclined to identify him with the stated author, gymnasium student Evgenii) is not so much addressing his peers as the older generation who bears responsibility for the children's moral upbringing. Moreover, the self-accusatory overtones we find in Lermontov and Nadson are conspicuously absent. The blame for youth's downfall is pinned on the "priests of printed vulgarity" (authors such as Artsybashev and Kamenskii) and the organizers of the "disgraceful league" but, above all, on the "fathers and mothers" whose negligence delivers their children straight into the hands of the first two groups of wrongdoers. The "children," then, are endowed with the vices generally attributed to them, but the blame lies with the "fathers."

Protests such as these permitted several journalists to reach the consoling conclusion that there also existed an *anti*-Saninist tendency among the students and that its salutary role could prove to be very significant.[63] "The young organism is ill," Vsevolod Azrum concluded in *Vestnik vospitaniia*, "but the first signs of its recovery can already be noticed." To illustrate his point, Azrum quoted a collective appeal of a group of female gymnasium students in Perm in which they called on their male colleagues to face their moral dissipation.[64] In the opinion of a reporter from *Poltavskii golos*, who also quoted the collective protest of a group of outraged gymnasium students, salvation from the *ogarki* should sooner be expected from the young people than from the older generation, which had yet to demonstrate any similar initiative.[65] Thus, side by side with the point of view that the *ogarki* represented a symptomatic phenomenon expressing the declining spirit of the age, there also existed another perspective, according to which it had spread only to an unrepresentative segment of youth.

The idea that the alarming phenomenon of *ogarchestvo* was, in fact, uncharacteristic of Russian youth in general was echoed by populist journalists who explained its occurrence exclusively in terms of class and descent. Convinced that sexual "aberrations" were caused by social factors, these opinion makers tried to explain the emergence of the *ogarki* as the product of a morally depraved elite hunting for extreme sensations. According to the well-known journalist Aleksandr Peshekhonov, the sexual excesses to which Artsybashev and Kuzmin devoted their work "sprang mostly from the center, from the milieu of the rich and the strong."[66] Another populist argued that, although *ogarchestvo* had also spread in the countryside, this was completely due to the influence of the big city. There the mushrooming of the free love leagues was caused by boredom and sensual saturation; in the countryside, it testified to the dissatisfaction of the youth, which had already acquainted itself with the urban life style.[67]

In his classical study of English youth culture in the 1960s, Stanley Cohen demonstrated that the coexistence of contradictory points of view is characteristic of the representation of social menaces in the organs of mass information. On the one hand, young people are presented as a "mirror" of society, directly reflecting all its illnesses and deficiencies. On the other, the organs of mass information often emphasize that society is dealing with a very small group of hooligans who should under no circumstances be identified with young people as a whole (what Cohen refers to as "the Lunatic Fringe theme").[68] Rumors concerning the free love leagues in the popular press were likewise subjected to contradictory interpretation, as a result of which the behavior of young people could be considered either "symptomatic" or "*un*representative." It is not surprising that the reports often concluded with a demonstrative declaration about the chastity prevailing among the majority of the student population.

However, it is crucial to bear in mind that, to a certain degree, young people themselves shared this idea of their unprecedented depravity. The discussion in the Oriol press in 1907 and the school students' collective protests bear witness to this. One can say that the students' reactions to the rumors of the free love leagues embody the very same paradox that Cohen has described: the proposed conduct of the league members was perceived as atypical and provoked protests from those who considered themselves as members of the "chaste majority."[69] At the same time, the persistent opinion existed that open debauchery was practiced widely among young people and that on the whole, as one gymnasium student put it, "we have lived to see great shame."[70]

The following three factors were of extraordinary significance in the establishment of this complicated and partially contradictory image that the young people held of themselves: the "old" question of school and family, leading to the reforms of the system of secondary education; the literary stereotype of the debauched adolescent; and finally, the sensational discourse in the popular press, circulating rumors of the students' immorality. The history of the free love league is the history of the identity of young people that arose precisely at the intersection of these three discursive ranks.

Official Investigations

At the beginning of this chapter, I stated that official investigations into the rumors about the free love leagues did not produce any material evidence. Despite the fact that persons suspected of being involved in them were kept under observation by the police, secret sex clubs as described in the press were never discovered. As the governor of Oriol concluded at the end of his report to the minister of interior: "The existence of a society of *ogarki* is a pure invention."[71] Less than a year later, the governor of Minsk wrote a similar letter, saying that newspaper reports on the free love leagues had hardly any bearing on reality and were produced by the "idle fantasy of the local press."[72]

Minister Shvarts remained distrustful, however. Once apprised of the results of a special investigation into the matter of the free love leagues in Perm, he concluded that "Where there's smoke, there's fire."[73] In view of this conclusion, we may want to know, first, what the police discovered during their investigations and second, what action, if any, was undertaken. To answer these questions, we must return to the moment when the first rumors began to circulate, specifically in the city of Perm, which constitutes one of the best documented cases, and then turn to the Ministry of Enlightenment's recommendations for the moral improvement of youth formulated almost a year later.

Government anxiety over secret organizations of young debauchers arose in the second half of March 1908 as a direct result of a disturbing article published in *Novoe vremia*. The article spoke of a core of three people—a former member of the *zemstvo*, a former correspondent of the radical newspaper *Kamskii krai* (*The Kama Region*), and an "impoverished, provincial writer"—who were obsessed with the idea of publishing their own newspaper in Perm and, to this end, collected money by "keeping vigil," that is: by organizing nightly gatherings that were frequented by the ladies of Perm. As if the behavior of these "mature *ogarki*" was not disturbing enough, they also exerted a profoundly pernicious influence on local youth. "Outrageous facts" were taking place in Perm, *Novoe vremia* insisted, such as female gymnasium students visiting the bathhouse together with pupils of the *realshule*.[74] The article in *Novoe vremia* prompted Prime Minister Piotr Stolypin to inquire of the governor of Perm whether the information provided in the newspaper was correct.[75] The governor immediately ordered an investigation, the results of which he was able to present a week later. The author of the article in *Novoe vremia* turned out to be Vasilii Mutnykh, a journalist from Yekaterinburg known for his far from sober lifestyle (*netrezvyi obraz zhizni*). The three persons mentioned in his article were Udintsev, also a drunk and a former member of the *zemstvo*, who was suspected of misappropriation of funds, a man named Glushchuk, notorious for his leftist sympathies and his collaboration with the "tendentious" newspaper *Kamskii krai,* and finally, a certain Strizhev, who was not suspected of any misdemeanor in particular but was nonetheless considered "morally and politically unreliable." These three men had indeed attempted to start a local newspaper in Perm but lack of funding had thwarted their plans and apparently had put an end to their collaboration.[76] Their involvement in some society of mature *ogarki*, however, could not be established.

As for the influence of these morally depraved misfits on local youth, the governor was convinced that, even if the reports in *Novoe vremia* were inflated, there was every reason for concern. He ordered the police to search the houses of tens of secondary school students, an operation that produced as "evidence" a copy of the illegal journal *Uchashchiesia* (*Students*), containing an "appeal by the faction of the *ogarki*," a few revolutionary brochures, and several handfuls of candles and candle ends.[77] Although this material might be deemed suspicious, it was no more than circumstantial evidence at best. The conclusions presented by the head of the Perm police department arrived in his final and extensive report to the central authorities were, therefore, somewhat contradictory. On the one hand, Mutnykh had certainly exaggerated the situation in his article in *Novoe vremia*, "because [a society of *ogarki*] has not yet started to function in Perm." On the other, the head of the police admitted that the town had recently seen a few cases of teenage pregnancy among well-to-do female gymnasium students and that socially and sexually mixed visits to the bathhouse were also occurring more frequently than before. In sum, Perm was witnessing a serious deterioration of morals, which would nonetheless be stopped by the special measures already taken by the governor and the pedagogical staff of the city.[78]

The curator of the Orenburg district presented Aleksandr Shvarts with an even more reassuring analysis of the situation in Perm. In reaction to the rumors on widespread moral corruption in the Urals, the curator had set up special committees of inquiry, which had not discovered the unprecedented debauchery described in the press. Even if the moral standards of the youth had recently declined, there were sufficient indications that things were improving. By way of illustration, the curator attached a copy of a letter from the head of one of the committees, N. A. Bravin, the director of the First Gymnasium for Boys in Perm, who not only downplayed the assumed magnitude of the *ogarki* scandal but also noted the first signs of moral improvement: "My own observations tell me that recently the youth is coming to its senses," Bravin noted with confidence.[79] "The students are beginning to work

"A Pleasant Conversation," dialogue between a dignitary and some school children. "—What do you little rascals want? —[We want] to study. —Hmm. Do you really want to study that badly? —Of course! —Hmm. Perhaps you'd like to learn arithmetic? —Whatever Your Grace will teach us—anything will be fine! —Hmm. Would you rather learn arithmetic than botany? —How would we know? We are ignorant. Anything you'll teach us will be fine! —Hmm! But as soon as we begin teaching you, you'll probably form a Free Love League!" (*Satirikon* 11 [1908]. University of Helsinki, Slavonic Library)

more seriously criticizing youth's earlier enthrallment with the Sanin followers [*sanintsy*], the sexual question, and similar literary works of recent date."[80] With exams coming up, the pupils would surely drop the "worldly questions" they had occupied themselves with for the last few months and resume their study.[81]

Even if the outcome of the investigations had been relatively reassuring, the government proved more skeptical about the state of affairs than the local authorities. On the basis of the Perm report and similar documents received from other parts of the country that were rumored to be afflicted by secret sex clubs, Shvarts wrote an extensive letter to Stolypin in which he offered two causes for youth's nationwide moral decline. The first was grounded in the political situation of postrevolutionary Russia: secondary school students were attracted to unsavory reading matter, especially to pornography, as it promised them the strong impulses to which they had become accustomed after the shocking events of 1905. "[The students] ceased to study and started to play revolution and, when it abated, they switched to lechery, heavy drinking, and profligacy."[82] The second cause, related to the first, was the stunning lack of discipline both inside and outside the school walls. The abolition of the school uniform, the weakening of extramural surveillance, and the absence of parental authority were the reasons that school-going youth "had started to grow up in the streets, in front of shop windows, in the cinema, at various dubious dancing parties."[83] The rumors about the *ogarki* and the free love leagues might have been fabricated—"even in Perm where they had been closest to the truth"—but this did not diminish the need to restore discipline at all costs. One way to achieve this goal, Shvarts believed, was to dissolve the parents' committees so as to reestablish the leading role of the school in the pupil's moral education.

Stolypin also considered the situation sufficiently alarming to undertake further action. On July 14, 1908, he wrote a confidential letter to all governors and mayors asking them to contact the local school administrations and urge them to develop a set of measures that would ensure the immediate restoration of discipline and order.[84] Obviously, the central authorities were to be kept abreast at all times. By choosing this line of action, Stolypin made it absolutely clear that the Ministry of Interior was in the driver's seat. The fight against moral depravity among young people was not only a problem of Shvarts's department, Stolypin wrote paternalistically, but also a matter of national security that "obliged the

Ministry of Interior to help the Education Department according to its ability."[85]

One of the first to report back to the Ministry of Interior was the curator of the St. Petersburg district. In a letter dated August 20, 1908, he set forth a large number of restrictive measures, placing a ban, for instance, on visiting cafés, parks, and cinemas (after 6 p.m.) as well as on attending socially "mixed" dancing parties, especially if they were not organized by the school itself. Attending political meetings was strictly forbidden, of course, as was the possession of indecent brochures and pictures.[86]

Some districts prided themselves on having taken measures even before the prime minister had urged them to do so. As early as December 1907, the curator of the Kazan district had established a permanent committee of school directors that had drawn up a protocol of measures for raising pupils' moral standing. Apart from listing the more predictable rules, such as the compulsory wearing of school uniforms and a complete ban on tobacco and alcohol, the document meticulously described the conditions under which a visit to the theater was allowed. Pupils had to ask for permission each time they fancied seeing a play, and the school would record each request so as be on top of it, should a suspicious pattern emerge. In the theater, seating in the gallery was strictly prohibited, since this was usually packed with "that part of the audience, which is the least inhibited in expressing its emotions." To monitor the behavior of pupils in the theater, a "special representative of all secondary educational institutions" would be given a year-long ticket for a free seat on the upper level.[87]

Not all of the measures taken or proposed had a prohibitive character. The curator of the Orenburg district stressed the importance of attending literary evenings and lectures on the dangers of tobacco and alcohol on the understanding that these activities were to be organized exclusively under the aegis of the school.[88] Astrakhan, on the other hand, announced measures to keep a close eye on lodging addresses and to put a stop to pupils sneaking into cafeterias, restaurants, and the local bicycle club.[89]

A few schools were annoyed at the prospect of having to check the whereabouts of their students and confined themselves to stating that there were no free love leagues active in the region. Consequently, there was no reason for extreme vigilance. Tobolsk and Tiumen promised they would be "more strict" but failed to specify exactly what steps would be taken.[90] The teacher seminary of Barnaul demonstrated even greater reluctance by simply stating that its students did not feel any sympathy for morally corrupting organizations such as the free love leagues.[91] An exceptional reaction came from the pedagogical council of the Omsk lower technical school, which declared that the phenomena described in Stolypin's confidential circular were unknown in Omsk, the school itself having been the acme of discipline and assiduity over the past few years.[92]

What did the central authorities do with this information? In the spring of 1909 the Ministry of Enlightenment created a Committee for Ways of Exerting Pedagogical Influence on Secondary School Students. Its task was to process the input received from the districts by selecting the most valuable suggestions and recommendations, which would then be distributed among the curators for implementation. At the first meeting, which took place on March 18, the committee merely took stock of the received recommendations for enlivening the curriculum and the teaching climate in general. The suggestions ranged from downsizing the classes, organizing summer camps and developing the pupils' aesthetic taste by taking them to museums to embellishing the classrooms with portraits of writers.

Yet the issue to which the committee returned time and again was the behavior of students outside the school walls, which, after all, had been the primary cause of all the anxiety. Characteristically, it was here that the committee demonstrated its utter impotence, as it contented itself with establishing that the widely ignored rules of comportment were, in fact, still valid. In his closing statement, Chairman L. A. Georgievskii formulated the committee's mission in surprisingly unambitious terms: "The task of this meeting was not to come up with something new but to review and emphasize what must be preserved of the existing rules."[93] One liberal-minded member of the committee ventured to disagree with Georgievskii, arguing that success in matters of moral upbringing depended on the entire education system rather than on demands and regulations. Clearly, the existing rules had not prevented the recent crisis from emerging. Another member, however, the director of the third *realshule* in St. Petersburg, was said to subscribe to the chairman's position. Although the rules of comportment had been in force during the chaos of 1905–6, many people had believed them to be abolished. For that reason, it was essential to "review and reaffirm the existing rules."[94]

Aftermath of the Scandal

By June 1908 the general agitation caused by the free love league had abated. Although official investigations had uncovered a disturbing decline in morality among students (in the opinion of Minister Shvarts) requiring the immediate restoration of discipline, they had never succeeded in proving the existence of societies of young people devoted to the practice of open debauchery.[95] Once acquainted with the results of the investigation, the editors of the *Minskii kur'er* limited themselves to a brief communication indicating that students of the town of Minsk "didn't participate in the league in any way."[96] While not denying the possible existence of the league, the newspaper apparently considered the theme exhausted and never returned to it again. In other cities also, the free love league ceased to be an object of interest.

The reassuring results of the investigations did not manage to convince everyone. In the autumn of the same year, *Russkaia shkola* (*Russian School*) published a long article in four parts (seventy-five pages in all) in which the author tried to prove the authenticity of the rumors and, in addition, ventured the opinion that the schools were attempting to squelch the story of the leagues.[97] No less characteristically, literary critics seized on one or another "pornographic" work and mentioned the leagues as though they were an absolutely genuine occurrence.[98] As late as 1913, the popular *Sinii zhurnal* (*Blue Journal*) published an article about the "love leagues" in prerevolutionary France, attempting to demonstrate their existence in contemporary Russia.[99] Although on rare occasions the opinion was voiced that in part the phenomenon of *ogarki* was in essence calumny directed against the emancipation movement, the veracity of the rumors was such that they exerted a significant influence both on the self-awareness of contemporaries as well as on the historical reputation of the decade 1907–17.

Considering this reputation, it might seem appropriate to juxtapose the free love leagues with the no less sensational rumors about suicide leagues, all the more so since the theme of suicide sometimes surfaced in connection with the *ogarki*. The conventional subject of a ruined young life that we find in reports on the *ogarki* assumed that the members of the leagues would be infected with syphilis or commit suicide. It is not a coincidence that, after the 1908 publication of his "social-fictional sketches" *The Secret Societies of Youth,* Roman Dobryi wrote a kind of continuation: *Why Do Young People End in Suicide?*

However, for all the seeming similarity between the rumors of the free love leagues and those of the suicide leagues, one should not forget that the latter also circulated in Western Europe and the United States.[100] The myth of the free love league, on the other hand, was a Russian narrative about secondary school youth, specifically about children of the Russian intelligentsia. As I have endeavored to show, young people themselves played a substantial role in the development of this narrative. Without wishing to negate the universal aspects that were undoubtedly present in the history of the free love league (we need merely recall the witches' Sabbath of the Middle Ages), one should emphasize that this history, by virtue of its political coloration, is rooted in the stereotypes of Russian cultural history, in part, the history of the Russian intelligentsia. It seems that it is precisely here that the specific character of the myth of the free love league lies.

The most noteworthy aspect of this entire affair may well be that it entered the collective memory as a sad, but by no means imaginary, episode of the Silver Age. References to the *ogarki* can be encountered in the memoirs of both Khodasevich and Mikhail Osorgin.[101] One can also find fleeting, though intentionally sordid, descriptions of the free love leagues in several books on the history of the revolutionary movement.[102] Temporal distance from the scandal apparently merely eliminated the last doubts of memoirists and researchers and managed to transform rumors into historical "facts."

7

Muscles for Money
Sanin as Ex-student

As we have seen, critics speculating on the significance of Vladimir Sanin as a contemporary type stressed the importance of his former involvement in the liberation movement. Whether he had eventually betrayed the revolution or instead represented its ultimate manifestation, opinion makers considered him a "hero of our time" because of what he was and what he had been. In other words, in order to understand Sanin completely, one also needed to understand his past.

But what exactly do we know about Sanin's past? And how different is it from the life he is leading in the novel? The narrator does not tell us very much about Sanin's background, and neither does Sanin himself. From his lengthy conversation with Soloveichik in chapter 32, we can infer that Sanin has spent at least a couple of years at university, though we are not told what he studied or with what result.[1] Apparently, the only thing worth mentioning is the rift with his former teacher Vladimir Lande, which, in retrospect, marks the beginning of a new and more mature stage in Sanin's personal development that continues beyond the closing scene of the novel (the open ending, which offended critics and readers alike).

Glimpses of Sanin's past can also be found in the first chapter, which describes his unexpected homecoming. In this scene, the focus is very much on Sanin's mother, who is displeased with her son because of his lowly status in society. His sister is disappointed too when she finds out that her brother is a quite ordinary young man whose life is not plagued by some "gloomy, sinister fate," as Lida's "dreamy feminine soul had desired."[2] Typically, Artsybashev is less interested in heaping praise on his hero than in exposing the hypocrisy and falsehood of those who surround him. Nevertheless, the reunion scene contains some vital information about Sanin's past, even if the narrator's flat tone (conveying Lida's disappointment with her brother) is meant to bring out the supposed mundaneness of it all: "Sanin related how life had tossed him from one place to another, how often he'd had to go hungry or roam around, how he'd taken part in the dangerous political struggle and had abandoned it when he'd had enough.... The more he said, the clearer it became that the life [Lida had] imagined in such glowing terms was in fact common and ordinary. There was something unusual about it, but Lida couldn't identify exactly what it was. Meanwhile, it emerged as very simple, boring, and, it seemed to her, even banal. Sanin lived wherever he happened to be, did whatever happened to come his way, worked a bit, loafed without a goal, apparently liked to drink, and knew a lot of women."³

These lines have often been adduced as proof of Sanin's unprincipled attitude ("loafed without a goal"), his "disappointment" with the revolution (which he abandoned "when he'd had enough"), and, in particular, his yearning for sensual pleasure ("liked to drink" and "knew a lot of women"). Yet the account of what he had been up to also contains bits of information that contradict such a negative reading. A womanizer and a political deserter, Sanin apparently also did "whatever happened to come his way" and, perhaps even more significantly, "worked a bit." As becomes clear in the course of the novel, other supposedly more high-minded (ex-)students, such as Iurii Svarozhich and Semionov, are not even capable of doing that.

At first sight, Sanin's identity as a former student may not look all that important, as it is brought up only once in the entire novel. Moreover, as a member of the radical intelligentsia, it would seem almost inevitable that Sanin had been a student at some point in time. How could he possess the nihilistic DNA of Mark Volokhov and Evgenii Bazarov and *not* have been a student as they had been? And yet I believe we should not take this particular detail for granted, if only because Artsybashev was peculiarly preoccupied with Russia's student community and particularly with its work ethos, which he found lacking. Echoes of this preoccupation, I argue, can be detected not only in *Sanin* and other fictional works of his but also in interviews and public statements that Artsybashev made about student poverty and the possible solutions to this problem. In short, Sanin's sometimes provocative comportment is more than a catalyst that exposes the untenability of certain outlived conventions; it is part of a larger behavioral paradigm that Artsybashev consciously promoted.

It is with these considerations in mind that I offer a reading of *Sanin* as a narrative of economic self-determination, a narrative that espouses self-reliance and physical strength instead of the intelligentsia's more traditional imperatives of group solidarity and self-abnegation.[4] In putting forward this alternative program, the novel intersected with a more general debate on student destitution that I discuss at the outset. Subsequently, I return to Artsybashev to scrutinize his statements on student poverty in the press and to discuss the ways in which he treated the problem of daily sustenance in his fictional work. Finally, I explore the figure of the "muscular student" in Russian fiction, an alternative role model that can be found especially in Nikolai Breshko-Breshkovskii's immensely popular novels about wrestlers. As I hope to demonstrate, the vaguely Darwinian notion of "struggle for life" (*bor'ba za sushchestvovanie*) and the growing popularity of bodybuilding, particularly wrestling as a martial art (*bor'ba*), blended into a single idealized image of the student wrestler (*student-borets*) that appeared frequently on the pages of sport journals and cheap popular weeklies. An adumbration of this image, I contend, is the athletic figure of the ex-student Vladimir Sanin.

Poverty and Dignity

During the interrevolutionary period, student poverty was a major issue, not only in the flourishing student press but also in medical literature and a variety of popular journals. Although it was widely recognized as a traditional phenomenon going back at least to the time of the Great Reforms, the problem of student destitution had, a majority of observers agreed, only recently acquired truly alarming dimensions. Ever larger numbers of students were expelled from university for not paying their tuition and thus were often forced to abandon all hopes of graduating. Even those who received tuition waivers or some other form of financial aid were sometimes hardly able to make ends meet.[5]

This deterioration of students' material situation was directly connected to the loosening of admission restrictions in 1906. As the student population grew, so did the pressure on available financial resources. In St. Petersburg and Moscow, the situation was particularly bad, since these cities seemed to promise more part-time work than the provinces and, consequently, attracted more students.[6] Yet, apart from increasing the demand for financial aid even further, the popularity of the central universities was also detrimental to the job market. With so many students offering to give lessons, parents could hire tutors at any price and sometimes get away with not paying them at all.[7] In addition, those who lacked the necessary connections and were forced to look for other work faced fierce competition from nonstudents as well.[8]

According to P. Ivanov, author of a 1903 study entitled *Students in Moscow: Daily Life, Social Mores, and Types* (*Studenty v Moskve: Byt, nravy i tipy*), probably the most detailed account of student culture in pre-revolutionary Russia, the "struggle for life" among students became an increasingly palpable phenomenon in the first years of the twentieth century. Not only did the competition for lucrative jobs intensify as a corollary of rising enrollments but the substantial reduction of classical languages in the curriculum of the gymnasia in 1901 made many a student tutor redundant. Although he was convinced that tutoring would remain the most important source of extra income for needy students, Ivanov acknowledged that the current crisis in tutoring forced them to look for less traditional forms of part-time work, such as doing simple calculations for a credit company, riding bicycles as part of a publicity campaign, or even sitting for a painter.[9] "Even if we haven't gone as far as America—ordinary physical work is not customary among students—the 'intellectual nature' of their work should now be interpreted very broadly," Ivanov concluded.[10]

The "struggle for existence," as this chapter of Ivanov's book is called, reveals a certain uneasiness on the part of the author to accept these changes and accept students' attempts to adapt to them. Ivanov frowned on students earning an extra ruble by singing in a church choir or playing in a band in some cheap *café chantant*. Working as a bookmaker at the horse races he considered completely inappropriate for students, though he admitted that it was one of the best paid jobs around and that competition for it was huge. Giving lessons to gymnasium students was far less profitable, paying only thirty rubles a month for five hours each day—a bit more than the "average" student budget—yet Ivanov clearly favored this work over other part-time jobs, referring to it respectfully as "intellectual student labor."[11] Lamenting the fact that few jobs were in keeping with students' vocations, he mentioned the well-paid, but non-traditional, jobs only in passing and devoted most of the chapter to the dwindling market for tutoring.[12]

After the strikes of 1905 and the resumption of academic studies the following year, many of the preoccupations we find in Ivanov's account on student poverty became topics in their own right. Students and opinion makers questioned or defended the primacy of intellectual work over physical labor and promoted or disputed the notion that the latter was incompatible with student dignity. Pivotal to this debate was the question of whether student poverty was different from poverty among other social groups and what student poverty meant in terms of practical behavior. Were students entitled to an exceptional position, as some of them claimed, arguing that society was obliged to support them. Or should they earn their own keep, if necessary by doing dirty work? Academic as this discussion may seem, it affected the public image of the student, bringing to the fore his bodily features in an unprecedented way. Alongside more traditional representations of students' bodies that drew on the paradigms of indigence and disease, new images of corporal demeanor emerged in which the body reassumed its more "primitive" function as a tool.

Poverty in the Student Press

Although the number of students doing physical labor may have been quite substantial toward the end of the decade, a mere look at the student press reveals that it was still perceived as something unusual. Convinced that the "cold statistics" on student poverty needed further illustration, one commentator adduced examples of students working as porters at a marketplace or as coachmen by night—the ultimate proof, he believed, that "hunger and unemployment had reached their final limit."[13] For him, the unusual image of a student engaged in physical labor was more telling than "mere" figures according to which more than half of the student population went hungry.

In an article in the Odessa journal *Studencheskoe delo* (*Student Matter*), N. A. Skvortsov employed similar rhetoric. After producing a few "highly characteristic" figures on growing poverty among students, he repudiated the accusation that they were unwilling to accept physical labor: "On the contrary, the impoverishment of the student community has gone so far that its needy elements no longer feel ill-disposed to any kind of dirty work." To buttress his argument, he quoted two ads in which students offered to stock icehouses or sew underwear.[14] In the end, it was not the "great many numerical data" on poverty, which

Skvortsov explicitly said to ignore, but the concrete image of a student dragging lumps of ice that served to illustrate how desperate the situation had become.

Behind these expressions of indignation lurked the charge that society wrongly equated students with ordinary workers and, in doing so, condemned them to poverty and even to death. Competing with each other for every tutoring opportunity and with the common folk for even the paltriest of jobs, students seemed to merge with society's growing army of paupers and share their miserable fate. In an article published in the right-wing journal *Vesti studencheskoi zhizni* (*News of Student Life*), A. Kazakov made the comparison explicit, suggesting that students formed a proletariat of their own. They were not only increasingly treated as ordinary workers but also paid accordingly, receiving no more than a few kopecks for their lessons. In fact, factory workers were better off, Kazakov maintained, as they were physically equipped for their jobs, whereas students ruined their health by having to study and work at the same time. No matter how little tutoring paid, however, Kazakov considered physical labor only a final resort for students. Aside from the fact that their poor constitutions would not allow it, heavy work also impinged on their "traditional self-image" (*samoliubivaia traditsiia*). As a poignant illustration that students were sometimes forced to break this taboo and "cast off their intellectual appearance," Kazakov cited an ad in a newspaper in which a student offered his services as a gatekeeper.[15]

A devoted member of the conservative academist movement, Kazakov attributed society's "indifference" to the fate of students to the one-sided and essentially distorted image it had of them as inveterate troublemakers. Although the majority had proven receptive to political propaganda in the past, students now kept aloof from politics, Kazakov assured his audience, and were concentrating on their studies again. Society ought to reward students for this return to purely academic pursuits by supporting them financially and thus putting a stop to the epidemic of student suicide. Moreover, it was in society's own interest to do so. By leaving youths to their own devices, as it was doing now, society pushed them back again into the arms of the opposition that was anxious to exploit their poverty and frustration for political means.

As these comments make clear, the issue of student destitution also had a more public dimension in that it raised the question of society's responsibility toward the student community. Did society have a moral obligation to support the nation's intellectual proletariat? Many students believed that it did. As one contributor to a collection of essays and letters on student poverty put it in 1911: "To diminish the need, to deliver the student population from the worst consequences of its poverty and the horror of degeneration, to eradicate death from starvation—*that* is society's duty."[16] Calling the students the "arteries that nourish our whole future," this commentator envisioned the ideal relation between educated youth and society as one of mutual dependence and support.

Not everyone was inclined to blame society for the alleged pauperization of the student community, of course. Commentators of various persuasions pointed to the students' relatively privileged position in comparison with the even harder circumstances under which unskilled workers had to eke out a living. Yet this was only one of the many arguments that was put forward to deny students the exceptional position to which some of them laid claim. Moral corruption and physical degeneration, in short the quintessential maladies of the fin de siècle, were advanced even more frequently to attack the students' traditional work ethos and to propose a more "manly" attitude instead.

Making Ends Meet the American Way

Regularly resurfacing in this context was the image of the American student who, as we have just seen in Ivanov's study, was believed to have no qualms about doing unskilled work. If, in 1903 the differences between the work ethic of Russian and American students had seemed considerable, judging by Ivanov's account, at the turn of the decade a number of commentators defended an "American-style" struggle for existence as a viable alternative to the traditional demand for financial support and "intellectual" jobs such as tutoring and copying. One student, for example, argued that the whole system of providing financial help to students through charitable institutions should be abandoned because it corrupted students and made them rely on donations even when they could manage without. Labeling charity a "disgrace for healthy young men," he gave the counterexample of a one-armed American who supported himself by copying documents at night. In America, he added, society helped only those who were "absolutely unable to work."[17] Part of the blame, however, went to Russian society, this student maintained. If it would conceive of students simply as workers and hire them for jobs other than tutoring, charitable deeds would not be needed at all. In contrast to Kazakov, then, who considered charity a crucial means by which to preserve the student community as a distinct social group, this author criticized society for not treating students as ordinary workers and thereby furthering their impoverishment.

Of all the participants in the debate on student poverty, it was Artsybashev who had the most outspoken view. In response to an opinion poll on the desirability of a separate community center for students in Moscow, he attacked the *studenchestvo* for what he saw as its lack of stamina and self-reliance. Unlike most young people who flocked to the city in search of employment and who also faced destitution and poor housing, students could apply for financial aid from one of the numerous charitable organizations specifically designed for them. The real problem, according to Artsybashev, was that students were being coddled and pampered too much and, as a result, were unaware of how seriously this affected their dignity. Declaring himself an opponent of any form of philanthropy, Artsybashev also referred to the United States, where students were less fastidious about doing unskilled work: "In America it is not a rare thing when students work as waiters in a restaurant. To the Russian ear it is somewhat strange, and I would not recommend it instead of other forms of work, but I find it equally strange that healthy, young men, who have democratic principles written on their banner, in search of work keep going round in circles of tutoring and copying because they consider any physical labor humiliating for themselves and find it humiliating to descend from their intellectual heights into the depths of an ordinary worker's life."[18]

Artsybashev's slightly patronizing tone is meant to suggest that he was not particularly interested in the topic or, at least, did not consider the problem of student destitution all that important. Yet the stereotype of the poor and emaciated student plays a considerable role in his fiction, especially as a negative counterpart to the muscular, self-supporting hero (often an ex-student) that we encounter in *Sanin* and a number of other works. Apparently, the topic interested Artsybashev far more than he wanted to admit. It is feasible that this preoccupation was informed by his own experience of moving to St. Petersburg from the Ukraine at the age of nineteen. Though he associated with students in the early 1900s and was even arrested during the famous student demonstration at Kazan Square in 1901, as a gymnasium dropout, Artsybashev never really belonged to the student community. Not eligible to enroll at university and to apply for financial aid, he had to earn his own keep by writing short stories and drawing caricatures for the yellow press.

How is Artsybashev's unsentimental attitude toward student destitution expressed in *Sanin*? Is the theme of economic self-reliance really all that important? Earlier we saw that some critics interpreted the hero as an adumbration of the predatory capitalist, the strong and selfish type of man that was firmly established in the United States but was only just emerging in Stolypin's "new" Russia of unhindered entrepreneurship (see chapter 2). To these opinion makers, at least, the connection between Sanin's philosophy of life and the changes in the nation's economy were only too obvious. Yet to determine the importance of the economic theme in *Sanin* with more precision, let us start with a comparison between the hero and Iurii Svarozhich, specifically between the ways in which they organize their lives upon their return home at the beginning of the novel. Clearly, the situation in which they find themselves is more or less similar. Both men are (ex-)students, have a revolutionary background, and are reunited with their families after a substantial period of absence. Their daily routines, however, are quite different, as we are about to see.

Artsybashev's Fictional Students

Sanin's conversation with his sister in the opening chapter is followed by a dialogue with his mother in which she addresses the issue of economic self-reliance head-on by inquiring about his plans for the future. Sanin's insouciant reply that he plans to live "somehow or other" (*kak-nibud'*) has far broader implications than purely practical ones, as the narrator does not fail to point out, and so even if we take these words literally as meaning "earning money somehow or other," their evocative charge is not to be denied. It is thus not surprising that most of Artsybashev's contemporary critics focused all their attention on Sanin's pursuit of sensual pleasure and so failed to notice his repeated, albeit modest, attempts to find some kind of employment, that is, to "work a bit."[19] In chapter 28, for example, we encounter him writing an application letter to a newspaper for which he used to work. Bored with his family, he considers leaving town again and taking up his old job as a writer. In chapter 35, we learn that Sanin has taken a position as a clerk with an insurance agent. Finally, Sanin enjoys physical labor (in chapter 2 we see him working on the flower beds in his mother's garden), and he even knows how to sew, a skill that he claims to have mastered when he was completely broke and couldn't afford a tailor to mend his clothes (chapter 1).

These minor but telling details acquire additional significance when compared to the conspicuous lack of independence that Iurii Svarozhich displays throughout the novel. If Sanin visits his family for no particular reason, Iurii moves in with his father on purely material grounds. Expelled from Moscow, he has been granted the right to choose his place of residence and, consequently, can settle wherever he likes. But for Iurii, who has lived "all his life without having to work," this is a frightening prospect.[20] Knowing deep in his heart that he is incapable of supporting himself, he sees no alternative but to return to his parental home. Making the comparison with Sanin almost explicit, Artsybashev then permits us to witness a painful conversation between Iurii and his father, in which the latter reproachfully inquires about his son's plans for the future. Iurii's answer ("Nothing for the moment") is only intended to irritate his father, but it clearly echoes Sanin's reply in the negative.[21] If Sanin plans to live "somehow or other" without being a burden to anyone, Iurii intends to "do nothing," thus continuing to hang his arms around his father's neck.

Sanin's capability to cope with material need is further suggested by overt references to his physical strength and his proximity to nature. Repeatedly, the narrator mentions his "iron hands" and "iron muscles." When Sanin tries to revive the plants in his mother's garden, he admits to "loving everything green."[22] In this connection, the very name "Sanin" appears highly suggestive, as various scholars have noted, evoking associations with the Latin *sanus*, "healthy."[23] Judging by a 1908 caricature of Artsybashev that plays on the Latin saying *mens sana in copore sano* and depicts the author as a frail intellectual surrounded by muscular torsos, the semantic link must have been immediately apparent to his more astute contemporaries. Psychologically superior to the other characters and blessed with an impressive physique, Sanin, then, could be seen as embodying (or, on the contrary, as profaning) that very same proverb.

It does not take a particularly penetrating reader to find the physical details by which Artsybashev enhances the opposition between Iurii and Sanin. An inventory would include, among other things, Iurii's "thick black hair" (Sanin is fair haired), his estrangement from nature, and various instances of body language that betray his hurt ego. However, if we confine ourselves to the theme of economic self-reliance and its expression through images of bodily deployment, then it is not Iurii (who is physically healthy) but the consumptive student Semionov who emerges as Sanin's antithesis. Characteristically, when introducing him in chapter 4, the narrator gives a concise description of him that

Caricature of Mikhail Artsybashev. The caption reads: "His motto is 'In copore sano, mens sana,' but having given Sanin a 'corpor sanus' [sic], he neglected the 'mens sana,' forgetting that ancient statues were not beautiful because they were headless." (*Satirikon* 14 [1908]. International Institute of Social History, Amsterdam)

packages both Semionov's poor health and his means of existence into an almost caricatural image of student poverty: "Semyonov was a consumptive university student who'd been living in town for several months, giving lessons. He was very plain-looking, gaunt, and weak; the barely perceptible but terrible shadow of imminent death could be seen in his prematurely aged face."[24] We may feel tempted to put aside the commonsensical consideration that Semionov is physically incapable of doing any other job and to posit instead that he is ill *because* of the one-sided nature of his work. Thus, on a deeper level, "giving lessons" becomes a signifier of an "unhealthy" way of life in which the balance between body and mind is distorted.

A glance at some earlier works by Artsybashev adds to the suspicion that, in his fiction on students, the juxtaposition of an independent, healthy character to one or more weak, unhealthy ones often carries economic overtones. Even if the contrast is not as protrusive as with Sanin and Iurii Svarozhich, material poverty and disease are likely to denote a poverty of spiritual resources rather than the ennoblement traditionally associated with asceticism and self-abnegation. In the story "Morning Shades" ("Teni utra" [1905]), for example, the characterization of the protagonists as either "weak" or "strong" clearly presupposes their (in)capacity to sustain themselves. Representing the "weak" characters is the seemingly selfless student Afanas'ev, who raves about serving "the people" and thus succeeds in persuading the provincial girls Dora and Liza to enroll in medical school in St. Petersburg ("Now that's what the people need most of all").[25] Suggestive of the hopelessness of this enterprise is the fact that Afanas'ev himself never reaches the capital, as he intended to, but dies—in typical fashion—of tuberculosis. Without having really suffered for humankind, Afanas'ev has prematurely died the death of a true revolutionary martyr.[26]

The gruff student Andreev—the "strong" character in the story—differs sharply from Afanas'ev and his infatuated followers in that his revolutionary activities are dictated by his own zest for life rather than by vague idealism. Just like Sanin, whom he evidently prefigures, he rejects the intelligentsia's traditional cult of self-abnegation, giving preference instead to his own needs and desires. More importantly still, Andreev's attitude is indicative of his self-esteem (asserts Andreev himself) that stems, in part, from his flexibility and resourcefulness. Having always earned his own money, he knows life "not only from books."[27] As in *Sanin*, physical strength, economic independence, and enjoyment of life combine to establish a new ethos that challenges traditional images of student identity.

At this point, it may be instructive to return to Artsybashev's reply to the opinion poll in which he expressed his dismay with the *studenchestvo* for their alleged aversion to physical labor. It is worth noting that in defining the possible functions of the community center in Moscow, Artsybashev explicitly argued for the foundation of a "house of labor" (*dom truda*) in which students could not only prepare for their exams but also master skills other than those required for "lessons" and "copying." As a result, Artsybashev conjectured, society would enjoy the benefits of a more versatile workforce while students' increased employability would save them from living on the alms of "dancing ladies" and "idle megalomaniacs." He therefore deemed it essential that the community center encourage students to do "varied labor at the largest possible scale."[28]

In putting these opinions forward, Artsybashev was clearly reiterating one of the central ideas of *Sanin*—the need for man's all-round development or, more specifically, the need to restore the balance between mind and body. Though this position was hardly original from a philosophical point of view, the articulation of it in a debate on student poverty is symptomatic of a paradigmatic shift in the public image of the student. As I show in the next section, this shift entailed a new vision of the body as a powerful instrument, or indeed a weapon, in the struggle for life. This is to argue neither that the more familiar representation of students as emaciated paupers became obsolete nor that the notion of students and physical power was completely new. Images of muscular students can be found in Dostoevsky's *The Possessed* (the boxer Keller) and, of course, in Chernyshevsky's *What is To Be Done?*, which features the "new man" Rakhmetov as an accomplished bodybuilder. However, the tendency to promote a more vigorous image of the student as a strongman became manifest only near the end of the first decade of the twentieth century. The significance of the economic theme in *Sanin* and Artsybashev's comments on student work ethics testify that the novel marks an important stage in this development.

In Search of the Student Wrestler

The rise of a vigorous and physically imposing image of the student after the revolution of 1905 was not attributable to economic factors alone. It was partly dictated by a more general preoccupation with the improvement of health and hygiene that can be observed throughout turn-of-the-century Europe. Among artists and other members of the educated classes, there was a growing interest in physical education, bodybuilding, nudism, and alternative forms of nutrition. This was also the time when intercollegiate sports became organized on a national scale in the United States and Protestant churches were promoting competitive sports with the aim of creating a Christian ideal of manliness, popularly known as "muscular Christianity."[29] In Russia too, sport, either as spectacle or as a leisure activity, became ever more popular, a tendency that was reflected in the rise and rapid expansion of a specialized sport press between 1907 and 1914.

The growing popularity of various forms of outdoor recreation and physical exercise often met with critical reactions from members of the Russian intelligentsia, however. In their perception, these activities signified a form of political escapism or a lack of spirituality. Populist critics tended to reject sport altogether as a "narrow" specialization that did not contribute to the "wholeness" of the individual.[30] Bicycling was repeatedly associated with flippancy and moral degeneration. After the turmoil of 1905, the more radical elements of the *studenchestvo* employed the more predictable argument that sport distracted students from the political struggle and thus contributed to their embourgeoisement. In 1908 the well-known student leader Aleksei Lozina-Lozinskii noted with dismay that students had given up politics for "Bal'mont, no Kuzmin, . . . no football."[31] Elsewhere he characterized the history of the Russian *studenchestvo* as one in which ideological and political consciousness had declined, moving from Marxism to "footballism."[32]

Even if the importance of physical education as such was never questioned, many contemporaries regarded the growing popularity of sport as proof of the educated classes' "unhealthy" thirst for strong sensations. Pondering the deeper significance of sport as a mass phenomenon, commentators often resorted to metaphors of disease and mental disorder to underline the unsoundness of the situation. As one contributor to the *Vestnik vospitaniia* put it, in typical fashion, "The diagnosis of sport fever, which holds the upper layers of our society in its grip, is confirmed by numerous symptoms."[33] As a result of the sickly proportions sport was acquiring, the traditional hierarchy of mind and body had become distorted. This was immediately reflected in the sight that magazines and shop windows offered: "Whereas recently the windows of art shops and stationery stores displayed portraits of writers, artists, and public figures, now they show photographs of wrestlers with gigantic torsos and monstrous muscles that attract masses of people.

Conversations about who 'floored' whom and employing which technique are now very common in those very same drawing rooms where previously music, literature, and politics were discussed."³⁴

Although these words express a deep anxiety over the sporting craze in general, it is not accidental that the author starts his enumeration of "symptoms of the sporting fever" with the hypermasculine sport of wrestling. Wrestling was one of the first professional sports in Russia enabling men to capitalize on their physical ability other than through unskilled labor. In other words, the value of men's physical capital increased, to use Pierre Bourdieu's terminology, whereas the conversion of cultural capital into income was felt to have become more problematic.³⁵ Many representatives of the intelligentsia, the contributor to *Vestnik vospitaniia* included, found this a disturbing development.

It is important for my argument to bear in mind that the crisis in the traditional job market for students coincided with the rise of professional sport and the growing popularity of wrestling in particular.³⁶ This is not to say either that the mere simultaneity of these developments was perceived as something significant or that every member of the student community was aware of it. I do argue, however, that the two intersected in a highly significant way in the lives of some contemporaries and even gave rise to a new role model: that of the student wrestler (*student-borets*) whose well-developed physique emblematized his ability to cope with economic hardship.

To a considerable extent, the popularization of the student wrestler as a role model can be attributed to the activities of writer, sport journalist, and art historian Nikolai Breshko-Breshkovskii, son of the "grandmother of the Russian revolution," Elena Breshko-Breshkovskaia. Although he was scorned by established literary critics such as Vladimir Korolenko, Breshko-Breshkovskii's sports novels were in great demand and not solely among semi-educated readers. An amateur wrestler himself, Aleksandr Kuprin was elated with Breshko-Breshkovskii's prose.³⁷ Aleksandr Blok, who regularly visited wrestling matches at the circus, admitted that he was fascinated with Breshko-Breshkovskii's "vulgar" novels about wrestlers and bullfighters.³⁸

In keeping with the didactic tradition of nineteenth-century literature, however, Breshko-Breshkovskii pretended to offer substantially more than mere entertainment. Like other representatives of the "boulevard," such as Evdokiia Nagrodskaia and Anastasiia Verbitskaia, he used his work as a vehicle for the advancement of a new behavioral ideal. In Breshko-Breshkovskii's fiction, this ideal is represented by a devoted and self-conscious sportsman (often a wrestler) who is given ample opportunity to expound his ideas in eloquent fashion. Although some of Breshko-Breshkovskii's wrestlers are characterized as innocent and almost naive, making them vulnerable to the sexual advances of female predators, on a number of occasions, the author almost turns them into ambassadors of wrestling who are in complete control of their own lives.[39] Intellectuals and athletes at the same time, these heroes proudly present themselves as the self-made men of the future.

One of Breshko-Breshkovskii's first attempts to offer such a success story of an educated wrestler can be found in a 1911 issue of *Sinii zhurnal*. It is not a fictional story but an article entitled "A Student Wrestler about Himself" ("Student-borets o sebe"), in which a certain A. Sh. tells about his "double life" as a student and an athlete. The somewhat unpolished language of the strongman A. Sh. is meant to suggest that his words are faithfully conveyed to the reader, but the numerous references to the supposedly uncomplicated attitude toward physical labor among Western students and the accompanying photograph showing

Writer Nikolai Breshko-Breshkovskii and student-wrestler A. Sh. (*Sinii zhurnal* 3 [1911]. University of Helsinki, Slavonic Library)

the weightlifting A. Sh. together with Breshko-Breshkovskii, leave the impression that the interview was written, or at least conducted and supervised, by the latter. In the interview, A. Sh. declared that "I am not a rich man, or, to put it correctly, I don't have a thing.... What do you want me to do? Run from one lesson to another and make fifty rubles at the most? No, thank you! As a wrestler I earn seven hundred and fifty rubles—almost a governor's salary. God gave me this build and strength; I've developed a good technique, why shouldn't I use all these attributes to my advantage? I beg your pardon, but in this respect we still have a purely Russian point of view, Russian rigorism. How is it possible to be a student and suddenly a wrestler? That's incompatible! A student should 'sow what is reasonable, honest, eternal.' To hell with these ideals, if they don't feed us. I don't want them."[40]

Subsequently, A. Sh. delivers the usual plea for physical labor as well as some gripping anecdotes that serve to illustrate the adventurous life of a wrestler. Of course, wrestling does not absorb A. Sh. entirely. Six months a year, he lives like an "ascetic," a "monk," devoting himself completely to his medical books. Only after an extended period of intellectual activity does he feel the need to live "without books and abstractions" and then the "savage" in him awakens: "And instead of my student room with its atlases, lectures, and a skeleton in the corner, there appears the dressing room in a theatre or in a circus."[41]

Whether or not the interview was entirely authentic, Breshko-Breshkovskii liked the student's scornful discard of Russian rigorism so much that he recycled A. Sh.'s monologue with only minor alterations in the 1914 short story "The Tattooed Wrestler." Published just before the outbreak of World War I (and clearly in anticipation of it), the story features a painter and wrestler by the name of Sokolov who succeeds in exposing his adversary (the title character) as an Austrian spy. This eventful story is only four pages long, but Breshko-Breshkovskii contrived to squeeze in quite an extensive statement by the hero in which he defends the moral and economic benefits of wrestling. The following words are directed to his nephew, Shepetovskii, who regards wrestling and art as incompatible: "'You don't understand a thing!' interrupted the artist Shepetovskii brazenly. '[It's a] wild, purely Russian view. We're afraid of everything. This shocks us and that shocks us, and so on. You should regard these matters in a much simpler way. Wrestling feeds me. It brings in twenty-five rubles a day. And as long as nobody will buy my paintings and I remain unknown, this sum is like a fortune to me.... Look at how it is in America. Ministers deliver lectures in *café chantants,* and it doesn't diminish them in the least. Poor students earn a loaf of bread by cleaning boots and later they become senators, highly placed public figures and billionaires.'"[42]

Just like Artsybashev, Breshko-Breshkovskii's fictional spokesman explains the problem of destitution among the educated youth as a corollary of the taboo on physical labor. He too evokes the image of the American student, whose alleged willingness to accept any kind of job guarantees him financial independence in the future. But Breshko-Breshkovskii goes a step further by concretizing the metaphor of the "struggle for existence" through the image of the part-time wrestler whose real ambitions lie elsewhere. Instead of delivering the obligatory eulogy on the benefits of sport, Breshko-Breshkovskii's hero admits to having become a wrestler on practical grounds: "Once the Lord has given me this figure and this force, why not use them?"

With his high-flown monologues Sokolov is a rather unconvincing figure who seems only designed to convey Breshko-Breshkovskii's own ideas. And yet, the almost oxymoronic image of the wrestling painter was not that far-fetched at all. The real-life prototype for Breshko-Breshkovskii's hero was Ivan Miasoedov (son of the well-known *peredvizhnik* Grigorii Miasoedov), who not only promoted nudism and weightlifting but also caused quite a sensation as a painter known for participating in wrestling matches. It is unknown whether he only fashioned himself in this way or was engaged in wrestling for financial reasons (or both), but Breshko-Breshkovskii was eager to exploit the latter scenario. Under his pen, Miasoedov's career became a moving story about a poor artist who overcomes his aversion to physical labor and makes a small fortune as a wrestler.[43]

Ivan Lebedev: A Student Wrestler Turns to Writing Fiction

A regularly recurring character in Breshko-Breshkovskii's novels about wrestlers is a referee by the name of Gusev in whom the readers could easily recognize the well-known wrestler, referee, and impresario Ivan Lebedev (1879–1950). Like his fictional counterpart, Lebedev usually wore a student uniform and hat, which earned him the nickname of "student" or "eternal student."[44] On the cover of Lebedev's numerous books about weightlifting and famous wrestlers, we see him wearing sports attire or a student uniform, the two outfits in which he was also invariably depicted in satirical journals. Significantly, Lebedev liked to call himself a "professor of athletics," a title probably invented to raise the status of wrestling among the intelligentsia. The sport journals *Gerkules* (*Hercules*) and *Krasota i sila* (*Beauty and Strength*), of which Lebedev was the main editor, published articles specifically intended for the student population that denounced the popularity of billiards among students and called on the *billiardsmeny* to devote their leisure time to sport.[45]

Lebedev also published a number of sentimental stories about destitute students whose introduction to wrestling marks the beginning of a new and fulfilling way of life. Yet, despite his own public image as a wrestler and eternal student, in his fiction he subordinated the socio-economic theme of student poverty to more general ethical questions. Lebedev's heroes appeal to us as fellow human beings, not as the members of a distinct social class.

Published in 1915, the story "The Murderer" ("Ubiitsa") introduces us to the student Petia Vyrubov, who spends most of his time "at the pool table or behind a pint of beer." Far from being bored with life, as his daily routine might suggest, Petia delights in leading the life of an idler: "By God, . . . there is beauty in the mist in which I find myself, there is a cheerful vapor about it."[46] After two years of heavy drinking and debauchery, however, Vyrubov decides to get a grip on himself and joins the circus where he soon establishes himself as the best wrestler in the country. The story reaches its climax when Vyrubov confronts the most fearsome opponent of his career: "fat" Franz Samson, an Austrian wrestler whose "pig's head" provides just enough room to store the concepts "money," "food," and "women."[47] Cheered on by an elated crowd who remind him that he is defending Russia's honor, Vyrubov not only defeats but also accidentally kills Samson. Although it was an accident and Vyrubov therefore cannot technically be deemed a murderer, he does consider himself guilty and determines to repent. He gives up wrestling and retreats to the monastery on the Solovki archipelago, where his extraordinary piety does not go unnoticed. Heavy with symbolism, the last paragraph describes Vyrubov's sunlit head and the impression it makes on his fellow monks: "But these sun rays cast such a friendly light on the monk Pitirim [i.e., Vyrubov] that it seemed as if the murder had not been committed at all."[48]

Echoing the parable of the prodigal son, Lebedev's story is essentially a paean to the Russian national character. It offered its readers the satisfaction of a victory over the Austrian enemy but simultaneously played on popular notions of the exceptional meekness of the Russian people. As in Breshko-Breshkovskii's story "The Tattooed Wrestler," in "The Murderer" World War I looms large. Therefore, although it would be quite a stretch to read Lebedev's story as a narrative of economic self-determination, its contours can still be discerned. After all, while student identity is no longer an issue, the hero of this story is an ex-student who has learned to overcome economic hardship. Just like Count Amori's sequel, *Sanin's Return,* Lebedev's "Murderer" is about a member of the intelligentsia whose development and spiritual growth is defined not in social or ideological but in moral and religious terms.

The Struggle for Life: From Metaphor to Role Model

At the beginning of the twentieth century, Russia's major cities witnessed a genuine boom in sport and outdoor recreation. Sport not only became a more "democratic" (i.e., less elitist) pastime than it had been before; it also received extensive coverage in the mass media, thus giving rise to the emergence of a specialized sport press. In this respect, Russia was not any different from Europe and the United States, where a similar development had manifested itself slightly earlier. Yet as Lozina-Lozinskii's expression of "footballism" demonstrates, in Russia the debate about the desirability of sport and physical education was highly politicized. Even if the Russian arguments *against* sport did not differ very much from those employed in the West (immoral waste of time, distraction from more spiritual matters), the context in which they were put forward was a different one, namely that of the "failed" revolution of 1905. Especially among left-wing students, the very idea of egotistically training and preserving one's body was contrasted negatively with the cliché of the consumptive student who ruins his health amid the struggle for life or sacrifices it for the revolutionary cause. The image of the muscular, self-sufficient student is worth taking notice of precisely because it challenged traditional notions of student identity and behavior.

Sanin and Artsybashev's public statements on student poverty played an important role in this development, even if Artsybashev could not have anticipated the ways in which Breshko-Breshkovskii and Lebedev would "poach"[49] the narrative of economic self-determination and use it for their own means. Already an important theme in *Sanin*, in the works of these two lowbrow authors the metaphor of "struggle for life" (*bor'ba za sushchestvovanie*) acquired a striking immediacy that resulted in a new role model: the student-wrestler who is master of his own fate.

Conclusion

When I had barely started my research on the myth of Saninism, an acquaintance asked me to go see some friends of hers in Moscow and present them with a copy of her recently published PhD dissertation on Marina Tsvetaeva. Although the thesis was written in Dutch and would therefore probably remain unread, I was struck by the solemnity with which the beneficiaries, three elderly women, accepted my delivery. Like my acquaintance, they were great admirers of the poetry of Tsvetaeva, and I understood that just the fact that another study of her work had been undertaken (especially by a good friend!) was perhaps more important to them than whether they could read it or not. When they asked me about my own research, and I told them that I was interested in the "pseudopornographic novel *Sanin*," one of the women remarked in a slightly resigned tone, "What couldn't you find at that time? There were even novels on homosexuality."

This meeting took place in the summer of 1997, almost six years after the collapse of the Soviet Union, by which time the master narrative of salvation through revolution had entirely lost its credibility. Yet, despite the fact that my three Tsvetaeva fans were ardent believers in the pre-Soviet story of the Silver Age and in all probability had always rejected the Soviet account of prerevolutionary history, they were also acutely aware of the period's "ugly face." Whether or not they had ever heard of Artsybashev, a few words about the reputation of his most infamous novel were sufficient to reactivate the all-too-familiar vision of fin-de-siècle hedonism and moral degeneration.

The choice of words and the additional allusion to the homoerotic novel *Wings* indicate that the speaker regarded the writing of Artsybashev and Kuzmin as symptomatic of the "spirit of the times." One of the goals of this book has been to argue the opposite, namely that the "spirit of the times" of the period 1907–17 is an ideological construct, a system of beliefs and assumptions that emerged partly as a result of the reception history of *Sanin*. In other words, the stir that the novel created and the spectacular but unsubstantiated rumors to which it gave rise were crucial in producing a certain conception of the prerevolutionary decade that subsequently came to be regarded as the historical "truth." Once this truth had been established, it was easy to label Vladimir Sanin a typical representative of the period's "degenerate" mentality, but, in fact, this mentality might never have been identified without Artsybashev's hero.

How is it possible that a literary character earns the reputation of being a "spokesman of the Russian intelligentsia" and a "role model for youth" with hardly anyone speaking out in favor of his message? This has been one of the central questions around which my discussion of Saninism has revolved. Although I acknowledge that the sources available to the historian may not accurately reflect the full spectrum of reader reactions, part of the answer lies in the mythology of the 1860s and the persistence with which it informed the perception of post-1905 reality. Critics' continuing search for epoch-making heroes, the conspicuous similarities between Sanin and the legendary nihilist Bazarov, who *did* become a role model of sorts, the existence of a subversive reading culture known to encourage an overly reverential attitude toward politically charged literature—all these factors contributed to the conviction that *Sanin* was devoured by readers who had found their ideal in the title character. Although the notion of a homogenously positive response has been called into question in a few scattered instances, other, sometimes even more recent, accounts revert to the old cliché of *Sanin* as a Bible for an entire generation.

This book has aimed at demonstrating that the reception of *Sanin* and the responses to perceived instances of Saninism in real life were more critical than has often been assumed as well as at bringing to light the very heterogeneity of these critical reactions. Indeed, looking over this episode in the history of Russian literature, one is struck by readers' inability to agree on the true nature of *Sanin*'s supposed success. Some believed the novel to be immensely popular among provincial readers incapable of savoring highbrow literature; others observed that its message resonated only with a tiny urban elite. A "fact of Russian reality" and a "hero of our time," Vladimir Sanin was simultaneously rejected as a "product of the author's fantasy" whose ties with reality were highly questionable. Critics were also divided on the question as to whose camp Sanin actually belonged. Was he a revolutionary, as the authorities feared, or did he represent the political reaction of Prime Minister Stolypin and his new economic course known as the "wager on the strong"? Finally, even after the court had banned the novel as a work of pornography, the question of its licentious character remained. While some readers noted its "titillating" and "hyperrealistic" effect, others considered its indebtedness to the *roman à thèse* incompatible with the very idea of sexual arousal.

Although most readers and critics were eager to dissociate themselves from *Sanin*, rumors about massive imitation of its hero instilled in school-going youth the belief that the novel's immediate influence actually extended to adolescents lacking in moral fortitude. In the perception of these students, the Saninist was not a political or social enemy but a fellow student gone astray, the sorry product of parental negligence and a victim of the police regime in secondary schools. Alcohol abuse, sexual license, and the strained relations between parents, children, and school—these issues had been addressed before in literature and pedagogical journals, but now they were perceived as the unmistakable signs of "Saninist" behavior. Whether Artsybashev had invented his hero or had portrayed a mentality that already existed, *Sanin* and the mythology of the 1860s provided a framework for interpreting juvenile debauchery.

The goal of this study has been neither simply to argue that *Sanin*'s reputation as a Bible was unfounded nor to find fault with other scholars, whose main interest lies elsewhere and who mention the novel in passing, for perpetuating this cliché. It would be somewhat condescending to cavil the authors of otherwise pioneering studies for "getting it all wrong" when dealing with *Sanin*. I do hope, however, that I have succeeded in demonstrating that Saninism was not an "ideology" but a complex of partly overlapping and sometimes mutually exclusive discourses that straddled the persistent traditions of realism and real criticism on the one hand, and the political and social concerns of early twentieth-century Russia, on the other. Contributing in no small measure to the unfavorable reputation of the years 1907–17 as the "most shameful and impudent decade in the history of the Russian intelligentsia," the reception history of Artsybashev's most notorious novel is, above all, indicative of the increased freedom of expression that Russians came to enjoy after the tumultuous events of 1905.

Appendix

Песнь санинцев

Мы санинцы—герои
Двусмысленных романов,—
Бульварных хулиганов
Развязней вдвое—втрое!

Морали сбросив гнет,
Укоров мы не слышим,—
За Куприна подпишем
Мы ресторанный счет...

Потребуйте с нас плату
При входе в аудиторию,—
Печальную историю
Готовим реферату....

Так! Истина в одном—
В романе Арцыбашева
Для просвещения нашего
Мы ходим табунком...

К искусству мы причастны,
И наша мощь—рецензии:
Поэты без претензии
Поистине несчастны!

Не попади нам в тон
Газета иль поэт:
Как бомба наш ответ—
Аршинный фельетон!

Мы—дети желтой прессы,
Мы, как она, развязны,—
Мы вечны, но мы разны,—
Мы—санинцы! Мы—бесы!
"Pesn' sanintsev," *Golos Moskvy*,
March 6, 1908, 2

Song of the Saninists

We Saninists are the heroes
Of suggestive novels
And we're twice, even three times, as shameless
As hooligans on the boulevard.

Having cast off the yoke of morality
We're immune to reproaches,
In a restaurant
We sign Kuprin's name on the check.

Just try and demand money from us
At the entrance to the hall,
We'll finish off
The speaker just like that . . .

That's right! The truth can only
Be found in Artsybashev's novel.
For the sake of our education
We wander around like a herd.

We're close to art,
Our power is the review:
Poets without pretensions
Are truly unfortunate.

Appendix

If we don't like the sound of
A newspaper or a poet:
We'll write our reply like a bomb:
A very long feuilleton.

We're children of the yellow press,
We're just as shameless,
We're eternal but different,
We're Saninists! We're demons!

Videant Consules!

Как в тине братья, сестры утопают;
Отцы и матери спокойно спят,
А дети их, в неведеньи считают
Любовью пошлый и гнилой разврат.

Забыты люди, ученье, книги,
Святыня попрана,—а совесть спит.
Забыто все—и длань позорной "лиги"
Над юностью веселою царит.

Молчите вы?! Иль мало жертв сгубила
Печатной пошлости толпа жрецов?
Иль ждете вы, чтоб общая могила
Покрыла родины младых сынов.

Когда пожар жилище истребляет,
Тогда на помощь все тушить бегут.
Здесь родины надежда погибает . . .
Что ж помощи к спасенью не несут?

Коль гибнет утлая ладья на море,
То с берега спешат на помощь ей . . .
Что-ж медлите? Иль ослепило горе,
Что гибели не видите своей?

Поменьше слов, бессильем не смущайтесь,
Иначе гибнет общество, семья.
Скорей на помощь гибнущим бросайтесь,
Пока не далеко еще ладья.

Гимназист Евгений

"Videant Consules," *Poltavskii golos,*
April 30, 1908, 3

Videant Consules!

As (our) brothers and sisters are drowning in the mire
(Our) fathers and mothers are sleeping soundly,
And their children in their ignorance regard
Rotten and vulgar debauchery as love.

People, learning, books are forgotten,
The sanctuary is defiled—while conscience is asleep . . .
Everything is forgotten—and the hand
   of the disgraceful "league"
Reigns over the merry young people.

You keep silent? Hasn't the mob of priests
Of printed vulgarity slain enough victims already?
Or are you waiting for a common grave
To cover the young sons of the fatherland?

When a fire is destroying a house,
People rush to extinguish the flames.
Here the hope of the fatherland is dying . . .
Why isn't someone coming to help?

When a frail boat is sinking at sea,
From the shore people hurry to the rescue . . .
Why are you taking so long? Or has grief blinded you
So that you don't see your ruin?

Fewer words, don't be embarrassed by your weakness,
Or else society, the family will perish.
Hurry to rescue those perishing,
Before the boat has sunk entirely.

Evgenii, a gymnasium student

Collective Letter to the Editor from a Group of Schoolgirls

Товарищи!

Мы, гимназистки, хотим с вами поделиться жгучим для нас вопросом. До сих пор мы мучились им каждая в отдельности, теперь же, когда в гимназии поднялся он открыто, мы хотим его вынести из стен ее.

Товарищи! Вопрос этот в разврате, который так сильно развит среди вас. Мы, ставя этот вопрос открыто, не хотим вас упрекать. Но хотим поделиться с вами нашими чувствами. Скажите, товарищи, думали ли вы когда-нибудь в какое положение вы ставите ваших будущих жен? Отчего она, чистая, не может требовать и от мужчины той же чистоты? Мы вас призываем к борьбе с развратом, который существует среди вас, к борьбе за чистое отношение к женщине. Вы не должны в ней видеть только самку, но—товарища. Гимназистки, которые с вами кокетничают, делают это бессознательно. Теперь же, когда в нас начинает пробуждаться сознание, вы тоже должны идти нам навстречу, чтобы будить сознание в наших подругах и среди вас. И мы требуем от вас также сознательного отношения к этому вопросу. Товарищи! объединяйтесь для борьбы с животным началом. Вы может быть будете смеяться над необычным призывом для современного "нравственного" общества. Но и в вас есть хорошее. Вы должны призадуматься над нашим призывом.

Мы верим, товарищи, что вы пойдете в этой борьбе с нами.

Группа гимназисток

Vsevolod Azrum, "Vinovaty li 'ogarki'?"
Vestnik vospitaniia 8 (1908): 123-24

Collective Letter to the Editor from a Group of Schoolgirls

Comrades!

We, *gimnazistki* [students of a girls gymnasium], want to share with you a burning issue. Hitherto each one of us has tormented herself with it individually, but now that it has been raised openly inside the gymnasium, we want to bring it out in the open.

Comrades! This issue is one of debauchery that is so prevalent among you. By raising this question, we do not want to reproach you. But we do want to share our feelings with you. Tell us, comrades, have you ever thought about the position in which you put your future wives? Why can't she, pure as she is, demand of a man the same purity? We call on you to start combating the debauchery among you, to start fighting for a pure attitude toward women. You should not see in her only a female of the species but a comrade. *Gimnazistki* who flirt with you are doing so unconsciously. Now that our consciousness is awakening, you should also come to join us in order to arouse the consciousness of our female friends among you. We demand of you a conscious attitude toward this issue. Comrades! Unite in the fight against the savage instinct. Perhaps you laugh at an appeal that is so extraordinary for modern "moral" society. But there is also something good in you. You should give our appeal serious consideration.

We believe, comrades, that you will join us in this fight.

A group of *gymnazistki*

Лиги любви в Киеве

Снова заговорили об обществе "Дарефа," которое было несколько лет тому назад довольно известно. Собственно "общества" не было. Существовал кружок ловеласов и негодяев, вовлекавших в свои сети подростков, преимущественно девушек, для низменных целей. В свое время фамилии этих "руководителей" были у всех на языке. Это было лица без определенных занятий, офицеры, чиновники и т.п.

К их услугам были женщины с темной репутацией, которые поджидали и выслеживали смазливеньких девушек и соблазняли их всякими приемами. Угощали конфетами, устраивали гулянья, и т.п. Приемы и способы обычные в подобных случаях. Одну из таких "дам" заметили, но благодаря ее связям с тогдашней полицией, она осталась без наказания. А после одного случая дело приняло в гимназиях огласку, в результате чего состоялось увольнение нескольких учениц—фамилии их нам точно известны, затем директор гимназии довел до сведения высшей администрации о поведении банды ловеласов, во главе с офицером, носившим кличку "Гри-гри," которому и было приказано не появляться в Киеве и не отлучаться с места стоянки его полка. Над остальными обещано было директору иметь строгое наблюдение.

Офицерик исчез с киевского горизонта, его приятели стали действовать осторожнее, а в гимназиях увольнение нескольких девушек, почти подростков, произвело страшный переполох.

Года два назад, говорят, было заложено основание новому "обществу." Среди кружков молодежи появилась некая девица, ставшая впоследствии центром незначительной группы очень юных последователей и последовательниц. Здесь занимались чтением Поль-де-Кока и похождений кавалера Фобласа и культивировались первые зародыши "свободной любви." В ту эпоху "Санин" еще не загромождал собою типографских станков, но принимая во внимание, что произведение это зачато еще в 1903 году, надо думать, что его духовное благословение всеуслопиет [sic] над этим ранним детищем и предтечей новейших настроений.

Но как бы там ни было, а литература отечественного производства—в подобном роде—еще обречена была на пребывание в самых пыльных углах библиотек и прилавков и могла быть усвоена в самый короткий промежуток времени. И потому все свободные идейные досуги основательница этого кружка, говорят, уделяла пропаганде иного рода, пропаганде не только вполне легальной, но и поощряемой. В настоящее время госпожа эта давно пошла по пути своего настоящего призвания, а зерна, посеянные в сердцах молодежи, успели дать довольно пышный посев. Ее участие, впрочем, являлось бы в дальнейшем совершенно излишним, так как ее последователи запаслись уже видным идеологом в лице "Санина."

Существующие теперь в Киеве кружки или лиги любви по одним версиям подобно минской и др. проповедуют ничем не прикрытый разгул, по другим базируют на идейном фундаменте. Поэтому слухи о циркулирующей среди них сугубо клубничной литературы—

согласно этой версии—не верны. У них есть одно евангелие: "Санин" и его евангелисты—в лице Арцыбашева, Каменского, Потемкина и Кузмина.

Утверждают, что текстами из этих писателей украшены все углы помещений, в которых совершаются радения лигистов. На их языке эти радения носят названия сеансов, и при встречах в одном из местных садов—они встречают друг друга со словами:

—Как вам спалось после вчерашнего сеанса?

Между прочим, этот сад является излюбленным местом свиданий местных нигилистов и в тоже время здесь завершается вербовка новых адептов.

Девушки вербуют мужчин, а гимназисты и реалисты девочек-подростков. Впрочем, здесь не только гимназисты. Во главе всей организации стоит, как уверяют, студент 3-ого курса, по прозванию, Генрих Красивый. Это—председатель.

Женщины составляют главный контингент среди член этого сексуального братства; наиболее многочисленные группы, над которыми простирается власть трехбунчужного падишаха Генриха Красивого, состоят из представительниц акушерских курсов и двух местных гимназий и не превышают возраста, относительно которого все суждения на Олимпе кончались одним решительным приговором:

—Так, розгами его . . .

Выше мы говорили, что вербовка новых лигистов совершается перекрестным путем: женщины вербуют мужчин, а мужчины улавливают женщин. Пропаганда развертывается по общему шаблону—применительно к психологии того и другого пола, как он дается в трактовании писателей-патронов. Девушки-агитаторши обыкновенно ходят попарно, и памятуя назидание Владимира Александровича [*sic*!] Санина, что они не более, как жирные, розовые и бесхвостые обезьяны или в лучшем случае хорошо раскормленные кобылицы, апеллируют, главным образом,—с позволения читателей,—к жеребцовым инстинктам своих жертв.

—А, хорошо нам живется!—Весело!

—О, да! поддерживает ее в тон другая. Раз в жизни молод бываешь, так бери, живи, пользуйся во всю!

Дело мужчины-агитатора гораздо сложнее. Тут уж требуется довольно подробное изучение "Санина"—во всей его психологической глуби, так сказать. Уменье подойти с аргументацией, от головного мозга идущей, дать хотя бы видимый антураж любви, воздвигнуть то идейное обоснование, без которого на первых порах уж никак невозможно.

Все усилия агитатора направлены к тому, чтобы доказать, что любовь есть крик голодной и будущей плоти, и нимало не связана с "душой." Из источника, заслуживающего доверия, нам передавали, что в пылу увлечения один вдохновленный агитатор, исчерпав весь запас модернистских аргументов, решил прибегнуть даже к содействию классиков и процитировал четверостишие Лермонтова:

> Делись со мною тем, что знаешь—
> И благодарен буду я.
> А ты мне душу предлагаешь—
> На кой мне черт душа твоя?

Впрочем, это исключительный случай. Из поэтов старой школы, кроме Баркова, господа нигилисты никого не признают.

Добившись теоретической подготовки, агитатор указывает адрес одного из клубов любви, где все оставшееся неясным и недосказанным разрешается в практическом постижении. Между прочим каждый член лиги снабжается билетом—на подобие контрмарки, выдаваемой в гардеробных—с обозначением номера.

Все эти сведения получены нами от лиц, глубоко возмущенных тем разложением, которое вносят лигисты в среду учащейся молодежи, и теперь держащих в руках только первые нити этих продуктов организованного распада. Как нам сообщают, всех лигистов в настоящее время около 100 человек. Для сеансов-радений у них имеется что-то 5 квартир. Внутренняя жизнь этих клубов разврата покамест еще не раскрыта в деталях.

Kievskaia mysl', April 28, 1908, 2

Love Leagues in Kiev

People have begun talking again about the Darefa society, which was quite well known a few years ago. It wasn't really a "society." There existed a circle of womanizers and scoundrels who tried to ensnare adolescents, primarily young women, for their base goals. Once the names of these "leaders" were on everybody's lips. It was people without specific occupations, officers, civil servants, etc.

At their disposal were women of shady reputation who were lying in wait for cute girls and seduced them using all sorts of devices. They presented them with candy, organized outings, etc. Such are the usual devices and methods in cases like these. One of these "ladies" was apprehended, but thanks to her connections with the police at that time, she remained unpunished. After another incident, the affair became known in the gymnasiums, as a result of which a few pupils were expelled—their names are known to us. And then the principal of the gymnasium informed the higher administration about the conduct of a gang of womanizers led by an officer nicknamed "Gri-gri," who was ordered not to show this face again in Kiev and not to leave the place where his regiment was camped. The principal was given assurance that the others would be kept under strict surveillance.

The officer disappeared from the Kiev horizon, his friends started to act with more caution, and in the gymnasiums the expulsion of a few girls, adolescents almost, caused a terrible stir.

They say that some two years ago the foundation was laid for a new "society." Among circles of young people, a certain damsel appeared who subsequently became the center of a small group of extremely young followers composed of both men and women. Here they engaged in reading Paul de Kock and the adventures of the cavalier Faublas, and the first seeds of "free love" were cultivated. In those days, the printing presses were not yet overloaded with *Sanin,* but bearing in mind that this work was begun back in 1903, we have to assume that its spiritual blessing extended to this early offspring and precursor of the latest trends.

Whatever the case, literature of national production—of this sort—was still doomed to lie around in the dustiest corners of libraries and shops and could be acquired in the shortest time. And this is why, they say, the founder of this circle dedicated all her spare mental time [and energy] to propaganda of a different sort, which was not only completely legal but even encouraged. This lady found the path of her true vocation long ago, and the seeds she planted in the hearts of the young have already yielded a rich harvest. Her further participation would have been absolutely superfluous, by the way, because her followers have ensured themselves of a prominent ideologue in the person of "Sanin."

According to some versions, the circles or love leagues now existing in Kiev profess unconcealed debauchery, like the league in Minsk and other organizations; according to other versions, they [the leagues in

Kiev] are based on a principled foundation. Therefore rumors about extremely juicy literature circulating among them—according to this version—are inaccurate. They have one gospel, *Sanin,* and its evangelists are Artsybashev, Kamenskii, Potemkin, and Kuzmin.

They maintain that all corners of the rooms, in which the rites of the league members take place, are adorned with these authors' texts. In their language, these rites are called "séances," and when they encounter each other in one of the local parks, they greet each other with the words:

—How did you sleep after yesterday's séance?

Meanwhile, this park is a favorite meeting place for local nihilists, and at the same time new followers are recruited here.

Young women recruit men while gymnasium students and students at the *realshule* recruit adolescent girls. Incidentally, there are not only gymnasium students here. The whole organization is headed, they maintain, by a third-year student nicknamed "Henry the Handsome." He is the chairman.

Women form the largest contingent among the members of this sexual fraternity; the most numerous groups, over which the power of sultan Henry the Handsome holds sway, consist of representatives of midwifery courses and two local gymnasiums and don't exceed the age about which all deliberations on Olympus were terminated with the decisive verdict:

—Well, wallop him good!

We said above that the recruitment of new league members is carried out across genders: women recruit men, men catch women. The propaganda follows a general pattern tuned to the psychology of one or the other sex, just as it is treated in the interpretations of author-patrons. Usually the female agitators walk in pairs and, heedful of Vladimir Aleksandrovich [sic!] Sanin's teaching that they're nothing more than fat, pink, and tailless monkeys or, in the best case, well-fed mares, they appeal mainly—with the reader's permission—to the stallion-like instincts of their victims.

—Ah, what a good life we have!—What fun!

—O, yes! agrees the other girl. "You're young only once, live and take full advantage of it!

The task of the male agitators is considerably more complicated. This requires a rather detailed study of *Sanin* in all its psychological depth, as it were. [It comes down to] the ability to approach [a girl] with an argument that springs from the brain, to create at least a perceptible appearance of love, to erect that principled foundation that one cannot do without during the first stage.

All the agitator's efforts are aimed at proving that love is a "cry of the hungry and future flesh" and not connected to the "soul" in the least. From a trustworthy source, word has reached us that one inspired agitator, in the heat of his enthusiasm, and having exhausted the entire supply of modernist arguments, even decided to resort to the help of the classics and quoted Lermontov's quatrain:

> Share with me you-know-what,
> And I'll be grateful.
> But you offer me your soul—
> What the hell do I need it for?

After these theoretical preparations, the agitator lists the address of one of the love clubs where all that has remained unclear and unsaid is resolved through practical understanding. By the way, every member of the league is supplied with a ticket—like a number handed out in a coatroom—with a number on it.

We have received all this information from people who are deeply shocked by the corruption the league members have introduced into the milieu of school-going youth and who hold in their hands only the first threads of these products of organized degeneration. We have been informed that, at present, there are about one hundred league members. For their rites of séance they have some five apartments at their disposal. The internal goings-on of these clubs of debauchery have not yet been revealed in all their detail.

Notes

Introduction

1. M. M. Dokshitskii, letter to Lev Tolstoi, February 4, 1908, Gosudarstvennyi muzei L. N. Tolstogo (hereafter cited as GMT), Moscow, f. 1, l. 1.

2. Lev Tolstoi, letter to M. M. Dokshitskii, February 10–11, 1908, in *Polnoe sobranie sochinenii*, 90 vols., ed. V. D. Chertkov (Moscow: Khudozhestvennaia literatura, 1928–64), 78:58–59. Tolstoy briefly referred to Dokshitskii's letter in an article on insanity that he started in 1910 but never completed. See Lev Tolstoi, "On Insanity" ("O bezumii"), in *Polnoe sobranie sochinenii*, 38:400.

3. It is not clear when Tolstoy read *Sanin* in its entirety for the first time. According to Dushan Makovitskii, he asked for a copy of *Sanin* on February 4, 1909, saying that he "would read it" (*skazal, chto prochtet ego*). This agrees with Makovitskii's diary entry from August 31, 1908, where it is stated that Tolstoy has not read *Sanin* yet (*U Tolstogo, 1901–1910: "Iasnopolianskie zapiski,"* 4 vols., ed. S. A. Makashin, M. B. Khrapchenko, and V. P. Shcherbina [Moscow: Nauka, 1979], 3:185. Yet Tolstoy's reply to Dokshitskii and other comments on *Sanin* made in the course of 1908 suggest that he had read some of it in the first half of 1908, probably only Sanin's monologues.

4. M. M. Dokshitskii, letter to Lev Tolstoi, February 10, 1908, GMT, f. 1, l. 2.

5. For the sake of convenience, I will stick to the more English-sounding "Saninism" and avoid *saninstvo* (*saninizm* and *saninstvo*, however, were both used). Although to the non-Russian ear, the first term seems to denote a teaching (commun*ism*) rather than a mood or state of mind, in Russian, the ending *-izm* is not necessarily restricted in its use to ideologies (cf. *idiotizm*, "idiocy"). Similarly, the ending *-stvo* in *saninstvo* does not contradict the idea of a teaching (cf. *khristianstvo*, "Christianity"). Dokshitskii, for example, used *saninstvo*, which he contrasted with *khristianstvo*. The unambiguously negative terms *saninshchina* and *artsybashevshchina* clearly connote a disease (analogous to Dobroliubov's *oblomovshchina*), not an ideology, but these were seldom used. Finally, I

will refer to Sanin's alleged imitators as "Saninists," though Artsybashev's contemporaries used the word *sanintsy* (as in *molodtsy* or *internetovtsy*, to use a term coined by the late Boris Yeltsin).

6. [Anonymous], "Russkaia kul'tura v Iaponii," http://www.japantoday.ru/books/biblioteka/VEHI/12.shtml (accessed December 10, 2008).

7. Vl. Kranikhfel'd, "Stavka na sil'nykh," *Sovremennyi mir* 5 (1909): 75.

8. Galina Rylkova, *The Archaeology of Anxiety: The Russian Silver Age and Its Legacy* (Pittsburgh: University of Pittsburgh Press, 2007), 15–17.

9. "Doklad A. M. Gor'kogo o sovetskoi literature," in *Pervyi vsesoiuznyi s"ezd sovetskikh pisatelei—1934*, ed. Ivan Luppol, Mark Rozental', and Sergei Tretiakov (Moscow: Khudozhestvennaia literatura, 1934), 12.

10. Ibid.

11. There is something contrived about the whole epilogue, and one suspects that Klimov was hoping to add just enough political correctness to mislead the censors. Unfortunately, the film was deemed ideologically inappropriate and remained "on the shelf" until 1987. See Valerii Fomin and Liliia Mamova, "Agoniia," in *Rossiiskii illiuzion*, ed. L. M. Budiak (Moscow: Materik, 2003), 607–8.

12. Vladislav Khodasevich, "Muni," in *Nekropol': Literatura i vlast'; Pis'ma B. A. Sadovskomu* (Moscow: SS, 1996), 74. The translation is Rylkova's (*Archaeology of Anxiety*, 54). For the moment, it is best to conceive of *sanintsy* and *ogarki* as synonyms. The exact meaning of *ogarki* is explained in chapter 6.

13. Contrary to popular belief, it was not Nikolai Berdiaev but the minor poet and critic Nikolai Otsup who, in 1933, was the first to apply the term "Silver Age" to the last decades before the revolution. See Omry Ronen, *The Fallacy of the Silver Age in Twentieth-Century Russian Literature* (Amsterdam: Harwood Academic Publishers, 1997), 21, 42–49.

14. Rylkova, *Archaeology of Anxiety*, 63–64.

15. Egyptologist Jan Assmann distinguishes between "communicative" and "cultural" memory. Communicative memory refers to the recent past and is shaped by concrete memories of eyewitnesses and other contemporaries, who are responsible for processes of exclusion and canonization. Cultural memory or "gelled" memory, on the other hand, relates to the more distant past; it does not so much store "factual" history (*faktische Geschichte*) as "historical" events that are remembered as such, that is, as "historic" events. At this point, history is transformed into a myth offering an all-encompassing explanation for the existing order and the way in which it has come about. With regard to *Sanin*, one can say that the memory of its assumed success was still alive during the 1920s and early 1930s but that it had been largely excluded from collective memory by the time the myth of the Silver Age was fully established. See Jan Assmann, *Das kulturelle Gedächtnis: Schrift, Erinnerung und politische Identität in frühen Hochkulturen* (Munich: Beck, 2005), 50–52.

16. One notable exception is the 1969 facsimile edition of *Sanin*, which was published by Bradda Books as no. 10 of its Rarity Reprints series. Of course, I am not referring to translations of *Sanin*, which continued to be published even after World War II (see chapter 4).

17. I use the term "modernism" in a broad "Russian" sense to denote all the schools and directions of early twentieth-century Russian literature that distanced themselves from the aesthetics of realism. This includes not only symbolism and acmeism but also the Russian branch of the historical avant-garde. In the context of Western European literature, the avant-garde is usually considered at odds with the skeptical world outlook of such quintessentially modernist authors as Marcel Proust, Robert Musil, Virginia Woolf, James Joyce, and Franz Kafka.

18. *Birzhevye vedomosti*, June 5, 1908, 6. Of all nineteenth-century Russian writers Artsybashev considered Lev Tolstoy to have exerted the strongest influence on him as a writer ("Ot 'malogo' nichtozhnym," in *Zapiski pisatelia: D'iavol; Sovremenniki o M. P. Artsybasheve*, ed. Timofei Prokopov [Moscow: Intelvak, 2006], 49).

19. Here I am referring to what Tynianov wrote about the disintegration of genres when they start shifting from the "center" of the literary system to its "periphery": "In this way, the adventure story came to belong to the boulevard [*bul'varnyi*], [and] in this way, the psychological story becomes 'boulevard' too" ("Literaturnyi fakt," in *Literaturnyi fakt*, ed. Olga Novikova [Moscow: Vysshaia shkola, 1993], 124).

20. Edith W. Clowes, *The Revolution of Moral Consciousness: Nietzsche in Russian Literature, 1890–1914* (DeKalb: Northern Illinois University Press, 1988), 7–9.

21. Jeffrey Brooks, *When Russia Learned to Read: Literacy and Popular Literature, 1861–1917* (Princeton, NJ: Princeton University Press, 1985), 160–62.

22. Another example of this approach is Alla Gracheva's article "Early Twentieth-Century Best-Sellers and the Aesthetics of Mass Consciousness," in *Twentieth-Century Russian Literature: Selected Papers from the Fifth World Congress of Central and East-European Studies*, ed. Karen L. Ryan and Barry P. Scherr, 16–24 (New York: St. Martin's Press, 2000).

23. According to Vladimir Piast, the symbolists did not respect realism (*realizma ne pochitali*) and did not read realist authors (*realistov i ne pochityvali*) (*Vstrechi* [Moscow: Novoe literaturnoe obozrenie, 1997], 52). Mikhail Kuzmin found fault with Artsybashev for his style and "lack of taste and subtlety" on several occasions, trashing, among other works, his short story "An Old Story" ("Staraia istoriia" [1912]), the novel *At the Last Frontier* (*U poslednei cherty* [1910–12]), and his essay on Chekhov ("O smerti Chekhova" [1906]). See "Zametki o russkoi belletristike: 2," in Kuzmin, *Kriticheskaia proza*, vol. 10 of *Proza*, ed. George Cheron et al. (Oakland, CA: Berkeley Slavic Specialties, 1997), 44; "Zametki o russkoi belletristike: 3," in *Kriticheskaia proza*, 56; "Zametki o russkoi

belletristike: 6," in *Kriticheskaia proza*, 75; "Zametki o russkoi belletristike: 9," in *Kriticheskaia proza*, 100. These reviews were originally published in the journal *Apollon* in 1910.

24. A. A. Blok, "Literaturnye itogi 1907 goda," in *Sobranie sochinenii*, 8 vols., ed. V. N. Orlov, A. A. Surkov, and K. N. Chukovskii (Moscow: Gosudartsvennoe izdatel'stvo khudozhestvennoi literatury, 1960–63), 5:228; A. V. Lavrov, "Blok i Artsybashev," in *Al. Blok i revoliutsiia 1905 goda*, Blokovskii sbornik 8 (Tartu: Tartu University, 1988), 54–60. According to Lavrov, Artsybashev solicited Blok's collaboration in order to lend *Sovremennyi mir* more prestige (54–55).

25. See, for example, an interview with Kuzmin in which the journalist assumes a causal connection between the poet's work and youth's depravity (*Moskovskaia gazeta*, October 4, 1911, 3).

26. Viktor Erofeev, *Russkii apokalipsis* (Moscow: Zebra E, 2006), 40. I owe this reference to Arie van der Ent.

27. Günther Seehaus, *Frank Wedekind in Selbstzeugnissen und Bilddokumenten* (Reinbek bei Hamburg: Rowohlt, 1974), 47–48.

28. Michael Squires, *The Creation of Lady Chatterley's Lover* (Baltimore, MD: Johns Hopkins University Press, 1983), 201.

29. For Artsybashev's claim that he never read Nietzsche, see his *The Millionaire*, trans. Percy Pinkterton (London: Martin Secker, 1915), 9. See also Nicholas Luker's article "Artsybashev's *Sanin*: A Reappraisal," in his *In Defence of a Reputation: Essays on the Early Prose of Mikhail Artsybashev* (Nottingham: Astra Press, 1990), 80. For an overview of Nietzsche's influence in Russia, see, for example, the collection of essays *Nietzsche in Russia*, ed. Bernice Glatzer Rosenthal (Princeton, NJ: Princeton University Press, 1986).

30. Beth Holmgren and Helena Goscilo, introduction to Anastasya Verbitskaya, *Keys to Happiness*, trans. and ed. Beth Holmgren and Helena Goscilo (Bloomington: Indiana University Press, 1999), xvii.

31. "Sanin in a skirt" is the title of an article on *Keys to Happiness*. The expression refers to the novel's main character, Mania El'tsova. See Tan [Vladimir Bogoraz], "Sanin v iubke," *Utro Rossii*, December 31, 1909, 3.

32. A seminal study on this topic is, of course, Laura Engelstein's *The Keys to Happiness: Sex and the Search for Modernity in Fin-de-Siècle Russia* (Ithaca, NY: Cornell University Press, 1992).

33. Mikhail Artsybashev, *Sanin: A Novel*, trans. Michael R. Katz, introduction by Otto Boele, afterword by Nicholas Luker (Ithaca, NY: Cornell University Press, 2001), 83.

34. Report of April 15, 1908, Rossiiskii gosudarstvennyi istoricheskii arkhiv, St. Petersburg, f. 777, op. 11, d. 67, 1. 11. The perceived similarities between *Sanin* and *What Is to Be Done?* are discussed in more detail in chapter 2.

35. "Artsybashev," in *Russkie pisateli, 1800–1917: Biograficheskii slovar'*, 5 vols., ed. P. A. Nikolaev and V. N. Baskakov (Moscow: Sovetskaia entsiklopediia, 1989), 1:114.

36. For a biographical account, see Nicholas Luker, "Mikhail Artsybashev: A Biographical Sketch," in *In Defence of a Reputation*, 1-11. See also "Artsybashev," in *Russkie pisateli, 1800-1917*, 1:113-15.

37. For a positive review of the first volume of Artsybashev's collected work, see Dmitrii Ovsianiko-Kulikovskii, "Literaturnye besedy: M. Artsybashev," *Nasha zhizn'*, August 3, 1905, 2-3.

38. Artsybashev submitted "Pasha Tumanov" to Mikhailovskii in 1901; in 1903 it was finally published in the third issue of the monthly *Obrazovanie*. For details, see *Russkie pisateli, 1800-1917*, 1:113.

39. Artsybashev attempted to commit suicide at the age of sixteen. He married at twenty, but the marriage soon failed. The significance of the economic theme forms the subject of chapter 7.

40. Ecclesiastes 7:29.

41. Peter Ulf Møller, *Postlude to "The Kreutzer Sonata": Tolstoj and the Debate on Sexual Morality in Russian Literature in the 1890s*, trans. John Kendal (Leiden: Brill, 1988), 2. The similarities in style were already pointed out by D. S. Mirsky in 1926: "Artsybashev's preaching proceeds direct from Tolstoy—only it is Tolstoy the other way around, and Tolstoy without genius" (*Contemporary Russian Literature, 1881-1925* [London: Routledge and Sons, 1926], 140).

42. *Sanin* was serialized in the course of 1907, the year in which Prime Minister Stolypin revoked many of the reforms that had been implemented in 1905. For a detailed discussion of these reforms and their revocation, see chapter 2.

43. *Sanin*, 259.

44. Hans Robert Jauss, *Literaturgeschichte als Provokation* (Frankfurt am Main: Suhrkamp, 1974), 169.

45. I cannot exclude the possibility that the novel was reprinted during the period of Lenin's new economic policy, but my searches in the most elaborate database available, the Electronic Union Catalog of the Nineteenth-Century Russian Book, yielded no results. Obviously, the purges of the school and public libraries in the 1920s severely limited the availability of Artsybashev's work. See Evgenii Dobrenko, *Formovka sovetskogo chitatelia: Sotsial'nye i esteticheskie predposylki retseptsii sovetskoi literatury* (St. Petersburg: Akademicheskii proekt, 1997), 179.

46. Jauss, *Literaturgeschichte als Provokation*, 194-99. I am much indebted to J. J. Kloek's thought-provoking discussion of Jauss's ideas. See Kloek's published doctoral dissertation, *Over Werther geschreven: Nederlandse reacties op Goethes Werther 1775-1800; Proeve van historisch receptie-onderzoek* (Utrecht: Hes Uitgevers, 1985), 45-55.

47. Zorkaia also quotes Gorky's characterization of the decade 1907-17 as "the most shameful and impudent decade in the history of the Russian intelligentsia" (*Na rubezhe stoletii: U istokov massovogo iskusstva v Rossii 1909-1910 godov* [Moscow: Nauka, 1976], 151, 156).

48. See "Reading as Poaching" in de Certeau's well-known study *The Practice*

of Everyday Life, trans. Steven F. Rendall (Berkeley: University of California Press, 1984), 165-76.

49. Iu. M. Lotman, "O Khlestakove," in *Izbrannye stat'i,* 3 vols. (Tallinn: Aleksandra, 1992), 1:363. See also Lidiia Ginzburg in the introduction to her well-known study *O psikhologicheskoi proze* (Moscow: Inrada, 1999), 26-27. As Boris Gasparov put it succinctly in the introduction to *The Semiotics of Russian Cultural History*: "'Psychological prose' is not a secondary reflection or description of actual human consciousness; it is a highly organized artistic model with a powerful reverse influence on society's self-consciousness" (*The Semiotics of Russian Cultural History: Essays by Iurii M. Lotman, Lidiia Ia. Ginsburg, Boris A. Uspenskii,* ed. Alexander D. Nakhimovsky and Alice Stone Nakhimovsky (Ithaca, NY: Cornell University Press, 1985), 18. Another classical study in this field is Irina Paperno's *Chernyshevsky and the Age of Realism: A Study in the Semiotics of Behavior* (Stanford, CA: Stanford University Press, 1988). I will return to Paperno's book in chapter 1.

50. Jean-Noël Kapferer, *Rumeurs: Le plus vieux média du monde* (Paris: Seuil, 1987), 85-103.

51. Stanley Cohen, *Folk Devils and Moral Panics: The Creation of the Mods and Rockers* (Oxford: Martin Robertson, 1980), 77-85.

Chapter 1. From Onegin to Bazarov

1. Barbara Heldt, *Terrible Perfection: Women and Russian Literature* (Bloomington: Indiana University Press, 1992 [1987]), 14-15.

2. Michel Foucault, *The History of Sexuality: An Introduction,* vol. 1, trans. Robert Hurley (New York: Vintage Books, 1990 [1978]), 11.

3. Introduction to M. Iu. Lermontov, *Geroi nashego vremeni,* in *Sobranie sochinenii,* 4 vols., ed. I. L. Andronikov, D. D. Blagoi, and I. G. Oksman (Moscow: Gosudarstvennoe izdatel'stvo khudozhestvennoi literatury, 1957-58), 4:8.

4. V. G. Belinksii, "Geroi nashego vremeni," in *Polnoe sobranie sochinenii,* 13 vols. (Moscow: Akademiia Nauk SSSR, 1953-59), 4:265.

5. See, for example, Chernyshevsky's famous essay "Russkii chelovek na rendez-vous," in *Polnoe sobranie sochinenii,* 16 vols. (Moscow: Gosudarstvennoe izdatel'stvo khudozhestvennoi literatury, 1939-53), 5:156-74.

6. Armed with only a rusty sabre, Rudin storms the government troops when the fighting is already over. The timing of his desperate attack and his inaccurate armament have been interpreted as the ultimate proof of his ineffectiveness.

7. M. V. Avdeev, *Nashe obshchestvo v geroiakh i geroiniakh literatury za piat'desiat' let,* 2nd ed. (St. Petersburg: Sklad u knigoprodavtsa I. P. Perevoznikova, 1907), 70. Nikolai Shelgunov, himself a representative of the radical left, expressed similar views when, in 1869, he wrote that Rudin had been judged too harshly. The men of the 1840s had indeed been "dreamers," but, during the dark years of Nicholas I, this was the only form of resistance possible ("Liudi

sorokovykh i shestidesiatykh godov," in *Literaturnaia kritika* [Leningrad: Khudozhestvennaia literatura, 1974], 61).

8. N. A. Dobroliubov, "Chto takoe oblomovshchina?" in *Voprosy, zadannye zhizn'iu* (Moscow: Sovetskaia Rossiia, 1986), 49–52.

9. In the 1860s Herzen would object to the inclusion of Onegin in this list, arguing that the Decembrist, not Pushkin's hero, was the typical representative of the 1820s. Herzen's modification did not catch on and Onegin continued to figure as a superfluous man in the debates on the Russian intelligentsia ("Eshche raz Bazarov," in *Sobranie sochinenii*, 30 vols. [Moscow: Pravda, 1975], 8:307).

10. D. I. Pisarev, "Bazarov," in *Polnoe sobranie sochinenii*, 6 vols. (St. Petersburg: F. Pavlenkov, 1897), 2:395.

11. Rufus W. Mathewson, *The Positive Hero in Russian Literature*, 2nd ed. (Stanford, CA: Stanford University Press, 1975), 51.

12. D. I. Pisarev, "Oblomov," in *Polnoe sobranie sochinenii*, 1:187.

13. D. I. Pisarev, "Novyi tip: Po povodu romana Chernyshevskogo *Chto delat'?*" in *Izbrannye proizvedeniia* (Leningrad: Khudozhestvennaia literatura, 1968), 558.

14. N. A. Dobroliubov, "Kogda zhe pridet nastoiashchii den'," in *Voprosy, zadannye zhizn'iu* (Moscow: Sovetskaia Rossiia, 1986), 340–41.

15. N. A. Dobroliubov, "Chto takoe oblomovshchina?" 59–60.

16. Ibid.

17. Mathewson, *The Positive Hero in Russian Literature*, 51.

18. Following Western studies of the radical intelligentsia by Daniel Brower and Michael Confino, Peter Pozefsky argues that the convenient picture of a social divide between the "aristocratic idealists of the 1840s" and the "non-aristocratic radicals of the 1860s" is, in fact, misleading. The very notion of a class conflict, introduced by the influential critic Nikolai Mikhailovskii, obscures the fact that in the 1860s most members of the radical intelligentsia were still of gentry origins (*The Nihilist Imagination: Dmitrii Pisarev and the Origins of Russian Social Radicalism (1860-1868)* [New York: Peter Lang, 2003], 11–12). Likewise, Elise Kimerling Wirtschafter has pointed out that it would be a mistake to attribute the radicalization of the intelligentsia in the 1860s to the "arrival" of the *raznochintsy* on the historical scene; they had been "visual participants" in social unrest long before (*Structures of Society: Imperial Russia's "People of Various Ranks"* [DeKalb: Northern Illinois University Press, 1994], 128).

19. For a discussion of this parallel, especially in the work of Turgenev, see Iurii Lotman's article "Siuzhetnoe prostranstvo russkogo romana XIX stoletiia," in *Izbrannye stat'i*, 3 vols. (Tallinn: Aleksandra, 1992), 3:98–101. See also Ellen Rutten, "Unattainable Bride Russia: Engendering Nation, State and Intelligentsia in Twentieth-Century Russian Literature" (PhD diss., University of Groningen, 2005), 36–38.

20. See Irina Paperno's study *Chernyshevsky and the Age of Realism: A Study in the Semiotics of Behavior* (Stanford, CA: Stanford University Press, 1988).

21. Richard Stites, *The Women's Liberation Movement in Russia: Feminism, Nihilism, and Bolshevism, 1860-1930* (Princeton, NJ: Princeton University Press, 1991 [1978]), 113.

22. Although the term "nihilist" was sometimes used as a kind of honorary nickname by members of the left-wing intelligentsia (see, for example Sof'ia Kovalevskaia's autobiographical novel *The Female Nihilist* [*Nigilistka* (1899)]), the term never entirely lost its negative ring. In *What Is to Be Done?* (written in response to *Fathers and Children*), there is no mention of "nihilism" or "nihilists." Pisarev also preferred more positive designations such as "new people," "realists," and "members of the thinking proletariat" (Pozefsky, *The Nihilist Imagination*, 12).

23. Paperno, *Chernyshevsky and the Age of Realism*, 13-14. See also the commentary in the complete edition of Turgenev's collected work: *Polnoe sobranie sochinenii i pisem*, 28 vols. (Moscow: Nauka, 1960-68), 8:589-611.

24. D. I. Pisarev, "Bazarov," 2:380, 395. For a recent discussion of "Bazarov," see Pozefsky, *The Nihilist Imagination*, 57-71.

25. D. I. Pisarev, "Realisty," in *Polnoe sobranie sochinenii*, 4:5-6.

26. Peter Kropotkin, *Memoirs of a Revolutionist*, ed. James Allen Rogers (London: Cresset Library, 1988 [1962]), 197, 266.

27. Nina Malysheva, "Obraz Bazarova v obshchestvenno-politicheskoi polemike 1908-1910 gg.," *Československá Rusistika* 31 (1986): 118.

28. Pisarev, "Bazarov," 427.

29. For a discussion of Bazarov's tragic and "superfluous" traits, see Wolf-Heinrich Schmidt, *Nihilismus und Nihilisten: Untersuchungen zur Typiesierung im russischen Roman der zweiten Hälfte des neunzehnten Jahrhunderts* (Munich: Fink, 1974), 87-88, and David Lowe, *Turgenev's "Fathers and Sons"* (Ann Arbor, MI: Ardis, 1983), 66-69.

30. D. N. Ovsianiko-Kulikovskii, *Istoriia russkoi intelligentsii: Chast' vtoraia; Ot 50-x do 80-x godov*, in *Sobranie sochinenii*, 9 vols. (The Hague: Mouton, 1969 [1909-13]), 8:75-79.

31. D. I. Pisarev, "Realisty," 89.

32. Paperno, *Chernyshevsky and the Age of Realism*, 14-15.

33. Ibid., 18.

34. M. V. Avdeev, *Nashe obshchestvo v geroiakh i geroiniakh literatury* (St. Petersburg: K. V. Trubnikov, 1874). The essays that make up the book were originally published in 1873 in the periodicals *Birzhevye vedomosti* and *Nedelia*.

35. Avdeev's line of reasoning can be traced back at least to Pisarev's essay on Bazarov, if not earlier. In that respect, his work is not particularly innovative. However, its significance lies in the fact that it is the first attempt to present a complete overview of Russian literature's "heroes of our time." It is the scope of Avdeev's book, rather than its content, that gives it its historical value.

36. I. [I. N. Ignatov], "*Sanin*, roman M. Artsybasheva," *Russkie vedomosti*, June 14, 1907, 3.

37. Viktor Zhivov, "Marginal'naia kul'tura v Rossii i rozhdenie intelligentsii," *Novoe literaturnoe obozrenie* 37 (1999): 49.

38. *Nashe obshchestvo v geroiakh i geroiniakh literatury*, 129.

39. R. D., "Novoe literaturnoe pokolenie: Chast' II," quoted in *Gospoda kritiki i gospodin Chekhov: Antologiia*, ed. Stiven Le Flemming (St. Petersburg: Letnii sad, 2006), 218. Originally published in *Nedelia* 15 (1888): 480–86.

40. R. D., "Novoe literaturnoe pokolenie: Chast' I," in *Gospoda kritiki i gospodin Chekhov*, 217. Originally published in *Nedelia* 13 (1888): 419–22.

41. Ibid., 218. Disterlo considered the following writers and poets typical exponents of the 1880s: Anton Chekhov, Eronim Iasinskii, Vladimir Dedlov, Kazimir Barantsevich, and Konstantin Fofanov.

42. See Shelgunov's essay "Liudi sorokovykh i shestidesiatykh godov," 39–209.

43. N. V. Shelgunov, "Peterburg i ego novye liudi," in *Ocherki russkoi zhizni* (St. Petersburg: O. N. Popova, 1895), 563–67.

44. N. K. Mikhailovksii, "Opiat' ob ottsakh i detiakh," in *Polnoe sobranie sochinenii*, 8 vols. (St. Petersburg: N. N. Mikhailovskii, 1906–14), 6:964.

45. Ibid., 956.

46. N. K. Mikhailovskii, "Ob ottsakh i detiakh i o g. Chekhove," in *Literaturno-kriticheskie stat'i* (Moscow: Goslitizdat, 1957), 596.

47. Ia. V. Abramov, "Stoit li rabotat' v derevne?" *Nedelia* 41 (1885): 1412. For a relatively recent discussion of Abramov's ideas, see V. V. Zverev, "Evoliutsiia narodnichestva: 'Teoriia malykh del,'" *Otechestvennaia istoriia* 4 (1997): 86–94.

48. V. I. Lenin, "Chto takoe 'druz'ia naroda'?" in *Polnoe sobranie sochinenii*, 5th ed., 55 vols. (Moscow: Izdatel'stvo politicheskoi literatury, 1967–70), 1:252, 264.

49. For a discussion of Abramov's ideas and their effectiveness, see Sergej V. Utechin, *Russian Political Thought: A Concise History* (London: Dent, 1964), 135–36.

50. See, for example, Veresaev's evocatively titled stories "Off the Road" ("Bez dorogi" [1895]), "Tendency" ("Povetrie" [1897]), and "At the Turn" ("Na povorote" [1901]). Artsybashev paints an extremely negative portrait of the unassuming toiler in his 1905 story "Morning Shades" ("Teni utra").

51. I. N. Potapenko, "Na deistvitel'noi sluzhbe," in *Derevenskii roman i drugie povesti i rasskazy iz dukhovnogo byta* (St. Petersburg: A. F. Marks, n.d.), 6–141.

52. I. N. Potapenko, "Ne geroi," in *Sochineniia*, 10 vols. (Petrograd: A. F. Marks, n.d.), 5:461.

53. Ibid., 469.

54. A. I. Reitblat, "Roman literaturnogo krakha," *Novoe literaturnoe obozrenie* 25 (1997): 99.

55. Dmitrii Strunin, "Kumir devianostykh godov," *Russkoe bogatstvo* 10 (1891): 162.

56. It is certain that Abramov was familiar with Potapenko's work, even if he does not seem to have valued him as a writer. In a June 1898 article published in *Knizhki Nedeli*, he observed that Chekhov's short stories contained

an "abundance of material" that would be enough for a "more calculating writer, such as Boborykin or Potapenko, to produce ten huge novels" ("Nasha zhizn' v proizvedeniiakh Chekhova," quoted in *Gospoda kritiki i gospodin Chekhov*, 20).

57. V. V. Vorovskii, "Lishnie liudi," in *Stat'i o russkoi literature* (Moscow: Khudozhestvennaia literatura, 1986), 102.

58. Ibid., 138.

59. In applying the term "new man" to Bazarov, I am alluding to Dmitrii Pisarev's positive reinterpretation of Turgenev's hero as an emerging historical type. As we have seen, the first reactions to *Fathers and Children* in the camp of radical critics were far less favorable.

60. D. N. Ovsianiko-Kulikovskii, *Istoriia russkoi intelligentsii*, 7:38-39.

61. The established pattern is somewhat reminiscent of Turgenev's distinction between Hamlet (contemplative) and Don Quixote (energetic), but nowhere does Ovsianiko-Kulikovskii refer to him.

62. Laevskii is one of the main characters in the story "The Duel" ("Duel'" [1891])—an alcoholic misfit who likes to compare himself to Evgenii Onegin. Asorin is a petty meddler in the story "The Wife" ("Zhena" [1892]), a "Russian foreigner," as Ovsianiko-Kulikovskii calls him, because he is incapable of appreciating anything Russian (*Istoriia russkoi intelligentsii*, 9:124).

63. Ovsianiko-Kulikovskii mentions one positive exception, the eponymous hero of Piotr Boborykin's novel *Vasilii Terkin* (1892). Terkin is a democrat-*Kulturträger* in whom practical shrewdness and efficiency go hand in hand with a certain moral and ideological maturity. Criticizing Russian literature for not having paid sufficient attention to this type (with the exception of Boborykin), Ovsianiko-Kulikovskii admits that it occurs only very sporadically in Russian society (*Istoriia russkoi intelligentsii*, 9:171).

64. Ovsianiko-Kulikovskii, *Istoriia russkoi intelligentsii*, 9:212-15. The novel by Boborykin is *The Pass* (*Pereval* [1894]).

65. Ovsianiko-Kulikovskii, *Istoriia russkoi intelligentsii*, 8:198. The parallel between Veresaev's village doctor and Rudin was drawn by an anonymous critic, "Periodicheskie izdaniia," *Russkaia mysl'* 9 (1895): 527.

66. Roman Disterlo, "Kriticheskie zametki," quoted in *Gospoda kritiki i gospodin Chekhov*, 222.

Chapter 2. Sanin

1. Abraham Ascher, *The Revolution of 1905: Russia in Disarray* (Stanford, CA: Stanford University Press, 1988), 85-92.

2. Abraham Ascher, *The Revolution of 1905: Authority Restored* (Stanford, CA: Stanford University Press, 1992), 364-65.

3. M. P. Artsybashev, letter to Anastasiia Krandievskaia (written between May 9 and 15, 1907), Rossiiskii gosudarstvenny arkhiv literatury i isskustva, Moscow, f. 251, op. 2, ed. khr. no. 1, l. 5.

4. *Sovremennyi mir* 7-8 (1907), table of contents. Contrary to Artsybashev's later claims that he had finished the manuscript long before its serialization, the delay in publication clearly suggests that, in May 1907, he was still working on it, perhaps even thoroughly rewriting it. If he had finished it, the entire manuscript would have been at the editorial office of *Sovremennyi mir* at the time of his detention.

5. A. A. Blok, "Literaturnye itogi 1907 goda," in *Sobranie sochinenii*, 8 vols., ed. V. N. Orlov, A. A. Surkov, and K. N. Chukovskii (Moscow: Gosudarvstvennoe izdatel'stvo khudozhestvennoi literatury, 1960-63), 5:228.

6. P. Dmitriev, "Zhurnal'noe obozrenie," *Obrazovanie* 3 (1907): 79.

7. *Knizhnaia letopis' glavnogo upravleniia po delam pechati*, December 1, 1907, 21:3; April 5, 1908, 14:2.

8. Vl. Votsianovskii, "Eshche kentavr," *Rus'*, October 27, 1907, 2.

9. See Artsybashev's comments in the preface to the English translation of his play *Voina* (*War: A Play in Four Acts*, trans. Thomas Seltzer [New York: Knopf, 1916], viii). In a personal letter to one L'dov (perhaps Konstantin), written between 1908 and 1914, Artsybashev claimed to have written *Sanin* as early as 1902 (Rossiiskaia natsional'naia biblioteka, f. 124 [sobr. P. L. Vakselia], ed. khr. no. 129, 1.1).

10. P. M. Pil'skii, "Reaktsiia zamuzhem," in *Problema pola, polovye avtory i polovoi geroi* (St. Petersburg: Osvobozhdenie, 1909), 112.

11. Apparently, Artsybashev made a statement to that effect in an interview published shortly after he had completed the novel, but I have not been able to retrieve the source. In an article published in the emigrant daily *Novoe Russkoe slovo* (*The New Russian Word*) in 1927, Artsybashev's old friend Evgenii Agafonov maintains that the novel's structure was completely changed around as a result of Artsybashev's revaluation of some of his convictions following his exile from St. Petersburg in 1901 (for participating in a student demonstration at Kazan square). For details, see the article on Artsybashev in *Russkie pisateli, 1800-1917: Biograficheskii slovar'*, 5 vols., ed. P. A. Nikolaev and V. N. Baskakov (Moscow: Sovetskaia entsiklopediia, 1989), 1:114.

12. Ia. Danilin, introduction to *"Sanin" v svete russkoi kritiki* (Moscow: Zaria, 1908), 6.

13. Evgenii Trubetskoi, "Konets revoliutsii v sovremennom romane," in *"Sanin" v svete russkoi kritiki*, 40-46.

14. V. Vorovskii, "Lishnie liudi," in *Stat'i o russkoi literature* (Moscow: Khudozhestvennaia literatura, 1986), 102.

15. Artzibashef, *War*, ix.

16. For a recent discussion of the tendentious novel, see Russel Scott Valentino's *Vicissitudes of Genre in the Russian Novel: Turgenev's "Fathers and Sons," Chernyshevsky's "What Is to Be Done?," Dostoevsky's "Demons," Gorky's "Mother"* (New York: Peter Lang, 2001), 43-85.

17. Peter Kropotkin, *Memoirs of a Revolutionist* (London: Cresset Library, 1988), 195.

18. Sigrid Nolda, "M. P. Arcybaševs Roman *Sanin*: Zur Aktualität eines vergessenen Skandals," *Zeitschrift für Slavische Philologie* 43 (1983): 395.

19. Nikolai Chernyshevsky, *What Is to Be Done?* trans. Michael R. Katz (Ithaca, NY: Cornell University Press, 1989), 376.

20. See 2.9, 3.1, 3.14, and 3.19 of *What Is to Be Done?*

21. Ibid., 2.9.

22. A. I. Kuprin, *Iama*, in *Sobranie sochinenii*, 9 vols. (Moscow: Pravda, 1982), 4:165.

23. For a more extensive exploration of the theme of incest in the work of some of Artsybashev's contemporaries, notably in Anatolii Kamenskii's story "Four" ("Chetyre" [1907]), see my article "'Why Pretend?' The Search for Authenticity in the Works of Volodymyr Vynnyčenko and Anatolij Kamenskij," *Russian Literature* 54 (2003): 67–84.

24. Elena Koltonovskaia, "Nasledniki Sanina," in *Kriticheskie etiudy* (St. Petersburg: Prosveshchenie, 1912), 70.

25. With the exception of Zinaida Hippius's novel *A Devil's Doll*, I ignore other "Saninist" fiction. It is not my intention to take stock of Sanin-like heroes or reconstruct some sort of "master narrative" underlying *Sanin*-like novels and stories. For the purpose of the present discussion, it suffices to know that Artsybashev's contemporaries believed that Sanin was not unique.

On the Sanin-type in Hippius's prose, see Elena Koltonovskaia, "Nasledniki Sanina." In this article, Koltonovskaia also discusses the work of Vynnychenko and O. Mirtov (pseudonym of Olga Kotyleva). The similarities between Sanin and Vynnychenko's hero, Myron Kupchenko, were noted by other critics as well. See, for example, K. I. Arabazhin, "Liubov' i brak v sovremennoi literature," in *Etiudy o russkikh pisatel'iakh* (St. Petersburg: Prometeo, 1912), 189. A more extensive scholarly comparison of Sanin and Kupchenko can be found in Andrew Kaspryk, "Volodymyr Vynnychenko's Nietzschean Revolutionary Hero" (PhD diss., University of Illinois at Chicago, 2000), 302–12. See also Vladimir Kranikhfel'd's article "Stavka na sil'nykh" (*Sovremennyi mir* 5 [1909]: 71–92), which dwells on Vikentii Veresaev's 1908 novella *To Life* (*K zhizni*) and Boris Savinkov's novel *The Pale Horse* (*Kon' blednyi* [1909]). One critic mentioned the appearance of the Sanin-type in Timkovskii's story "The Family Nal'chin" ("Nal'chiny" [1909]). See V. Bronin, "N. Timkovskii, *Povesti i rasskazy*," *Novyi zhurnal dlia vsekh* 1 (1910): 124.

26. V. L'vov, "Mirosozertsanie Sanina," in *"Sanin" v svete russkoi kritike*, 58.

27. V. Burenin, "Kriticheskie ocherki," *Novoe vremia*, November 2, 1907, 4.

28. Graf Amori [I. P. Rapgof], *Vozvrashchenie Sanina* (Riga: Gramatu Draugas, 1931), 24.

29. Report dated April 15, 1908, Rossiiskii gosudarstvennyi istoricheskii arkhiv, f. 777, op. 11, d. 67, l. 11.

30. Peter Pozefsky, *The Nihilist Imagination: Dmitrii Pisarev and the Origins of Russian Social Radicalism (1860–1868)* (New York: Peter Lang, 2003), 102.

31. To my knowledge, this is the only time when Sanin was compared explicitly to Chernyshevsky's heroic creation, Rakhmetov.

32. S. Petropavlovskii, "*Sanin*: Roman Artsybashev," *Minskoe slovo*, April 2, 1908, 3-4.

33. A. Trifonovich, "K kharakteristike sovremennogo russkogo obshchestva," *Molodye poryvy* 4 (1908): 26.

34. Apparently, the parallel between Sanin and Bazarov was so obvious that the critic Aleksandr Izmailov wrote a short parody on *Sanin* in which the main hero was called *Ba*sanin. See Aleksandr Izmailov, "M. P. Artsybashev," in *Russkaia literaturnaia parodiia* (Ann Arbor, MI: Ardis, 1980), 177-78.

35. G. S. Novopolin [Grigorii Semenovich Neifel'd], *Pornograficheskii element v russkoi literature* (Ekaterinoslav: Tipografiia L.I. Satanovskogo, 1909), 127.

36. Fiodor Dan, "Geroi likvidatsii," in *Na rubezhe (k kharakteristike sovremennykh iskanii)* (St. Petersburg: Nashe vremia, 1909), 86-87.

37. V. V. Vorovskii, "Bazarov i Sanin: Dva nigilizma," in *Literaturnaia kritika* (Moscow: Khudozhestvennaia literatura, 1971), 197, 211.

38. Ibid., 210.

39. Ibid., 217.

40. *Sanin*, trans. Michael R. Katz (Ithaca, NY: Cornell University Press, 2001), 82.

41. Novopolin, *Pornograficheskii element v russkoi literature*, 128-30.

42. S. L. Frank, "Etika nigilizma (k kharakteristike nravstvennogo mirovozreniia russkoi intelligentsii)," in *Vekhi: Intelligentsiia v Rossii, 1909-10* (Moscow: Molodaia gvardiia, 1991), 177.

43. Quoted in George Tokmakoff, *P. A. Stolypin and the Third Duma: An Appraisal of the Three Major Issues* (Lanham, MD: University Press of America, 1981), 44.

44. Kranikhfel'd, "Stavka na sil'nykh," 75.

45. Ibid., 76.

46. B. Kaplan, "Dva mira," *Molodye poryvy* 4 (1908): 34.

47. A. Rossov, "Sanin i ego ucheniki," *Russkoe slovo*, March 19, 1908, 2.

48. F. Dan, "Geroi likvidatsii," 85-86.

49. Ibid., 97.

50. Ibid., 104.

51. Ibid., 105.

52. Sidney Monas, "The Twilit Middle Class of Nineteenth Century Russia," in *Between Czar and People: Educated Society and the Quest for Public Identity in Late Imperial Russia*, ed. Edith W. Clowes, Samuel D. Kassow, and James L. West (Princeton, NJ: Princeton University Press, 1991), 29-30. Monas points out that the autocracy tended to be hostile to any signs of a budding bourgeoisie as well (31).

53. Kol-Oman, *Kto-zhe, nakonets, Sanin? Opyt materialisticheskogo tolkovaniia "problemy pola"* (Odessa: kommercheskaia tipografiia B. Sapozhnikova, 1908), 13.

54. Ibid., 16.

55. M. Greidenberg, *"Sanin": Itogi proshlogo i problemy budushchego* (Khar'kov: Russkaia tipo-litografiia, 1908), 1.

56. Ibid., 2.

57. Ibid., 16.

58. Arskii, "*Sanin* M. P. Artsybasheva," *Novosti dnia*, October 1, 1907, 3-4.

59. On the antinihilist novel, see Valentino, 49, I. P. Smirnov, "Nigilizm, antinigilizm i *Besy* Dostoevskogo," in *Russische Literatur an der Wende vom 19. zum 20. Jahrhundert*, ed. Rainer Grübel (Amsterdam: Rodopi, 1993), 71-91, and Charles A. Moser, *Antinihilism in the Russian Novel of the 1860s* (The Hague: Mouton, 1964).

60. The term countertext is explained in the introduction to chapter 3.

61. For a discussion of the relationship between Hippius and Savinkov, and the confusion over the authorship of *Kon' blednyi*, see V. Kranikhfel'd, "Stavka na sil'nykh," 78.

62. Viktor Chernov, "Literaturnye vpechatleniia," *Sovremennik* 5 (1911): 324-26. Savinkov himself also considered this to be the novel's main shortcoming. For details, see Marina Mogil'ner, *Mifologiia "podpol'nogo cheloveka"* (Moscow: Novoe literaturnoe obozrenie, 1999), 113-14.

63. Chernov, "Literaturnye vpechatleniia," 306; Dikii, "Na zloby dnia: O chertovykh kuklakh i troebratsakh, o mysliakh, otdaiushchikh zapakhom 'kholodnykh koshek,' i prochee," *Znamia truda* 36 (1911): 6; Koltonovskaia, "Nasledniki Sanina," 79. For a discussion of Artsybashev's work in Hippius's criticism, see Temira Pachmuss, *Zinaida Hippius: An Intellectual Profile* (Carbondale: Southern Illinois University Press, 1971), 331-39.

64. Anton Krainii [Zinaida Gippius], "Razocharovaniia i predchuvstviia," *Russkaia mysl'* 11 (1910): 179.

65. Zinaida Gippius, "Chitateliam," *Chertova kukla/Roman-czarevich* (Munich: Fink, 1972 [1911]), iv.

66. Ibid.

67. Zinaida Gippius, *Chertova kukla*, in *Chertova kukla: Proza, Stikhotvoreniia, Stat'i* (Moscow: Sovremennik, 1991), 288.

68. Hippius was not the first to use the bicycle as a signifier of frivolous behavior. It also occurs in Chekhov's story "Man in a Suitcase" ("Chelovek v futliare" [1898]) and Tolstoy's play *The Fruits of Enlightenment* (*Plody prosveshcheniia* [1891]).

69. *Chertova kukla*, 354.

70. *Sanin*, 83.

71. Compare, for example, Iurii Dvoekurov's insistence on the need to "consciously strive for happiness" (*Chertova kukla*, 351) and the following words by Sanin: "I know one thing. . . . I live life and I don't want it to be miserable" (*Sanin*, 83).

72. *Chertova kukla*, 352.

73. *Sanin*, 232.
74. A. E. Red'ko, "Predvideniia i nabliudeniia v belletristike," *Russkoe bogatstvo* 2 (1911): 92-93.
75. A. E. Red'ko, "O chertovoi kukle—mertvoi krasote," *Russkoe bogatstvo* 7 (1911): 170.
76. E. Koltonovskaia, "Naslednikí Sanina," 78-79.
77. V. Chernov, "Literaturnye vpechatleniia," 306.
78. Ibid., 323.
79. Pachmuss, *Zinaida Hippius: An Intellectual Profile*, 55, 170.
80. *Roman-czarevich*, 278.
81. Temira Pachmuss, introduction to *Chertova kukla/Roman-czarevich*, vii.
82. Zinaida Gippius, "Chitateliam," ibid., iv.
83. Veniamin Popov, "Modnyi roman (*Sanin* M. Artsybasheva)," in *O veianiiakh vremeni* (St. Petersburg: Tvorchestvo, 1908), 51.
84. Piotr Olenin, *Vakkhanka (Vampuka liubvi)* (St. Petersburg: Zhurnal teatr i iskusstvo, 1912), 45.
85. G. R., "Russkii sport i uchashchaiasia molodezh," *Vestnik vospitaniia* 9 (1909): 162.
86. B. Frommett, "Osnovnye momenty istorii russkogo studenchestva," *Vestnik studenchestva: Zhurnal demokraticheskogo studenchestva* 2 (1917): 18.

Chapter 3. Counterliterature

1. *Kievskie vesti*, May 18, 1908, 3.
2. V. L'vov [-Rogachevskii], "Satiry i nimfy," *Obrazovanie* 4 (1908): 44.
3. In his fascinating study on the reception of *The Kreutzer Sonata*, Peter Ulf Møller uses the term "counterliterature" to "designate, quite specifically, the literary works that were written as clear parallels to *The Kreutzer Sonata* in the choice of title, plot or characters, for example, and which at the same time contained a clear polemic intent directed against the ideas of the work. At a certain point the similarity ceases, and the story takes a different turn, thus permitting an alternative sexual morality to come to expression in contrast to that of *The Kreutzer Sonata*" (*Postlude to "The Kreutzer Sonata": Tolstoj and the Debate on Sexual Morality in Russian Literature in the 1890s*, trans. John Kendal [Leiden: Brill, 1988], 163). Obviously, my aim in this chapter is rather similar to that of Møller, who also devotes a chapter to the counterliterature written in reaction to Tolstoy's famous novella.
4. Anonymous, *"Sanin": Stseny iz romana*, ms., Sankt-Peterburgkaia gosudarstvennaia teatral'naia biblioteka (hereafter cited as SPTB), St. Petersburg, 32. It was rejected by the censor on March 10, 1908.
5. According to at least one critic, the theater was even more strictly censored after 1905. See Viktor Ryshkov, "Dramy teatra (chast' pervaia)," *Teatr i iskusstvo* 50 (1910): 972.

6. G. A. Grigor'ev, *Sanin: P'esa v 5-i stsenakh,* ms., SPTB (rejected March 10, 1908); anonymous, *Sanin: P'esa v 4-kh deistviiakh,* ms., SPTB (rejected March 13, 1908); A. V. B. and R. A. Ch[erepanov?], *Tri stseny iz romana "Sanina,"* ms., SPTB (rejected March 31, 1908); N. Kiselev, *Sanin: P'esa v 5-i aktakh,* ms., SPTB (rejected December 13, 1908); I. I. Kondrat'ev, *Sanin: Svobodnaia liubov': P'esa v 5-i deistviiakh i 8-i kartinakh,* ms., SPTB (rejected June 10, 1910).

7. "Eshche i eshche o Sanine," letter signed Natan B., *Minskii kur'er,* April 30, 1908, 2.

8. Dukh-Banko, "Iz"iatyi Sanin," *Kievskie vesti,* May 4, 1908, 3.

9. The manuscript does not state the name of the authors, but the handwriting suggests that it was written by two persons (*"Sanin": Fars v trekh deistviiakh s kupletami* [1908], SPTB, 34).

10. E. Khizhniakov, *"Sanin": Roman Artsybasheva v kratko-iumoristicheskom ocherke* (Khar'kov: Kommercheskaia tipografiia, 1908).

11. A. V. Amfiteatrov, "Protest V. P. Sanina," in *Protiv techeniia* (St. Petersburg: Prometei, 1909), 112.

12. One notable exception is an account by one of Tolstoy's sons, Sergei L'vovich, who attended a lecture by Artsybashev in Yalta. In his opinion, the writer did look like Sanin: "[He is] strong, a pale face, impertinent, clever, unpleasant, a repulsive voice" (Dushan Makovitskii, *U Tolstogo, 1901-1910: "Iasnopolianskie zapiski,"* 4 vols., ed. S. A. Makashin, M. B. Khrapchenko, and V. P. Shcherbina (Moscow: Nauka, 1979), 3:185 (entry of August 31, 1908).

13. *Birzhevye vedomosti,* August 15, 1909 (evening edition), 3-4.

14. Vsevolod Borisov, "V gostiakh u avtora *Sanina,"* *Vestnik literatury* 4 (1908): 74-75.

15. Beth Holmgren, *Rewriting Capitalism: Literature and the Market in Late-Tsarist Russia and the Kingdom of Poland* (Pittsburgh: University of Pittsburgh Press, 1998), 139-40.

16. Vasilii Rozanov, "Na knizhnom i literaturnom rynke [Artsybashev]," in *O pisatel'stve i pisateliakh,* ed. A. N. Nikoliukin (Moscow: Respublika, 1995), 280-86.

17. Skitalets, "Reaktsiia i literatura upadka posle 1905 goda: Artsybashev," in *Povesti i rasskazy: Vospominaniia* (Moscow: Moskovskii rabochii, 1960), 455.

18. Ibid., 456.

19. "O. Sh.," *"Sanin,"* g. *Artsybashev i zhenshchina* (St. Petersburg: A. A. Ulybina, 1908), 10.

20. Ibid., 26.

21. Ibid., 32.

22. Ibid., 9.

23. Ibid., 5.

24. Rossiiskii gosudarstvennyi istoricheskii arkhiv, St. Petersburg, f. 776, op. 16, d. 1779, l. 1.

25. Graf [Count] Amori [Ippolit Rapgof], *Final: Roman iz sovremennoi zhizni; Okonchanie proizvedeniia "Iama" A. I. Kuprina*, 3rd. ed. (St. Petersburg: n.p., 1914), 4.

26. Rapgof's full name was Ippolit Pavlovich Rapgof (1860-1918?). For a biographical account, see E. T. Iaborova's article "Graf Amori," in *Russkie pisateli, 1800-1917: Biograficheskii slovar'*, 5 vols., ed. P. A. Nikolaev and V. N. Baskakov (Moscow: Sovetskaia entsiklopediia, 1989), 2:12-13. Information on Count Amori's activities after the 1917 revolution is scarce and contradictory. Jay Leyda and Richard Stites maintain that he adapted remarkably well to the new situation, playing a prominent role in the early Soviet film industry. Iaborova, on the other hand, conjectures that, in 1918, Count Amori was one of the cofounders of an anarchist state in Rostov-na-Donu, which lasted only one day. He was reportedly shot immediately after the city was seized. See Jay Leyda, *Kino: A History of the Russian and Soviet Film*, 3rd ed. (London: Allen and Unwin, 1983), 163, and Richard Stites, *Russian Popular Culture: Entertainment and Society since 1900* (Cambridge: Cambridge University Press, 1992), 27-28. For a description of some of Rapgof's screenplays, see *Velikii kinemo: Katalog sokhranivshikhsia igrovykh fil'mov Rossii, 1908-1919* (Moscow: Novoe literaturnoe obozrenie, 2002), 239, 275, 333, 337, 371, 405. A more extensive discussion of Count Amori's notorious sequels can be found in my article "Melodrama as Counterliterature? Count Amori's Response to Three Scandalous Novels," in *Imitations of Life: Two Centuries of Melodrama in Russia*, ed. Louise McReynolds and Joan Neuberger (Durham, NC: Duke University Press, 2002), 99-126.

27. According to Jeffrey Brooks, Count Amori was able to sell "tens of thousands" of copies of his ending to Verbitskaia's *Keys to Happiness*. *The Finale*, the ending to Kuprin's novel *The Pit*, appeared in three editions totaling seventeen thousand copies. Some of his original installment novels were published in editions of fifty thousand copies (*When Russia Learned to Read: Literacy and Popular Literature, 1861-1917* [Princeton, NJ: Princeton University Press, 1985], 154, 161). Unfortunately, I do not have any exact figures on *Sanin's Return*, but the fact that it was republished in Latvia as late as 1931 suggests that its commercial potential had not yet been exhausted. One can therefore safely assume that the number of prerevolutionary copies of this work at least approximated that of the other sequels.

28. Iurii Tsivian, "Vvedenie: Neskol'ko predvaritel'nykh zamechanii po povodu russkogo kino," in *Velikii kinemo*, 9.

29. Graf Amori, *Vozvrashchenie Sanina*, 10.

30. Ibid., 10.

31. Ibid., 11.

32. Ibid., 16.

33. Ibid., 16-17.

34. Ibid., 156.

35. Count Amori explicitly labeled Sanin a "hero of our time" and ranked him with Chatskii, Onegin, and Pechorin (*Vozvrashchenie Sanina*, 6).

36. Ibid., 13.

37. Ibid., 9.

38. This lack of social specificity in the boulevard novel and Dostoevsky's work was first pointed out by Mikhail Bakhtin. See M. M. Bakhtin, *Problemy tvorchestva Dostoevskogo* (Moscow: Sovetskaia Rossiia, 1979), 119-20.

39. My discussion of the specifically melodramatic qualities of Count Amori's work relies on the following works: Peter Brooks, *The Melodramatic Imagination: Balzac, Henry James, Melodrama, and the Mode of Excess* (New Haven, CT: Yale University Press, 1995 [1976]), 15-22; Marvin Carlson, *Theories of the Theatre: A Historical and Critical Survey, from the Greeks to the Present* (Ithaca, NY: Cornell University Press, 1984), 214; and *Sisters of Gore: Seven Gothic Melodramas by British Women, 1790-1843*, ed. John Franceschina (New York: Garland, 1997), 2. See also Louise McReynolds and Joan Neuberger's introduction to *Imitations of Life*, especially their discussion of the concept of poetic justice (1-24).

40. Brooks, *The Melodramatic Imagination*, 16.

41. *Vozvrashchenie Sanina*, 82, 136.

42. Brooks, *The Melodramatic Imagination*, 202.

43. Ibid., 20.

44. *Vozvrashchenie Sanina*, 176.

45. On the significance of this pattern, see Iurii Lotman's article "Siuzhetnoe prostranstvo russkogo romana XIX stoletiia," in *Izbrannye stat'i*, 3 vols. (Tallinn: Aleksandra, 1993), 3:91-106, esp. 102.

46. Brooks, *The Melodramatic Imagination*, 15.

47. In playing on the moral indignation of his readers, Count Amori resorted to a specific kind of voyeurism that one would normally associate with the tabloids and their willful disrespect of privacy. As Joan Neuberger has argued about Russia's thriving boulevard press at the turn of the century, "The boulevard newspapers' reporting of scandalous crimes, outrageous behavior, and the private lives of public figures supplied engrossing reading but also offered readers unforgettable examples of improper behavior, defined the parameters of the acceptable, and reassured readers of their own superiority for never sinking so low" (*Hooliganism: Crime, Culture, and Power in St. Petersburg, 1900-1914* [Berkeley: University of California Press, 1993], 18). Just like the tabloids, Count Amori's sequel performed a double function in that it offered entertainment and at the same time was reassuring and morally uplifting.

48. Lande is merely mentioned in *Sanin*. The consumptive student Semionov is the only character to appear in the story and the novel.

49. Matthew 5:39-40.

50. Despite their different views on life, Sanin judges Lande very mildly in his conversation with Soloveichik, saying that he loved Lande "because he was sincere" (*Sanin*, trans. Michael R. Katz [Ithaca, NY: Cornell University Press,

2001], 194). An article by Iakov Levchenko discusses the striking similarities between the personalities of Sanin and Lande, rather than the differences, which critics have traditionally highlighted ("Ob odnom personalisticheskom tipe v proze M. P. Artsybasheva," in *Russkaia filologiia (Sbornik nauchnykh rabot molodykh filologov)* [Tartu, 1995], 68-77).

51. See, for example, A. S. Glinka-Volzhskii's review "O rasskazakh gg. B. Zaitseva, L. Andreeva i M. Artsybasheva," *Voprosy zhizni* 1 (1905): 282.

52. V. L'vov-Rogachevskii, "Satiry i nimfy," 43-44.

53. *U poslednei cherty, Zemlia,* issues 4, 7, and 8 (1910-1912).

54. Interview with Artsybashev, *Utro Rossii,* January 16, 1911, 5.

55. M. P. Artsybashev, letter to Evsei Aspiz, in "Pis'ma M. P. Artsybasheva," *Voprosy literatury* 11-12 (1991): 364.

56. The "suicide epidemic" is discussed by Susan K. Morrissey, *Suicide and the Body Politic in Imperial Russia* (Cambridge: Cambridge University Press, 2006), and Irina Paperno, *Suicide as a Cultural Institution in Dostoevsky's Russia* (Ithaca, NY: Cornell University Press, 1997), 75-104.

57. Sergeev-Tsenskii reports that Artsybashev threw into the Black Sea the table of the box office girl and reimbursed her for the loss by paying 150 rubles ("Mikhail Artsybashev," in *Radost' tvorchestva: Stat'i, Vospominaniia, Pis'ma* [Simferopol: Krym, 1969], 178).

58. E. M. Aspiz, "Vospominaniia o M. P. Artsybasheve," *Voprosy literatury* 11-12 (1991): 357-58.

59. M. P. Artsybashev, letter to Aspiz, 367.

60. Artsybashev repeated these ideas in a 1912 opinion poll on the suicide epidemic: "Not condoning, nor approving of suicide, I look at it with calmness, just as at each death. I know death is inevitable and the only sensible attitude toward it is to take it as a fact without being a coward" ("Samoubiistvo (nasha anketa)," *Novoe slovo* 6 [1912]: 2).

61. Mikhail Artsybashev, *U poslednei cherty,* in *Sobranie sochinenii,* 3 vols. (Moscow: Terra, 1994), 2:60.

62. Ibid., 444-45. This part of Mikhailov's monologue draws heavily on the autobiographical story "The Wife," Artsybashev's first work to raise the issue of free love. For a synopsis of this story, see the introduction.

63. Ibid., 479, 445.

64. A. Izmailov, "Bankrotstvo idealov (literaturnyi portret M. P. Artsybasheva)," in *Pestrye znamena: Literaturnye portrety bezvremen'ia* (Moscow: I. D. Sitina, 1913), 32.

65. V. L'vov-Rogachevskii, "Oderzhimyi," in *Snova nakanune: Sbornik kriticheskikh statei i zametok* (Moscow: Knigoizdatel'stvo pisatelei, 1913), 61.

66. Ibid., 66.

67. This view is put forward by Lev Voitolovskii in his *Ocherki istorii russkoi literatury XIX i XX vekov* (Moscow: Krasnyi proletarii, 1925-28), 236-38.

68. Artsybashev's biography in the *Dictionary of Russian Writers* follows the

same line of reasoning. There is mention of Artsybashev's turning to theater and cinema, but his later fictional prose is not dealt with at all (*Russkie pisateli, 1800-1917*, 1:115).

69. Artsybashev, letter to Viktor Muizhel' (March 26, 1913), Rossiiskaia natsional'naia biblioteka, f. 497 (V. V. Muizhel'), ed. khr. no. 4, l. 3. On his productivity, see Nicholas Luker's bibliography of Artsybashev's work in his *In Defence of a Reputation: Essays on the Early Prose of Mikhail Artsybashev* (Nottingham: Astra Press, 1990), 129-47.

Chapter 4. The Pornographic *Roman à Thèse*

1. "Artsybashev," in *Literaturnaia entsiklopediia*, vol. 1 (Moscow: Kommunisticheskaia akademiia, 1929), 265.

2. *Istoriia russkoi literatury*, vol. 10 (Moscow: Akademii Nauk SSSR, 1954), 618-19; *Istoriia russkoi literatury*, vol. 3 (Moscow: Nauka, 1964), 775.

3. "Artsybashev," in *Kratkaia literaturnaia entsiklopediia*, vol. 1, ed. A. A. Surkov (Moscow: Sovetskaia entsiklopediia, 1962), 335.

4. *Istoriia russkoi literatury*, vol. 4 (Leningrad: Nauka, 1983), 586.

5. *Sanin* (Moscow: Sovmestnoe sovetsko-zapadnogermanskoe predpriiatie Vsia Moskva, 1990).

6. M. P. Artsybashev, *Teni utra: Roman, povesti, rasskazy* (Moscow: Sovremennik, 1991).

7. M. P. Artsybahsev, *Sobranie sochinenii*, 3 vols. (Moscow: Terra, 1994).

8. That *Sanin*'s reputation as a pornographic novel was undeserved dawned earlier on readers who had the opportunity to reread it in exile. In a 1934 letter to his wife, the artist Konstantin Somov writes how amazed he is with the "naive" and "modest" character of Artsybashev's pornography (letter to A. A. Mikhailova [July 11, 1934], in Konstantin Somov, *Pis'ma: Dnevniki: Suzhdeniia sovremennnikov* [Moscow: Iskusstvo, 1979], 420).

9. Lynn Hunt, "Obscenity and the Origins of Modernity, 1500-1800," in *The Invention of Pornography: Obscenity and the Origins of Modernity, 1500-1800*, ed. Lynn Hunt (New York: Zone Books, 1993), 10.

10. Chukovskii, quoted in Laura Engelstein, *The Keys to Happiness: Sex and the Search for Modernity in Fin-de-Siècle Russia* (Ithaca, NY: Cornell University Press, 1992), 386.

11. Daniel Balmuth, *Censorship in Russia, 1865-1905* (Washington, DC: American University Press, 1979), 135; Charles A. Ruud, *Fighting Words: Imperial Censorship and the Russian Press, 1804-1906* (Toronto: Toronto University Press, 1982), 224-26.

12. Artsybashev, letter to Anastasiia Krandievskaia, Rossiiskii gosudarstvenny arkhiv literatury i isskustva, Moscow, f. 251, op. 2., ed. khr. 1, l. 5.

13. Rossiiskii gosudarstvennyi istoricheskii arkhiv (hereafter cited as RGIA), f. 776, op. 9, d. 1496, l. 9.

14. *Sanin*, trans. Michael R. Katz (Ithaca, NY: Cornell University Press, 2001), 194.

15. RGIA, f. 776, op. 9, d. 1496, l. 9.

16. This appears to be in line with the general policy of the press affairs committees. As Paul Goldschmidt notes: "Obscenity did not seem of much concern to the censors. Most banned works from the period were connected with politics, and particularly with Marxist notions. The laws were used to deal with immediate political threats, not potential challenges to social morals" (*Pornography and Democratization: Legislating Obscenity in Post-Communist Russia* [Boulder, CO: Westview Press, 1999], 95).

17. André Villard, introduction to *Ssanin*, trans. André Villard and S. Bugow (Munich: Georg Müller, 1909), lxxii. This edition also contains an introduction by André Villard, a preface by publisher Georg Müller, the six reviews that led to *Sanin*'s confiscation and its subsequent release, and the decisions of the courts.

18. RGIA, f. 776, op. 9, d. 1496, l. 13.

19. RGIA, f. 776, op. 9, d. 1496, l. 18.

20. RGIA, f. 776, op. 9, d. 1496, l. 22.

21. RGIA, f. 776, op. 9, d. 1496, l. 23.

22. It is only characteristic of the committee's political fears that a far more explicit story like Anatolii Kamenskii's "Leda" (1906) was never censored. Featuring a defiant heroine parading naked before her "bourgeois" guests, the story does not contain any references to political activism or the revolution of 1905.

23. Aleksei Achkasov, *Artsybashevskii "Sanin" i okolo polovogo voprosa* (Moscow: Knizhnyi magazin D. P. Efimova, preemnitsa A. D. Drutman, 1908), 36; Arkadii Gornfel'd, *Knigi i liudi: Literaturnye besedy* (St. Petersburg: Zhizn', 1908), 26.

24. Dneprov, "Kuval'da i Artsybashev," *Minskoe slovo*, April 13, 1908, 4.

25. Goldschmidt, *Pornography and Democratization*, 164.

26. Zaimar Mseriants, ed., *Zakony o pechati: Nastol'naia spravochnaia kniga dlia avtorov, perevodchikov, izdatelei i soderzhatelei tipografii*, 8th rev. ed. (Moscow: I. N. Kushnerev, 1899), 254.

27. Piotr Tkachev, *Izbrannye sochineniia na sotsial'no-politicheskie temy*, 6 vols. (Moscow: Vsesoiuznoe obshchestvo politkatorzhan i ssylnoposelentsev, 1932–37), 2:375. For a discussion on the task of the critic, see Deborah Hardy, *Piotr Tkachev: The Critic as Jacobin* (Seattle: University of Washington Press, 1977), 219–25.

28. Achkasov, *Artsybashevskii "Sanin" i okolo polovogo voprosa*, 9.

29. "Literaturnye protsessy," *Nasha gazeta*, February 18, 1909, 2.

30. Iurii Aleksandrovich, "Nashi moralisty," in *Posle Chekhova*, 2 vols. (Moscow: Obshchestvennaia pol'za, 1908–9), 1:179.

31. G. S. Novopolin [Grigorii Semenovich Neifel'd], *Pornograficheskii element v russkoi literature* (Ekaterinoslav: Tipografiia L. I. Satanovskogo, 1909), 49.

32. Ibid., 103-4.
33. Piotr Pil'skii, *Problema pola, polovye avtory i polovoi geroi* (St. Petersburg: Osvobozhdenie, 1909), 112; Aleksandrovich, "Nashi moralisty," 169.
34. "Pornografiia i ekzameny (Beseda s tovarishchem ministra narodnogo prosveshcheniia L. A. Georgievskim)," *Peterburgskii listok,* May 6, 1908, 2.
35. Novopolin, *Pornograficheskii element v russkoi literature,* 43.
36. Ibid., 244.
37. E. Koltonovskaia, "Problema pola i ee osveshchenie u neo-realistov," *Obrazovanie* 1 (1908): 24.
38. Ibid., 125.
39. M. A. Voloshin, "Propoved' novoi estestvennosti," *Apollon* 3 (1909): 43.
40. Chukovskii, quoted in Engelstein, *The Keys to Happiness,* 386.
41. *Kievskaia mysl',* April 28, 1908, 2.
42. Iakov Falevich, "Itogi tomskoi studencheskoi polovoi perepiski: Doklad, chitannyi 18 fevralia 1910 g. na zasedanii Pirogovskogo studencheskogo meditsinskogo obshchestva pri tomskom universitete," *Sibirskaia vrachebnaia gazeta* 22 (1910): 259.
43. A. G. Gornfel'd, *Knigi i liudi,* 26.
44. L. Frappier-Mazur, "Truth and the Obscene Word in Eighteenth-Century French Pornography," in Hunt, *The Invention of Pornography,* 217.
45. Hunt, "Obscenity and the Origins of Modernity, 1500-1800," 37.
46. In a rudimentary form this chapter was presented as a paper at the Conference on Russian Pornography held at the University of Southern California in 1999. During the discussion following my presentation Eliot Borenstein questioned whether the criteria of explicitness and obscene language could be applied to the Russian situation at all. He pointed out that modern Russian pornography shows a conspicuous predilection for more or less "neutral" words like *chlen* and *grud'* and avoids using coarser expressions. Borenstein's remark is very much to the point and shows that definitions of pornography based on Western literature should not be applied to Russian material unreservedly. Still, I believe that Frappier-Mazur's observations on the fetishizing properties of (French) pornography can help us to understand the almost physical repulsion that a critic like Gornfel'd seems to have experienced when he forced himself to quote Artsybashev's use of the word *grud'.* Although it is not obscene in itself, not even by the puritan standards of nineteenth-century literature, it is certainly very explicit and evocative. Therefore, strictly in terms of its immediate effect, the repetition of *grud'* in *Sanin* enables it to achieve the functional equivalence of obscene language.
47. Gornfel'd, *Knigi i liudi,* 27.
48. Ibid., 28.
49. The classical argument that sexual excitement is incompatible with the "tranquil, detached involvement evoked by genuine art" was convincingly done away with by Susan Sontag. She emphasized that whereas pornography

possesses only one intention (to arouse the reader sexually), a "genuine valuable work of literature" has many (which may include the intention to arouse) ("The Pornographic Imagination," in Georges Bataille, *Story of the Eye* [New York: Penguin, 1986], 86–87).

50. Gornfel'd, *Knigi i liudi*, 30–31.

51. E. Koltonovskaia, "Problema pola i ee osveshchenie u neo-realistov," 127. The image of male and female as two parts of a whole is put forward by Aristophanes in Plato's *Symposium*.

52. E. Trubetskoi, "Konets revoliutsii v sovremennom romane: Po povodu *Sanina* Artsybasheva," in *"Sanin" v svete russkoi kritiki* (Moscow: Zaria, 1908), 42.

53. Ibid., 43; Koltonovskaia, "Problema pola i ee osveshchenie u neo-realistov," 127–28.

54. Sontag, "The Pornographic Imagination," 100.

55. Georg Müller, "Der *Ssanin* und Seine Schicksale in Deutschland," in *Ssanin*, vii.

56. "Arzibaschews *Sanin* konfiskiert," *Münchener neueste Nachrichten*, November 29, 1908, 3.

57. "Konfiskationsbeschluß," in *Ssanin*, xvi–xvii.

58. "Gutachten über den Roman *Sanin* von Artzibaschew von Professor Dr. Karl Boll," in *Ssanin*, xviii–xix.

59. This is, at least, what Georg Müller claimed, but he may have exaggerated the success for commercial reasons ("Der *Ssanin* und Seine Schicksale in Deutschland," vii).

60. "Gutachten von Professor Dr. Karl Brunner in Pforzheim," xxviii.

61. "Gutachten von Ludwig Ganhofer," in *Ssanin*, xxxxv–xxxxvi.

62. "Gutachten von Wilhelm Weigand," in *Ssanin*, lxviii.

63. Ibid., lxvii–lxviii.

64. "*Ssanin* freigegeben," *Münchener neueste Nachrichten*, March 28, 1909, 3.

65. The extras were translated into Russian and published that same year: *Sud'ba "Sanina" v Germanii: Postanovleniia suda kasatel'no konfiskatsii i sniatiia aresta s romana "Sanin" M. Artsybasheva; Mneniia sudebnykh ekspertov*, trans. V. I. Rotenshtern (St. Petersburg: V. I. Rotenshtern, 1909).

66. This is, at least, suggested by the title page of the edition I have used (seventeenth edition, year of publication 1909).

67. One edition, translated by one L. Wiebeck, was published in Berlin by B. Harz in 1919. This is in all probability a reprint of Lully Wiebeck's translation, which was originally published by Herman Seemann Nachfolger in Berlin and Leipzig in 1909. The other translation is by Stefania Goldenring and was published in Berlin by Schreitersche Verlagsbuchhandlung (year of publication unknown). Goldenring and Wiebeck were both active at the beginning of the twentieth century. Even for those editions that do not specify their year of publication, we can safely conclude they were published well before 1917.

68. *Ssanin*, trans. André Villard and S. Bugow (Vienna: Langen-Müller, 1971).

69. Neia Zorkaia, *Na rubezhe stoletii: U istokov massovgo iskusstva v Rossii 1900–1910 godov* (Moscow: Nauka, 1976), 165.

70. *Lydia Sanin* (Germany, 1923), director, Friedrich Zelnik. As far as I was able to establish the film has not been preserved. A brief synopsis of the plot can be found in *Paimann's Filmlisten: Wochenschrift für Lichtbild-kritik*, April 6, 1923.

71. *Ssanin* (Austria/Poland, 1924), director, Friedrich Fehér. Again a synopsis is all that remains. See *Paimann's Filmlisten: Wochenschrift für Lichtbild-kritik*, September 5, 1924, 173–74.

72. See the ad in *Der Kinematograph*, April 20, 1924, 49.

73. *Paimann's Filmlisten* also stated censorship restrictions. Advertised in April 1924, the film had met with no objections from the censor as late as September 5, 1924.

74. Maximilian Barck, *Juris Traum (Nach Motiven aus Michail Artzibaschews Roman "Ssanin")* (Berlin: Maldoror, 1993).

Chapter 5. *Sanin* and Its Readers

1. At this point, I must repeat that it is not my goal to reconstruct the "implied reader" and his or her "horizon of expectations" as some aesthetic response theorists have proposed (see the introduction). I am concerned with the concrete reactions of historical readers and the often ideologically charged image of "the" *Sanin* reader that we find in the writings of professional critics and other opinion makers.

2. D. S. Mirsky, *Contemporary Russian Literature, 1881–1925* (London: George Routledge and Sons, 1926), 139–40.

3. Abram Reitblat, *Ot Bovy k Bal'montu: Ocherki po istorii chteniia v Rossii vo vtoroi polovine XIX veka* (Moscow: MPI, 1991), 41.

4. See, for example, Grigorii Miasoedov's 1893 painting "Reading L. N. Tolstoy's *Kreutzer Sonata* ('New Truths')," Institute of Russian Literature (Pushkinskii dom), St. Petersburg.

5. N. A. Rubakin, "Russkie chitateli i ikh obstanovka," *Vestnik znaniia* 2 (1905): 142. The first part of this article was published in the first issue of that year (172–82).

6. I. Bachaldin, *Chto chitaiut v dukhovnoi shkole? (Anketa sredi uchashchikhsia)* (Vologda: Tipografiia gubernskogo pravleniia, 1912), 28.

7. Pupils of secondary schools sometimes outnumbered the regular readers for which a given public library was intended. In 1911 a journalist observed that among the 1,203 regular visitors to the library of the Society for Mutual Aid to Shop Assistants (Obshchestvo vzaimnogo vspomozheniia prikazchikam), only 168 were actually employed as such. The majority of readers belonged to the educated youth (934). See "Sovremennyi chitatel'," *Ogni,* October 22, 1911, 13. A contributor to the pedagogical journal *Russkaia shkola* (*Russian School*) made similar observations, noting with regret that small and large libraries alike did

not cater to the "people" but predominantly to juvenile readers (which he apparently did not take seriously). In Voronezh 36.7 percent of the regular visitors to the public libraries were underage; in Yekaterinaburg 46.1 percent were. See P. Zhulev, "Sovremennyi chitatel' iz naroda," *Russkaia shkola* 9-10 (1911): 1-19; 24-39. See also N. N. Zhitomirova, "Chitatel'skie zaprosy i krug chteniia uchashchikhsia srednei shkoly predrevoliutsionnoi Rossii (konets XIX i nachalo XX-veka)," in *Istoriia russkogo chitatelia: Sbornik statei* (Leningrad: LGIK imeni N. K. Krupskoi, 1976), 70.

8. I. Bachaldin, "Uchenik-chitatel': Anketa o chtenii v srednei shkole," *Russkaia shkola* 3-4 (1912): 110-34; 118-31.

9. There is a vast amount of critical literature on the importance of the written word in Russia. John McNair discusses the topos of the youth's self-education through literature in memoirs and fictional accounts on the *gimnaziia*; see his article "The School as Prison: The Myth of the *Gimnaziya* in Russian Literature," *Irish Slavonic Studies* 11 (1990-91): 64-65. The tradition of literature as a manual to life in the Soviet period is the subject of D. K. Ravinskii's article "Kniga— uchebnik zhizni?" in *Biblioteka i chtenie: Problemy i issledovaniia; Sbornik nauchnykh trudov* (St. Petersburg: Russkaia natsional'naia biblioteka, 1995), 154-56.

10. Olga Matich, "The Symbolist Meaning of Love: Theory and Practice," in *Creating Life: The Aesthetic Utopia of Russian Modernism*, ed. Irina Paperno and Joan Delaney Grossman (Stanford, CA: Stanford University Press, 1994), 40-44.

11. D. A. Funkendorf, *Liga svobodnoi liubvi*, ms., Sankt-Peterburgkaia gosudarstvennaya teatral' naia biblioteka, St. Petersburg.

12. The best-known literary character to display many of these characteristics is Evdoksiia Kukshina in Turgenev's *Fathers and Children*. For more examples, see Charles A. Moser, *Antinihilism in the Russian Novel of the 1860s* (The Hague: Mouton, 1964), 148-49.

13. "Liga liubvi v Kieve," *Kievskaia mysl'*, April 28, 1908, 2. Petr Potemkin (1886-1926) was a minor poet who gained some notoriety with his parodies of symbolist poetry. See his autobiographical description in *Russkaia poeziia serebriannogo veka 1890-1917: Antologiia* (Moscow: Nauka, 1993), 665.

14. Appalled at a letter to the editor that had expressed a genuine interest in the free love league of Minsk, one reader used the very words "evangelie" and "nastol'naia kniga" to describe how admirers referred to the work of Artsybashev, Kamenskii, and "other pornographers" (*Okraina*, April 12, 1908, 2).

15. Richard Stites, *The Women's Liberation Movement in Russia: Feminism, Nihilism, and Bolshevism, 1860-1930* (Princeton, NJ: Princeton University Press, 1991 [1978]), 187.

16. Edith W. Clowes, "Literary Reception as Vulgarization: Nietzsche's Ideas of the Superman in Neo-Realist Fiction," in *Nietzsche in Russia*, ed. Bernice Glatzer Rosenthal (Princeton, NJ: Princeton University Press, 1986), 324.

17. Laura Engelstein, *The Keys to Happiness: Sex and the Search for Modernity in Fin-de-Siècle Russia* (Ithaca, NY: Cornell University Press, 1992), 376.

18. Eric Naiman, *Sex in Public: The Incarnation of Early Soviet Ideology* (Princeton, NJ: Princeton University Press, 1997), 48. Writing about *Sanin*'s popularity, Naiman, in my view, relies too much on Piotr Pil'skii, who painted a rather exaggerated picture of readers' supposed enthusiasm. Pil'skii simply rehashed two sensational articles that had appeared in *Golos Moskvy* and *Russkoe slovo*. The populist critic Iakov Danilin, who claimed to have been an eyewitness, gave a far less spectacular account of the same event (see the section "Educated Youth: The *Sanin* Reader in the Popular Press" in this chapter). While Danilin had his own reasons to play down *Sanin*'s impact, there is every reason to take Pil'skii's descriptions with a grin of salt.

19. Referring to a 1908 article, which speaks of "hosts of Sanin imitators," Mogil'ner maintains that this is "not an exaggeration at all." The evidence she adduces, however, consists of one comment by a student who admitted that in theory he had been a Saninist for some time. Mogil'ner does not quote this student's additional remark that he had never really practiced Saninism (*Mifologiia "podpol'nogo cheloveka"* [Moscow: Novoe literaturnoe obozrenie, 1999], 126). For a more detailed discussion of Mogil'ner's book, see my review in the *Slavic and East European Journal* 44 (2000): 474-75.

20. E. A. D'iakova, "Belletristy 1900-1910-kh gg.," in *Russkaia literatura rubezha vekov (1890-e—nachalao 1920-x godov)* (Moscow: IMLI RAN, 2000), 675.

21. Makovitskii, *U Tolstogo, 1901-1910: "Iasnopolianskie zapiski,"* 4 vols., ed. S. A. Makashin, M. B. Khrapchenko, and V. P. Shcherbina (Moscow: Nauka, 1979), 3:80.

22. Ibid., 3:139.

23. Gol'berg, letter to Lev Tolstoy, November 20, 1909, Gosudarstvennyi muzei L. N. Tolstogo, f. 1, l. 1.

24. Zinaida Gippius, "Po Artsybashevu," in Mikhail Artsybashev, *Zapiski pisatelia; D'iavol; Sovremenniki o M. P. Artsybasheve* (Moscow: Intelvak, 2006), 725.

25. This marginalia was found in a copy of *Sovremennyi mir* in the Gorky State Library of Perm. I am grateful to Vladimir Abashev for sharing this information with me.

26. On Lidiia Charskaia and her readership, see Susan Larsen's article "Girl Talk: Lydiia Charskaia and Her Readers," in *Self and Story in Russian History*, ed. Laura Engelstein and Stephanie Sandler (Ithaca, NY: Cornell University Press, 2000), 141-67. See also Beth Holmgren's article "Why Russian Girls Loved Charskaia," *Russian Review* 54 (1995): 91-106.

27. A. A. Nikolaev, *Khleb i sveta! Material'nyi i dukhovnyi biudzhet trudovoi intelligentsii u nas i za granitsei (po dannym ankety "Vestnika znaniia")* (St. Petersburg: Vestnik znaniia, 1910), 28.

28. Viacheslav Vodarskii, "Chto i kak chitaiut ucheniki gimnazii (po dannym ankety)," *Rodnoi iazyk v shkole* 1 (1915-16): 14.

29. One researcher simply noted that students eagerly read *Sanin* alongside any books that came from Gorky's publishing house, Znanie. What they preferred remains unspecified (*K kharakteristike sovremennogo studenchestva, po*

dannym perepisi 1909-1910 g. v SPB-skom tekhnologicheskom institute, ed. M. V. Vernatskii [St. Petersburg: Nauchno-ekonomicheskogo kruzhka pri SPB-skom tekhnologicheskom institutie, 1910], 29).

30. Iakov Falevich, "Itogi tomskoi studencheskoi polovoi perepisi: Doklad, chitannyi 18 fevralia 1910 g. na zasedanii Pirogovskogo studencheskogo meditsinskogo obshchestva pri tomskom universitete," *Sibirskaia vrachebnaia gazeta* 22 (1910): 259.

31. E. P. Radin, *Dushevnoe nastroenie sovremennoi uchashcheisia molodezhi, po dannym Petereburgskoi obshchestvennoi ankety 1912 goda* (St. Petersburg: N. P. Karbasnikov, 1913), 59.

32. On the brother-sister model in *What Is to Be Done?* see chapter 2.

33. Naiman, *Sex in Public*, 50-51.

34. A query among female students in St. Petersburg conducted in 1912 appears to confirm Naiman's suspicion, for the respondents showed less interest in Artsybashev than the male readers polled two years earlier. Only 4.3 percent of the female students ranked Artsybashev among their "favorite authors and poets." On the other hand, the time gap separating these two polls may help to explain the difference in response. By 1912 *Sanin*'s cult status had considerably diminished, so it would be dangerous to conclude on the basis of this material that the novel appealed to an overwhelmingly male readership. The two queries are: Falevich, "Itogi tomskoi studencheskoi polovoi perepiski," 258, and *Slushatel'nitsy S.-Peterburgskikh vysshikh zhenskikh (Bestuzhevskikh) kursov* (St. Petersburg: n.p., 1912), 122, 124.

35. *Birzhevye vedomosti*, April 30, 1908, 5.

36. "Zhalkii geroi," *Molodye poryvy* 2 (1908): 12.

37. Engelstein, *The Keys to Happiness*, 148-50.

38. Verbitskaya, *Keys to Happiness*, trans. and ed. Beth Holmgren and Helena Goscilo (Bloomington: Indiana University Press, 1999), 28.

39. Vasilii Rozanov, "Na knizhnom i literaturnom rynke [Artsybashev]," in *O pisatel'stve i pisateliakh* (Moscow: Respublika, 1995), 281.

40. Ibid., 284.

41. Ibid., 281.

42. Ibid., 282.

43. Engelstein, *The Keys to Happiness*, 217.

44. O. Sh., *Sanin, g. Artsybashev i zhenshchina*, 9.

45. See Pil'skii's unflattering commemoratory published a month after Artsybashev's death: "M. Artsybashev," in Mikhail Artsybashev, *Sobranie sochinenii*, 3 vols. (Moscow: Terra, 1994), 3:768-72 (originally published in *Novoe russkoe slovo*, April 24, 1927).

46. P. M. Pil'skii, "Polovaia provokatsiia," in *Problema pola, polovye avtory i polovoi geroi* (St. Petersburg: Osvobozhdenie, 1909), 68.

47. P. M. Pil'skii, "Reaktsiia zamuzhem," in *Problema pola, polovye avtory i polovoi geroi*, 107.

48. Ibid., 106.

49. Ibid., 105.

50. Pil'skii, "M. Artsybashev," 769. Judging by a February 12, 1908, letter from the lawyer Iurii Gruzenberg to Maksim Gorky, Artsybashev was so annoyed by Pil'skii's degrading reviews that he considered suing him for libel (in *Gor'kii i russkaia zhurnalistika nachala XX veka: Neizdannaia perepiska* [Moscow: Nauka, 1988], 1002).

51. Ia. Danilin, introduction to *"Sanin" v svete russkoi kritiki* (Moscow: Zaria, 1908), 6.

52. Ibid., 8.

53. *Golos Moskvy*, March 4, 1908, 3.

54. *Russkoe slovo*, March 4, 1908, 4.

55. Ia. Danilin, introduction, 5.

56. For a discussion of the poetic feuilleton in local turn-of-the-century media, see Elena Vlasova, "Ural'skaia stikhotvornaia fel'etonistika kontsa XIX—nachala XX veka" (PhD diss., University of Yekaterinaburg, 2001).

57. Svirel', "Pesn' sanintsev," *Golos Moskvy*, March 6, 1908, 2. For the Russian text, see the appendix of this book.

58. Joan Neuberger observes that although women engaged in rowdiness, drunkenness, and street disturbances, female offenders were rarely referred to as "hooligans" (*Hooliganism: Crime, Culture, and Power in St. Petersburg, 1900–1914* [Berkeley: University of California Press, 1993], 36).

59. Roman Dobryi, *Pochemu molodezh' konchaet samoubiistvom: Sotsial'no-belletricheskie ocherki iz polovogo i inykh psikhozov poslerevoliutsionnogo perioda* (St. Peterburg: Obnovlenie, 1911). Roman Dobryi was a pseudonym of Roman Lukich Antropov (1876?–1913), son of the quite popular playwright Luka Nikolaevich Antropov. See Ivan Masanov, *Slovar' psevdonimov russkikh pisatelei, uchenykh i obshchestvennykh deiatelei*, 4 vols. (Moscow: Vsesoiuznaia knizhnaia palata, 1956–60), 1:345, and *Russkie pisateli, 1800–1917: Biograficheskii slovar'*, 5 vols., ed. P. A. Nikolaev and V. N. Baskakov (Moscow: Sovetskaia entsiklopediia, 1989), 1:95.

60. Dobryi, *Pochemu molodezh' konchaet samoubiistvom*, 7–8.

61. In this brief overview of the student movement, I have heavily relied on Susan Morrissey's persuasive and deeply researched book *Heralds of Revolution: Russian Students and the Mythologies of Radicalism* (Oxford: Oxford University Press, 1998).

62. *Sanin*, trans. Michael R. Katz (Ithaca, NY: Cornell University Press, 2001), 16.

63. Ibid., 228.

64. "Pis'mo studenta Don. Pol. In. A. S.," *Molodye poryvy* 3 (1908): 31–32.

65. Ibid., 31.

66. Morrissey, *Heralds of Revolution*, 130.

67. See the journal's "mission statement" on the rear cover of the November issue of 1908.

68. A. Makeev, "Zhalkii geroi," *Molodye poryvy* 2 (1908): 12–16.

69. B. Kaplan, "Dva mira," *Molodye poryvy* 4 (1908): 34.
70. "Protest," signed by a group of people who referred to themselves simply as "youth" (*Molodye poryvy* 2 [1908]: 28).
71. *Zhizn'* (*Life*) was Artsybashev's response to *Znanie*, Gorky's almanac, and Andreev's *Shipovnik* (*Rose Hip*). Apparently, Artsybashev's name was sufficient to label the collection pornographic.
72. "Beznravstvenno-li?" *Molodye poryvy* 4 (1908): 37.
73. "Da, beznravstvenno!" *Molodye poryvy* 5-6 (1908): 37.

Chapter 6. Hard-core Saninism

1. Rossiiskii gosudarstvennyi istoricheskii arkhiv (hereafter cited as RGIA), f. 733, op. 201, ed. khr. 112, l. 7-8. The letter is written in a most awkward style (*ustraivaiut* raznye orgii, *ustraivaia* kakie-to ligi svobodnoi liubvi), which I have tried to render as much as possible. The denunciatory nature of the collective letter relates to the fathers' attempt to besmirch the director, a married man, by accusing him of having a relationship with the teacher of French. Novokhopiorsk boasted two gymnasiums, one for boys and one for girls. Shostenko was the director of both.
2. I have stated my approach to rumors in the introduction.
3. According to one commentator who worked for the respectable journal *Vestnik vospitaniia*, the connection between *Sanin* and the free love leagues was beyond dispute. From the fact that these organizations had often started as illegal reading circles devoted to contemporary literature, one could conclude that *Sanin's* influence on educated youth was enormous. See G. R., "O 'nedugakh' sovremennoi molodezhi," *Vestnik vospitaniia* 8 (1908): 78.
4. On the censorships reform, see Louise McReynolds, *The News under Russia's Old Regime: The Development of a Mass-Circulation Press* (Princeton, NJ: Princeton University Press, 1991), 218-22.
5. On Russia's growing readership in the second half of the nineteenth century, see Abram Reitblat, *Ot Bovy k Bal'montu: Ocherki po istorii chteniia v Rossii vo vtoroi polovine XIX veka* (Moscow: MPI, 1991), 8-31. On the development of the popular press, see Daniel R. Brower, "The Penny Press and its Readers," in *Cultures in Flux: Lower-Class Values, Practices, and Resistance in Late Imperial Russia*, ed. Stephen P. Frank and Mark Steinberg (Princeton, NJ: Princeton University Press, 1994), 147-67.
6. Michel Foucault, *Discipline and Punish: The Birth of the Prison*, trans. Alan Sheridan (London: Penguin, 1991), 200.
7. Susan Morrissey, *Suicide and the Body Politic in Imperial Russia* (Cambridge: Cambridge University Press, 2006), 319.
8. Idef, "Liga svobodnoi liubvi," *Okraina*, April 6, 1908, 3.
9. Dneprov, "Liga svobodnoi liubvi," *Minskoe slovo*, April 6, 1908, 2.
10. Svengali, "Liga svobodnoi liubvi," *Minskoe slovo*, April 9, 1908, 3.

11. K-n., letter, *Okraina,* April 9, 1908, 2; Ours, "Nekotorye podrobnosti o 'lige svobodnoi liubvi,'" *Okraina,* April 8, 1908, 2.

12. K-n., letter, 2.

13. K-n., letter, 2.

14. G. Ozerov, "Liga svobodnoi liubvi," *Minskoe slovo,* May 2, 1908, 2.

15. A. Rudnitskii, "Bol'noi vopros," *Okraina,* April 8, 1908, 2.

16. "Ligi 'svobodnoi liubvi,'" *Poltavskii golos,* April 18, 1908, 2.

17. "Otdel 'ligi svobodnoi liubvi' v Poltave," *Poltavskii golos,* April 26, 1908, 3.

18. "Poltavskii otdel saratovskoi 'ligi svobodnoi liubvi,'" *Poltavskii golos,* April 27, 1908, 3.

19. Ibid.

20. "O lige 'Darefa,'" *Kievskie vesti,* April 27, 1908, 4.

21. "Poltavskaia liga," *Poltavskii golos,* April 29, 1908, 3; "Ligi liubvi v Kieve," *Kievskaia mysl',* April 28, 1908, 2.

22. RGIA, f. 776, op. 22, d. 49, l. 2, 4.

23. Ib-Globo Mikhailenko, "Tania," *Okraina,* April 17, 1908, 2.

24. Roman Dobryi, *"Ogarki." Tainye obshchestva molodezhi: Ocherki* (St. Petersburg: Iakov Balianskii, 1908); *Tainye obshchestva molodezhi: Ocherki Romana Dobrogo* (St. Petersburg: Stolichnoe knigoizdatel'stvo M. G. Voronova, 1908). These thin brochures (thirty and thirty-two pages, respectively) were both published in the summer of 1908, each with a print run of ten thousand copies (*Knizhnaia letopis'* 23, June 14, 1908, 6; *Knizhnaia letopis'* 26, July 5, 1908, 14). For the press affairs committee report, see RGIA, f. 776, op. 9, d. 1533, l. 2.

25. RGIA, f. 776, op. 26, ed. khr. 28, l. 309; f. 776, op. 26, d. 27, l. 143, 237. These materials contain reviews by the censor of the following plays: *The Free Love League* (*Liga svobodnoi liubvi* [1908]) by Anatolii Sergeev and *The Free Love League* (*Liga svobodnoi liubvi* [1908]) by S. R. Cherniavskii. The manuscripts can be found in the Sankt-Peterburgkaia gosudarstvennaia teatral' naia biblioteka (hereafter cited as SPTB).

26. Aleksandr Abelian, *Liga svobodnoi liubvi* (St. Petersburg: Tipografiia M. Volkovicha, 1911), 67.

27. "Ot redaktsii," *Okraina,* April 13, 1908, 2.

28. "Minskie radeniia," *Novoe vremia,* April 22, 1908, 3.

29. Aleksandr Etkind, *Khlyst: Sekty, literatura i revoliutsiia* (Moscow: Novoe literaturnoe obozrenie, 1998), 63.

30. "Ogarochnaia opasnost'," *Permskie vedomosti,* March 28, 1908, 4.

31. Etkind, *Khlyst: Sekty, literatura i revoliutsiia,* 73.

32. The very use of the word "league" in this context was probably dictated by the league for education (*liga obrazovaniia*), which was established out of disaffection with Russia's educational system. The league existed from 1906 until 1917.

33. N. A. Smurskii, *Deti XX veka (Ogarki)* (1908), 45, SPTB.

34. Skitalets, "Ogarki: Tipy russkoi bogemy," in *Rasskazy i pesni,* 2 vols. (St. Petersburg: Znanie, 1907), 2:25.

35. Ibid., 40.

36. The similarity between the *ogarki* and Gorky's tramps was also obvious to Aleksandr Blok, who nonetheless was impressed by the coarseness of Skitalets's heroes and, in general, liked the tale very much ("O realistakh," *Sobranie sochinenii*, 8 vols., ed. V. N. Orlov, A. A. Surkov, and K. N. Chukovskii [Moscow: Gosudartsvennoe izdatel'stvo khudozestvennoi literatury, 1962], 5: 110-11). According to Skitalets himself, the difference between Gorky's tramps and his own *ogarki* came down to the fact that the former were slipping into the lower depths of life, whereas the latter were *emerging* from them ("Avtory o sebe," *Zhurnal-zhurnalov* 15 [1916]: 14).

37. To a student of nineteenth-century Russian literature, this formulation conjures up the image of the superfluous man and yet nowhere does Skitalets allude to the *ogarki* as being superfluous. We may conjecture that Skitalets deemed the notion of superfluity incompatible with the proletarian roots of his heroes.

38. Skitalets, "Ogarki: Tipy russkoi bogemy," 57.

39. In one of Roman Dobryi's sketches, which mentions the ritualistic extinguishing of candles, a young mother, a "victim of the league of *ogarki*," takes stock of her own life pronouncing the following words: "My *ogarok* has burnt itself out [*moi ogarok dogorel*]. Consequently, I must have taken everything from life, which it could offer. Once the smell of smoke and soot starts to spread, one must hurry to extinguish one's *ogarok*" (*Pochemu molodezh' konchaet samoubiistvom?* 19).

40. On the mechanism of designating types of everyday behavior, see the introduction.

41. "Vnimaniiu roditelei i uchebnogo nachal'stva," *Orlovskaia rech'*, March 13, 1907, 3.

42. Zanoza, "Nashi 'ogarki,'" *Orlovskii vestnik*, March 17, 1907, 2.

43. "Avtoru 'Nashikh Ogarkov,'" *Orlovskii vestnik*, March 18, 1907, 2.

44. Morrissey, *Suicide and the Body Politic in Imperial Russia*, 324-25. On the image of the school as prison see John McNair, "The School as Prison: The Myth of the *Gimnaziya* in Russian Literature," *Irish Slavonic Studies* 11 (1990-91): 57-72.

45. I. A., "Eshche po povodu 'ogarkov,'" *Orlovskii vestnik*, March 21, 1907, 3; Tvoi znakomyi, "Tovarishchu gimnazistu, avtoru zametki ob 'ogarkakh,'" *Orlovskii vestnik*, March 24, 1907, 3.

46. "Voskresnyi fel'eton: Po povodu 'ogarkov,'" *Orlovskii vestnik*, March 21, 1907, 3.

47. A. V., "Opiat' pro 'ogarkov,'" *Orlovskii vestnik*, March 28, 1907, 1.

48. Parents' committees were established in early 1906 (although there were forerunners to them) with the aim of restoring order in secondary schools. The picture painted in the reactionary *Orlovskaia rech'* is extremely tendentious, of course, for it ignores the fact that these committees were organized by the director of the school and often included teachers as well. See Patrick Alston's seminal study *Education and the State in Tsarist Russia* (Stanford, CA: Stanford University Press, 1969), 177-79.

49. V. Brianskii, "'Vospitatel'nye' meropriiatiia nashikh roditel'skikh komitetov," *Orlovskaia rech'*, March 16, 1907, 3; "Printsy 'ogarchestva,'" *Orlovskaia rech'*, March 20, 1907, 3.

50. On the political agenda of Minister Tolstoi, see Alston, *Education and the State in Tsarist Russia*, 97.

51. *Sbornik postanovlenii i rasporiazhenii po gimnaziiam i progimnaziiam vedomstva ministerstva narodnogo prosveshcheniia* (St. Petersburg: n.p., 1874), 541.

52. John McNair, "The School as Prison: The Myth of the *Gimnaziya* in Russian Literature," 64.

53. A. S. Izgoev, "Ob intelligentnoi molodezhi (zametki o ee byte i nastroeniiakh)," in *Vekhi: Intelligentsiia v Rossii* (Moscow: Molodaia gvardiia, 1991), 191.

54. N. Ostanin, "Roditeli i ikh otnosheniia k uchashchimsia detiam (nabliudeniia i zametki)," *Vestnik vospitaniia* 3 (1903): 133-47; Nikolai Chekhov, "Kto vinovat (po povodu stat'i N. Ostanina 'Roditeli i ikh otnosheniia k uchashchimsia detiam')," *Vestnik vospitaniia* 5 (1903): 131-37.

55. A. Veselovskaia, "Neskol'ko slov o sovremennykh 'ottsakh i detiiakh,'" *Vestnik vospitaniia* 1 (1903): 76.

56. A new production of Naidenov's play premiered at the Maiakovskii Theatre in Moscow in 2000.

57. S. Zolotarev, "Deti revoliutsii," *Russkaia shkola* 3 (1907): 18; G. Agraev, "Fraktsiia 'ogarkov,'" *Russkaia shkola* 10 (1907): 101.

58. John Neubauer, *The Fin-de-Siècle Culture of Adolescence* (New Haven, CT: Yale University Press, 1992), 6.

59. Smurskii, *Deti XX veka (Ogarki)*.

60. S. R. Cherniavskii, *Liga svobodnoi liubvi (shkol'nye ogarki)* (Kharbin: n.p., 1908).

61. *Poltavskii golos*, April 30, 1908, 3. For the Russian original, see the appendix of this book. The formula "Videant consules ne res publica detrimenti capiat" ("Let the consuls see to it that the state suffer no harm") was pronounced by the Senate of ancient Rome to temporarily invest the consuls with semidictatorial powers during times of crisis.

62. See, for example, Lermontov's early "Monologue" ("Monolog" [1829]) and his well-known "Thought" ("Duma" [1838]). A typical example of Nadson's is his poem "Our Generation Does Not Know Youth..." ("Nashe pokolenie iunosti ne znaet..." [1884]).

63. "Melochi," *Ural'skaia zhizn'*, March 18, 1908, 3.

64. Vsevolod Azrum, "Vinovaty li 'ogarki'?" *Vestnik vospitaniia* 8 (1908): 123-24. For the full text of the students' appeal, see the appendix of this book.

65. "Poltavskaia liga," *Poltavskii golos*, April 30, 1908, 3.

66. A. Peshekhonov, "'Sanintsy' i 'Sanin,'" *Russkoe bogatstvo* 5 (1908): 130.

67. G. Agraev, "Nedug molodezhi," *Russkai shkola* 10 (1908): 110. For a discussion of the political discourse on sexual pathology, see Evgenii Bershtein, "'Psychopathis sexualis' v Rossii nachala veka: Politika i zhanr," in *Eros i*

pornografiia v russkoi kul'ture, ed. M. Levitt and A. Toporkov (Moscow: Ladomir, 1999), 414–41; see also Laura Engelstein, *The Keys to Happiness: Sex and the Search for Modernity in Fin-de-Siècle Russia* (Ithaca, NY: Cornell University Press, 1992), 165–211.

68. Stanley Cohen, *Folk Devils and Moral Panics: The Creation of the Mods and Rockers* (Oxford: Martin Robertson, 1980), 59–60.

69. See, for example, the following reaction in support of the Minsk students who objected to the activities of the free love league: "I subscribe to the group of secondary school students. I repeat: there are many people like me" (letter to the editor, signed "tozhe devushka," *Okraina*, April 16, 1908, 2).

70. Letter to the editor signed "Gimnazist S. Z-L.," *Minskii kur'er*, April 12, 1908, 3–4.

71. Report dated August 24, 1907, Gosudarstvennyi arkhiv rossiiskoi federatsii (hereafter cited as GARF), f. 102, op. 4-D 1907, d. 162 sh. 1, l. 2.

72. Report dated April 28, 1908, GARF, f. 102, 4-D 1907, d. 162 sh. 1, l. 17.

73. GARF, f. 102, op. 4-D 1907, d. 162 sh. 1, l. 40.

74. "Eshche raz ob ogarkakh," *Novoe vremia*, March 28, 1908, 6.

75. GARF, f. 102, op. 4-D 1907, d. 162 sh. 1, l. 5.

76. Letter from the governor of Perm to the police department dated April 8, 1908, GARF, f. 102, op. 4-D 1907, d. 162 sh. 1, l. 9.

77. Report of a house search conducted by village constable Oshchepkov on April 1, 1908 (Vladimir Kagelev and Nikolai Kuznetsov, suspects), Gosudarstvennyi arkhiv permskoi oblasti, f. 160, op. 1, d. 113. Unfortunately, the file does not contain any of the material evidence mentioned in the report. Thus it is impossible to ascertain whether the "appeal" in the journal *Uchashchiesia*, as Oshchepkov called it, could really be classified as such or whether it was merely a short, perhaps sympathetic note on the wasted lives of schoolchildren that mentioned the *ogarki* in passing. The assumed ritual of extinguishing candles followed by open debauchery was described in great detail in the *Permskie vedomosti* issue of April 28, 1908, 4.

78. GARF, f. 102, op. 4-D 1907, d. 162 sh. 1, l. 15 ob.

79. The First Gymnasium for Boys was on the eve of its centenary and could well do without the fuss over youth's assumed moral dissipation. See the article on Perm's official regional server at http://old.perm.ru/history/school/man1.html (accessed April 16, 2009).

80. Copy of a letter (April 24, 1908) by N. A. Bravin, the director of the First Male Gymnasium of Perm, to the head of the Orenburg education district, RGIA, f. 733, op. 196, d. 249, l. 47.

81. Not everybody in Perm shared Bravin's optimism. Three days before the director sent his report to the curator of the Orenburg district, Otilliia Tsimmerman, the headmistress of a private school for boys, wrote a desperate letter to none other than Lev Tolstoy. In it, she presented the rumors on the *ogarki* as established facts, noting the spectacular rise in teenage pregnancies. Although

her own pupils had not been involved in this organization, the headmistress stressed, she feared that eventually her boys might be tempted to join it. As she had recently found out, they were frequenting taverns, going on binges, and reading racy novels: "They engross themselves in *Sanin*; they say the hero's better than anyone else because instead of concealing his depravity, he openly and boldly expresses what others only think, yet dare not say" (letter to Tolstoi, April 15, 1908, Gosudarstvennyi muzei Tolstogo, f. 1, l. 4). Tolstoy never replied to Tsimmerman's letter, nor did he, as far as we know, comply with her request to write some edifying story. For a more detailed discussion of Tsimmerman's letter, see my introduction to Michael Katz's English translation of *Sanin* (Ithaca, NY: Cornell University Press, 2001), 1-2.

82. E. Shvarts, letter to Stolypin, June 19, 1908, GARF, f. 102, op. 4-D 1907, d. 162 sh. 1, l. 40 ob.

83. Ibid., l. 42.

84. Letter to the governors, mayors, and the head of the Warsaw police, signed by the head of the police department, Trusevich, July 14, 1908, RGIA, f. 733, op. 196, d. 249, l. 11.

85. RGIA, f. 733, op. 196, d. 249, l. 11.

86. RGIA, f. 733, op. 196, d. 249, l. 19.

87. RGIA, f. 733, op. 196, d. 249, l. 23.

88. RGIA, f. 733, op. 196, d. 249, l. 39.

89. RGIA, f. 733, op. 196, d. 249, l. 46.

90. RGIA, f. 733, op. 196, d. 249, l. 72, 76.

91. RGIA, f. 733, op. 196, d. 249, l. 77.

92. RGIA, f. 733, op. 196, d. 249, l. 78.

93. RGIA, f. 733, op. 201, ed. khr. 146, l. 16.

94. RGIA, f. 733, op. 201, ed. khr. 146, l. 4-5 ob.

95. E. Shvartz, letter to Stolypin, GARF, f. 102, op. 4-D 1907, d. 162 sh. 1, l. 42 ob.

96. "Dnevnik," *Minskii kur'er*, May 27, 1908, 2.

97. G. Agraev, "Nedug molodezhi," *Russkaia shkola* 11 (1908): 46. The article was published in nos. 7-8, 9, 10, and 11 of *Russkaia shkola*. See also Vsevolod Azrum's article "Vinovaty li 'ogarki'?" (published in December 1908), in which he asserted that the existence of the leagues had been confirmed by the students themselves and their parents (*Vestnik vospitaniia*, 8:123).

98. See, for example, Aleksei Achkasov, *Artsybashevskii "Sanin" i okolo polovogo voprosa* (Moscow: Knizhnyi magazin D. P. Efimova, preemnitsa A. D. Drutman, 1908), 5

99. "O ligakh svobodnoi liubvi," *Sinii zhurnal* 1 (1913): 5.

100. The case of the suicide leagues is analyzed in Marina Mogil'ner, *Mifologiia "podpol'nogo cheloveka"* (Moscow: Novoe literaturnoe obozrenie, 1999), 190-96. For a thorough discussion of the "suicide epidemic," see Susan Morrissey's *Heralds of Revolution: Russian Students and the Mythologies of Radicalism* (Oxford:

Oxford University Press, 1998), 178–205, and particularly her *Suicide and the Body Politic in Imperial Russia*, 301–5, and 315–24. See also Irina Paperno, *Suicide as a Cultural Institution in Dostoevsky's Russia* (Ithaca, NY: Cornell University Press, 1997), 94–104.

101. Mikhail Osorgin, "Vremena," in *Vremena* (Moscow: Sovremennik, 1989), 95.

102. Nikolai Konstantinov, *Ocherki po istorii srednei shkoly* (Moscow: Uchpedgiz, 1947), 135. See also Richard Stites, *The Women's Liberation Movement in Russia: Feminism, Nihilism, and Bolshevism, 1860–1930* (Princeton, NJ: Princeton University Press, 1991 [1978]), 186–87.

Chapter 7. Muscles for Money

1. "It was in my first year at university and I had a friend, a student of mathematics, Ivan Lande." *Sanin*, trans. Michael Katz (Ithaca, NY: Cornell University Press, 2001), 192.

2. Ibid., 17.

3. Ibid., 16–17.

4. I have borrowed the term "narrative of self-determination" from Edith Clowes's study *The Revolution of Moral Consciousness: Nietzsche in Russian Literature, 1890–1914* (DeKalb: Northern Illinois University Press, 1988), 83.

5. For a general discussion of the historical background, see Susan K. Morrissey, *Heralds of Revolution: Russian Students and the Mythologies of Radicalism* (Oxford: Oxford University Press, 1998), and Samuel Kassow, *Students, Professors, and the State in Tsarist Russia* (Berkeley: University of California Press, 1989).

6. Kassow, *Students, Professors, and the State in Tsarist Russia*, 68–70.

7. P. Ivanov, *Studenty v Moskve: Byt, nravy i tipy* (Moscow: Obshchestvo rasprostraneniia poleznykh knig, 1903), 88.

8. K. M., "O sovremennoi studencheskoi nishchete," in *"Na pomoshch' molodezhi": Sbornik statei, pisem i zametok o studencheskoi nuzhde i samoubiitsakh uchashchikhsia*, ed. T. L. Krivonosov (Kiev: Obshchestvo vzaimopomoshchi studentov kievskogo polit. in-ta imp. Aleksandra II, 1910), 238.

9. P. Ivanov, *Studenty v Moskve*, 81.

10. Ibid., 78.

11. Ibid., 3, 80.

12. Ibid., 79.

13. K. M., "O sovremennoi studencheskoi nishchete," 239.

14. N. A. Skvortsov, "V bitve s zhizn'iu," *Studencheskoe delo* 7 (1912): 156.

15. A. Kazakov, "Studencheskii proletariat," *Vesti studencheskoi zhizni* 1 (1910): 10.

16. K. M., "O sovremennoi studencheskoi nishchete," 239.

17. "Studencheskaia nuzhda," *Vestnik studencheskoi zhizni* 4 (1912): 22.

18. "M. P. Artsybashev o studencheskom dome," *Studencheskoe delo* 7 (1912): 152.

19. Omel'chenko, a socialist doctor, for example, interpreted Sanin's "somehow or other" exclusively in hedonistic terms, arguing that "amoral, degenerate declasses" like Sanin always live off other people (*Geroi nezdorovogo tvorchestva ("Sanin" roman Artsybasheva)* [St. Petersburg: Sever, 1908], 32-38).

20. *Sanin*, 35.

21. Ibid., 38.

22. Ibid., 19.

23. Daniel Schüman, *Die Suche nach dem "neuen Menschen" in der deutschen und russischen Literatur der Jahrhundertwende: Frank Wedekinds "Mine-Haha" und Michail Petrovič Arcybaševs "Sanin"* (Munich: Otto Sagner, 2001), 78.

24. *Sanin*, 39.

25. Artsybashev, "Teni utra," in *Sobranie sochinenii*, 3 vols. (Moscow: Terra, 1994), 3:721. Artsybashev's critically acclaimed story "The Death of Lande" follows a similar pattern.

26. On the tuberculosis victim as a martyr in radical fiction, see Katerina Clark, *The Soviet Novel: History as Ritual*, 3rd ed. (Bloomington: Indiana University Press, 2000), 64.

27. "Teni utra," 743.

28. "M. P. Artsybashev o studencheskom dome," 152.

29. On muscular Christianity see Clifford Putney's seminal study *Muscular Christianity: Manhood and Sports in Protestant America, 1880-1920* (Cambridge, MA: Harvard University Press, 2003).

30. Puritans in the United States expressed similar objections (albeit in a completely different context, of course), claiming that sports detracted from spiritual devotion. See Putney, *Muscular Christianity*, 44-47.

31. Aleksei Iarmolovich [Alekesei Lozina-Lozinskii], *Smert' prizrakov (nadgrobnoe slovo nad poslednimi sobytiiami v sankt-peterburgskom universitete)* (St. Petersburg: Luch, 1908), 8.

32. Ibid., 83.

33. G. R., "Russkii sport i uchashchaiasia molodezh'," 162.

34. Ibid., 163.

35. Pierre Bourdieu, "Sport and Social Class," *Social Science Information/Information sur les Sciences Sociales* 17 (1978): 819-40; Chris Chilling, *The Body and Social Theory* (London: Sage, 1993), 136-38; Nick Crossley, *The Social Body: Habit, Identity and Desire* (London: Sage, 2001), 109.

36. The popularity of wrestling in prerevolutionary Russia is discussed by Louise McReynolds in her book *Russia at Play: Leisure Activities at the End of the Tsarist Era* (Ithaca, NY: Cornell University Press, 2003), 131-50.

37. A. Kuprin, "N. Breshko-Breshkovskii: Etiud," in N. Breshko-Breshkovskii, *Zhutkaia sila* (Rostov-na-Donu: zhurnal Don, 1991), 3-6; "Breshko-Breshkovskii," in *Russkie pisateli, 1800-1917: Biograficheskii slovar'*, 5

vols., ed. P. A. Nikolaev and V. N. Baskakov (Moscow: Sovetskaia entsiklopediia, 1989), 1:327.

38. A. A. Blok, letter to his mother, February 21, 1911, in *Sobranie sochinenii*, 8 vols., ed. V. N. Orlov, A. A. Surkov, and K. N. Chukovskii (Moscow: Gosudartsvennoe izdatel'stvo khudozestvennoi literatury, 1962), 8:331.

39. See McReynolds, *Russia at Play*, 146–47.

40. A. Sh., "Student-borets o sebe," *Sinii zhurnal* 3 (1911): 14.

41. Ibid.

42. N. Breshko-Breshkovskii, "Tatuirovannyi borets," *Gerkules* 19 (1914): 14.

43. In the article "Borets o sebe," A. Sh. explicitly refers to Ivan Miasoedov as his main example.

44. See, for example, Breshko-Breshkovskii's novel *The Gladiators* (*Gladiatory*), in his *Roman torreadora* (Moscow: Sfinks, 1910), 165–322.

45. Eka, "Billiardsmeny," *Krasota i sila* 2 (1913): 10–11; A. P. Egorov, "Na puti," *Krasota i sila* 3 (1913): 9–10. This criticism was directed at billiards as a betting game, not at the sport itself.

46. I. V. Lebedev, "Ubiitsa," *Gladiatory nashikh dnei* (Petrograd: Rubikon, 1915), 77.

47. Ibid., 85.

48. Ibid., 89.

49. The term "to poach" is de Certeau's.

Index

Note: Page numbers in italics refer to figures.

Abramov, Iakov, 41–42, 46–47, 49, 215n56
"The Abyss" (Andreev), 107, 125
Achkasov, Aleksei, 103
acmeism, 209n17
adolescence: censorship and protection of adolescents, 111–12; generational dynamics and, 156–61; myth of Saninism and, 5; Saninism as frame for interpreting, 193. *See also* gymnasium students
Afanas'ev (character, "Morning Shades"), 181
Agony (*Agoniia*, film, 1974), 6
Amfiteatrov, Aleksandr, 79, 95
Amori, Count (pseud. Ippolit Rapgof), 83–90
Andree'v (character, "Morning Shades"), 181
Andreev, Leonid, 6, 107, 125
antinihilist novels, 55–56, 68, 121
anti-Saninism, 117; *Youthful Impulses* (literary journal) and, 138–42. *See also* countertexts to *Sanin*
Antonovich, Maksim, 35
Antropov, Roman Lukich. *See* Dobryi, Roman (pseud. Roman L. Antropov)
Arnol'di, Dr. (character, *At the Last Frontier*), 93, 94
Arskii (pseud. Nikolai Abramovich), 67

Artsybashev, Mikhail: biographical information, 14–17, 177, 211n39; caricature of, *180*; literary reputation of, 8–10, 12, 14, 15, 55, 125, 233n34 (*see also* specific *works of*); pictured, *9*; rejection of "small deeds" theory and philanthropy, 42; style of, 8, 11, 15, 69, 79, 108, 209n23, 211n41; work as vulgarization or popularization of existing genres, 8–10
Aspiz, Evsei, 92–93
Astrov, Dr. (character, *Uncle Vania*), 46–47
athletes and athleticism. *See* sports
At the Last Frontier (Artsybashev), 77, 92–96
Avdeev, Mikhail, 30, 37–39, 41, 214n35
"average readers": access to banned books by, 101, 118, 235n5; access to *Sanin* by, 117–19, 130–31; assessing response of, 19, 116–17; censorship and protection of, 118; general readership, 21; "horizon of expectation" and, 230n1; as intended audience for Amori's *Sanin's Return,* 89–90; journalistic exploitation of, 22; provincial readers, 129–32; reception of *Sanin* by, 24, 119–20, 122–26, 192; reputation of *Sanin* as frame for response of, 24, 27, 97–99, 116–17,

245

"average readers" (*continued*)
120, 123–24, 226n8; *Sanin* and asserted popularity with, 192; sensitization of the, 22; social class of, 8, 13, 84; statistical data regarding responses of, 124–25; vulgarization and taste of, 8–10; women as, 126–29, 233n34

Baklanov (character, "Not a Hero"), 43, 45–46
Barck, Maximilian, 115
Bazarov, Evgenii (character, *Fathers and Children*), 34–37, 192; as "contemporary type," 35–36; gender or sexuality related criticisms of, 35, 36; as heroic figure, 34–37, 121, 161; as "new man," 35–36, 216n59; Sanin compared to, 61–63, 65–67, 86, 103, 106, 121, 171, 192, 219n34; as "superfluous man," 36
Belinskii, Vissarion, 28–29, 30, 37
Bely, Andrei, 10, 75
Blok, Aleksandr, 10, 53–54, 184, 237n36
"Bloody Sunday," 51
the body: fetishlike preoccupation with, 108–9; physical strength as characteristic in Artsybashev's works, 91; student work ethos and physical labor, 25, 171–76; student wrestler ideal and, 172, 182–87; as tool, 174
Boll, Dr. Karl, 111–12
bolshevism, 6
boulevard literature, 20, 77, 84–85
boulevard press: free love leagues as reported in, 24–25, 110, 121, 145–51; pornography statute and censorship of, 148; reports on Saninism in, 5, 10, 54, 132–36; and *Sanin* as manual for living, 121; social anxiety fed or created by, 22
Bravin, N. A., 163–65
Breshko-Breshkovskii, Nikolai, 25, 172, 184–87, *185*, 189–90
Brooks, Peter, 88
Brunner, Karl, 112

capitalism: as predatory or rapacious, 64–65; Stolypin's economic reforms, 52

Catechism of a Revolutionary (Nechaev), 42
censorship, 14, 22; abolition of preliminary censorship as context for publication of *Sanin*, 99–100; Alexander III and political contexts of, 39; banning of *Sanin*, 24, 99–102, 111–15; confiscation of printed copies of *Sanin*, 99–102; of countertexts to *Sanin*, 82–83; German, 111–15; library collections and, 118; and literary reputation, 15; political motives for, 101–2; pornographic content as rationale for, 24, 82–83, 102–4; and protection of young readers, 118, 121
Certeau, Michel de, 20–21
Chaadaev, Piotr, 13–14
character analogy, 46–50, 58–61
"character crisis," 23–24
characterization. *See specific characters*
Chatskii (character, *Woe from Wit*), 37, 38
Chekhov, Anton, 30, 42, 46–47
Cherniavskii, S. R., 157–58
Chernov, Viktor, 73
Chernyshevsky, Nikolai, 13, 30, 57–58
Children of the Twentieth Century (Smurskii), 151, 157
Chukovskii, Kornei, 98–99, 102, 106–7
class, social: "embourgeoisement" of intelligentsia, 139; as frame for reception of *Sanin*, 24, 131–32; of the intelligentsia, 96, 139, 213n18; morality and, 90; *ogarki* as class-bound, 160; *raznochintsy*, 33, 36–37, 213n18; of readers, 8, 13, 84; Saninism as class-bound, 132; and secondary education, 33; students and social identity, 173–77, 181, 189; "superfluous man" and, 237n37
Clowes, Edith, 8, 122
Cohen, Stanley, 22, 160–61
"Collective Letter to the Editor from a Group of Schoolgirls," 199; translation, 200
conclusion of *Sanin*, 18–19, 76–77, 170; countertexts as reaction or remedy to, 83, 95–96
"contemporary types": Avdeev's formulation of, 37–39, 41, 214n35; behavioral

ideals presented in boulevard novels, 184–85; Belinskii's Pechorin, 29–33; character analogy and, 46–49, 58–61; contemporary critical debate regarding, 30; "contemporary hero of nonexistence" (impostor), 68–69, 74; critics and construction of concept, 23–24, 27–28; decline of, 23, 38–40, 54–55; "de-heroization" of literature, 38–39, 43–46, 54–55; as epoch-defining (*see* epoch-making heroes); female, 37–38, 45; Hippius and, 68–69; Lermontov's *A Hero of Our Time* and concept of, 28–29; "new man," 23, 29–36, 49, 55–56, 64–65, 68–69, 72, 139, 182, 216n59; non-heroes, 41–47, 49, 54–55; persistence of critical concept of, 54–55, 58–61; popular fiction as less concerned with, 87; realism and typicality, 28, 32; as role models, 36–39, 49–50, 120, 154, 192; Sanin as, 52, 59–68, 86–87, 142, 170, 192–93; and social function of literature, 37–39; "superfluous man," 21, 23, 27–31, 47, 49, 52, 59, 213n9; teleological evolution of, 28–31, 37–38, 86–87

Contemporary World (*Sovremennyi mir*, periodical), 10

countertexts to *Sanin*, 24; alternative endings proposed, 77, 83, 95–96; censorship of, 82–83; *A Devil's Doll* (Hippius), 68–74; *Sanin, Mr. Artsybashev, and Woman* (anon.), 81–83; *Sanin's Return* (Amori), 59, 83–90, 96, 136; satires or mock sequels, 77–81

critical reception: assessing reader response of critics, 19; boulevard press as influence on, 121–22; character analogy and, 48–50; critics as readers, 20–23; female readers as rationale in, 126–32, 129–32; in Germany, 111–12, 115; of literature with sexual themes, 11, 98–99, 107–11; provincial readers as rationale in, 129–32; serialization as factor in, 53–54. *See also specific works*

Dan, Fiodor, 36, 61, 65–66
dandyism, 31

Danilin, Iakov, 24, 132, 232n18; and class as frame for reception of *Sanin*, 24, 131–32; on reported Saninist disruptions at lecture, 133–34, 232n18

Dead Souls (Gogol), 74

"The Death of Lande" (Artsybashev), 90–91

descriptive realism vs. prescriptive romanticism, 21

designative function of realistic literature, 21

A Devil's Doll (Hippius): as countertext to *Sanin*, 68–74; critical reception of, 73–74

"Diary of a Superfluous Man" (Turgenev), 29

disease, metaphors of, 70, 81, 143, 174, 183, 207n5

Disterlo, Roman, 39–40

Dobroliubov, Nikolai, "new man" and, 30–33, 35

Dobryi, Roman (pseud. Roman L. Antropov), 135–36, 142, 148–49, 168–69, 237n39

Dokshitskii, Moisei, 3–4, 123

Dostoevsky, Fyodor, 71, 118, 125, 224n38

Dvoekurov, Iurii (character, *A Devil's Doll*), 69–74

Ecclesiastes, epigraph of *Sanin*, 16, 126

economics: commercial value of literary scandal and sensationalism, 84, 92, 98, 111, 113, 132–36; economic self-determination in *Sanin*, 25, 171–72, 178, 182, 189–90; health and illness linked metaphorically to, 179, 181; Stolypin's reforms as context for *Sanin*, 25, 52, 63–64, 66, 178; student poverty, 171–78

education, secondary, 5; class and, 33; *in loco parentis* role, 155–56, 166–67; reforms as reaction to nihilism, 155; as restrictive political-bureaucratic regime, 25, 144, 154, 155, 193; as theme in Artsybashev's works, 15, 177–78. *See also* gymnasium students

egotism, 5–6, 13, 61–65, 71, 113, 189
egotistical rationalism, 13, 33

embodiment: the body as instrument in "struggle for life," 182; gender equality and diminished physical difference, 57
Engelstein, Laura, 122, 129
epoch-making heroes: agency of, 55–56; Avdeev's formulation and canonization of, 30, 37–39, 41, 214n35; character analogy and, 46–49; "character crisis" and search for, 23–24, 28, 39–40; concept as frame for reception of Sanin, 27, 49–50, 192; "contemporary hero of nonexistence" as impostor, 68–69, 74; critical canonization and concept of, 37–38; de-heroization or decline of, 23–24, 38–39; generational differences and rejection of characters as potential, 39–43, 46; as role models, 36–37; Turgenev's Bazarov as last example of, 34–37, 49, 54–55; typicality and, 27–29 (*see also* "contemporary type" *for specific types of*)
Erofeev, Viktor, 11
erotic love: marriage as institutionalized form of, 16–17
"The Ethics of Nihilism" (Frank), 62–63
Etkind, Aleksandr, 150–51
Evgenii Onegin (Pushkin), 29

Fathers and Children (Turgenev), 34–37, 113; critical reception of, 37
February Revolution, 6, 21–22
film adaptations of *Sanin*, 113–15
Foucault, Michel, 28
Frank, Semion, 62–63
frankness, 56–57
Frappier-Mazur, Lucienne, 108
free love: erasure of individuality and, 109–10; gender and sexual ethic of, 127; as response to economic pressures, 67; in *Sanin*, 99. *See also* free love leagues
The Free Love League (Cherniavskii), 157–58
The Free Love League (Funkendorf), 121
free love leagues, 24; amateur plays and poetry about, 149, 151, 157–59; anonymous "confessions" and other "eye witness" reports, 147, 148, 153–55; boulevard press reports of, 24–25, 110, 121, 145–51; cartoon about school children and, 164; censorship of works concerning, 148–49; illegal reading circle linked to, 235n5; literature as inspiration for, 107, 144, 149–51; "Love leagues in Kiev" (*Kievskaia mysl'*), 200–206; as manifestation of generational alienation, 156–61; official investigations of, 161–67; ritualistic descriptions of "secret" meetings in the dark, 146–47, 150–51; rumors of, 143–45, 147–49, 161; suicide leagues as comparable phenomenon, 168–69; as urban phenomenon, 130; youth identity (collective self-image) and, 145, 151–56, 161. *See also ogarki*
Frommett, Boris, 75
Funkendorf, D. A., 121

Ganghofer, Ludwig, 113
gender, 27–28; Artsybashev's depictions of gender relations, 58; capitalism and enslavement of women, 64–65; female hero figures, 37–38; hooliganism as gender-specific term, 134, 234n58; inequality and social ambivalence about marriage or sexuality, 57–58; "new man" as gender neutral concept, 33–34; and reader reception of *Sanin*, 233n34; *Sanin* as mysoginistic work, 126; Saninism and, 81–82; Turgenev's Bazarov and relationships with women, 35, 36; women as readers, 126–29, 233n34; wrestling as hypermasculine, 184
generational conflict: as frame for perceived depravity of the young, 133, 140–41, 144, 155–61; and rejection of potential "epoch-making heroes," 39–43, 46; and the tendentious novel, 55–56; writers as "generations," 39–41
German idealism, 29
Germogen, Bishop, 14
Gogol, Nikolai, 13–14
Goldschmidt, Paul, 102, 227n16
Gorky, Maxim, 5–7, 10

Gornfel'd, Arkadii, 107-9
Goscilo, Helena, 12
gospels, literature as. *See* "manuals for living"
gradualism (*postepenstvo*), 41-42
Greidenberg, M., 67
gymnasium students: access to books by, 117-19, 230n7, 235n5; as anti-Saninist authors, 138-39, 157-60, 197-200; as constructed in the popular press, 132-36; heroic suicide and, 154, 157; literary stereotypes of, 125-26, 144-45, 161; literary works by, 157-60; reading and response to *Sanin* by, 117-19, 122-24, 125-27; self-image of, 25, 145, 154, 161, 193, 199-200; social anxiety about morality of, 132-33, 140, 162-63 (see also *ogarki*); stereotypes of, 135-36, 140, 144-45; as vulnerable to corruption, 143-44, 156-61, 200-206

heroes. *See* epoch-making heroes; *specific characters*
A Hero of Our Time (Lermontov), 28-29
Herzen, Aleksander, 35
Hippius, Zinaida, 10, 120, 124; critical reception of *Sanin* by, 69; *A Devil's Doll* as countertext to *Sanin*, 68-74
Holmgren, Beth, 12, 80
homosexuality, 11
hooliganism, 54, 133-34, 161
"horizon of expectation," 20, 230
"House of Love" (newspaper article), 148, 149-50
How to Live? (theater adaptation of *Sanin*), 79
Hunt, Lynn, 109

idealism, 29-31, 40, 46-47, 213n18; in Hippius's *A Devil's Doll*, 70, 74; nihilism and rejection of, 35, 55; "small deeds" theory and, 42-43; in Turgenev's *Rudin*, 29-30
ideology: modernism and, 13; and reaction to *Sanin*, 13-14; realism and, 13; Saninism as, 4, 13, 56, 86, 88, 120-22, 131, 134, 137-38, 141, 193, 207n5

idleness, 30-31, 33, 139, 171, 188
incest, 57, 85, 88
individualism, 74, 130; generic nature of "new people" as literary characters, 34; self-reliance and economic self-determination, 171-72; sexual transgression or nonconformism and, 12. *See also* egotism
individuality: free love as erasure of, 109-10
"In Real Service" (Potapenko), 43, 46
Insarov (character), 31-33
intelligentsia: abandonment of ideals after revolution of 1905 by, 5-6, 7, 103, 116, 193, 213; class and, 96, 139, 213n18; "embourgeoisement" of, 139; and evolution of hero figures in fiction, 38, 39, 41-43; "hero of our time" and "superfluous man" in discourse of, 28; ideological fragmentation of, 38; marginalization anxiety of, 45; political and economic change linked to loss of authority of, 22; reading and reception of *Sanin* by, 132, 136, 139; *Sanin* as attack on values of, 17-18, 137; Saninism myth as narrative of, 132-33, 169; small deeds or gradualism and, 41-43; sport and the, 183-84, 188; as voice of common people, 132
intelligentsia as fictional characters, 87, 89, 91, 189; "middle type," 42, 46, 47, 48; Sanin, 103, 136, 139, 171; as types, 33-39, 43-46, 213n9
"In the Fog" (Andreev), 107, 125
Iser, Wolfgang, 20
Iurii's Dream (Barck), 115
Ivanov (Chekhov), 48, 49
Ivanov, P., 173-74
Izmailov, Aleksandr, 94-95, 219n34

Jauss, Hans-Robert, 20

Kalymov (character, "Not a Hero"), 45
Kamenskii, Antolii, 8, 10, 106, 109, 121, 130-31, 149
Kamskii krai (*The Kama Region*, newspaper), 162-63

Kapferer, Jean-Noël, 22
Kaplan, B., 139
Karsavina, Zinaida (character), 18, 64, 77–78, 111, 126
Katkov, Mikhail, 35
Kazakov, A., 175, 177
Keys to Happiness (Verbitskaia), 8, 12
Khesia (character, *A Devil's Doll*), 70, 72
Khodasevich, Vladislav, 6–7
Kievskie vesti (*Kievan News*, newspaper), 148
Klimov, Elem, 6
Knorr (character, *A Devil's Doll*), 70, 72
Kol-Oman, 67
Koltonovskaia, Elena, 73, 106, 109–10
Krainii, Anton (pseud. Hippius). *See* Hippius, Zinaida
Krandievskaia, Anastasiia, 53
Kranikhfel'd, Vladimir, 5, 63–64
The Kreutzer Sonata (Tolstoy), 110–11
Kropotkin, Piotr, 35–36, 56
Kuzmin, Mikhail, 10, 121

Lady Chatterley's Lover (Lawrence), 11–12
Lande, Ivan (character, "The Death of Lande"), 90–91, 224n50
Lawrence, D. H., 11
Lebedev, Ivan, 25, 187–90
Lermontov, Mikhail, 28–29, 159
Lialia (character), 18
libraries, readers' access to books, 130–31
literary evolution, 8
Lombroso, Cesare, 127
Lopukhov (character, *What Is to Be Done?*), 33–34, 57–58
Lotman, Iurii, 21
Lozina-Lozinskii, Aleksei, 183
"Lunatic Fringe," 160–61
L'vov-Rogachevskii, Vasili, 76–77, 91, 94–95
Lydia Sanin (film adaptation, 1923), 113–15

Makovitskii, Dushan, 123, 207n3
"manuals for living": behavioral ideals presented in boulevard novels, 184–85; Chernyshevsky's *What Is to Be Done?*, 120; didactic tradition and, 120; free love leagues as inspired by literature, 149–50; provincial readers and enthusiasm for, 131; *Sanin* as "Gospel," 21, 81–82, 106, 117, 120–22, 192; *Sanin* as relatively unpopular with average readers, 124–26
marriage, 15–17, 93–94, 211n39
martyrdom, "superfluous man" and, 29
Marxism and Marxist criticism, 24, 39, 46–47, 55, 62–63, 65–66, 67, 76–77, 105, 132; and reception of Turgenev's Bazarov as heroic figure, 35–36
materialism, 34–35, 62–63, 69, 73
Mathewson, Rufus, 31
Matich, Olga, 120
McNair, John, 155–56
melodrama, 12, 87–88, 151; Amori's *Sanin's Return* as, 83, 86–90
Memoirs of a Revolutionist (Kropotkin), 56
Merezhkovskii, Dmitrii, 10, 120
Miasoedov, Ivan, 187
middle-brow literature, 8, 77, 84
Mikhailov, Sergei (character), 93–94, 96
Mikhailovskii, Nikolai, 15, 40–41, 42, 211n38, 213n18
Minskii kur'er (*Minsk Courier*, newspaper), 148, 168
Minskoe slovo (newspaper), 146–47
Mirsky, D. S., 7–8, 117, 122, 142, 211n41
modernism: Artsybashev and, 10; critical rejection of, 6–7; realism vs., 8
Møller, Peter Ulf, 16, 221n3
morality: appeal to moral indignation as frame for sensationalism, 90, 224n47; literature and affirmation of social norms, 224n47; social or political unrest and moral decline, 105. *See also* pornography
"Morning Shades" (Artsybashev), 181
Morrissey, Susan, 137, 138, 145, 154
mortality, as theme in *At the Last Frontier*, 92–95. *See also* suicide
Moskovskii golos (*The Moscow Voice*, newspaper), 133–34
Müller, Georg, 111, 112, 113
"Murderer" (Lebedev), 188–89

Nadson, Semion, 159
Nagrodskaia, Evodkiia, 12, 184
Naidenov, Sergei, 156-57
Naiman, Eric, 122, 126-27, 232n18, 233n24
Naumov (character, *At the Last Frontier*), 92, 93, 95
Nechaev, Sergei, 42
Nedelia (periodical), 39-42
Neuberger, Joan, 224n47, 234n58
"new man": conventional norms challenged by, 56; heroic agency and, 31; Hippius's use of, 68-69, 72; productive agency and the, 33-34; Sanin as, 23, 55-56, 64-65, 139; spiritual loneliness and, 36; vs. "superfluous man," 36
Nietzsche, Friedrich, or Nietzscheanism, 8, 12, 122, 130
nihilism, 34-35, 214n22; Bazarov as nihilist, 34-35; educational reform as response to, 155; Sanin and, 56-57
nonconformism, authenticity and, 16
nonviolence, 90-91
"Not a Hero" (Potapenko), 43-46, 56
Notes of Iasnaia Poliana (Makovitskii), 123
Novoe vremia (*New Times*, newspaper), 128, 149-50, 162-63
Novopolin, G. S., 62, 105-6

objectivity: obscene language and hyperrealism, 108; and realist aesthetics, 99, 103-4; and representation of the contemporary type, 32, 35, 59, 73, 104
Oblomov (character), 30-31, 46
Oblomov (Goncharov), 30-33, 46
Obnovlenskii (character, "In Real Service"), 43, 46, 49
obscenity: censorship and, 11-12, 100, 101, 112, 227n16; fetishlike quality of obscene language, 108-9, 228n46; *Sanin* as obscene work, 102, 108-9, 112
October Revolution, 5
Ogarchestvo. See ogarki; Saninism
ogarki: decadence (syphilis and suicide) and, 150; generational dynamics as context for concerns regarding, 156-60; vs. Gorky's tramps, 237n36; *Ogarchestvo* as class-bound phenomenon, 160; political anxiety and investigation of *Ogarchestvo*, 160, 162-63; rumors of, 146, 152, 153, 158-59, 163, 165, 169, 239n81; vs. "superfluous man," 237n37; use of term, 150-52, 237n39, 239n77
Okraina (*The Outskirts*, newspaper), 145-47, 148, 149
On the Eve (Turgenev), 31, 33
originality, Artsybashev as derivative, 8-12, 20, 23-24
Orlovskaia rech' (*Oriol Speech*, newspaper), 153, 155
Orlovskii vestnik (*Oriol News*, newspaper), 153, 155

Pachmuss, Temira, 74
The Pale Horse (Savinkov), 69
Paperno, Irina, 36-37
parodies. *See* countertexts to *Sanin*
"Pasha Tumanov" (Artsybashev), 15, 16, 211n38
Pavlovna, Vera (character), 33-34
Pechorin, Grigorii (character), 28-29, 31, 38, 59, 86-87
Peterburgskii listok (newspaper), 105
Pil'skii, Piotr, 99, 130
Pisarev, Dmitrii, 31-32, 35-36, 46, 66
politics: Artsybashev and rejection of political readings of *Sanin*, 54; political connotations of *Sanin* scandal, 12; "superfluous man" in context of, 29
Poltavskii golos (*Voice of Poltava*, newspaper), 146, 158-60
populism, or populist criticism, 38-45, 48, 157, 160, 232n18; generational guilt and, 140; in Potapenko's works, 43-46, 56; and reception of *Sanin*, 24, 54, 56, 132; and reception of Turgenev's Bazarov as heroic figure, 35-36; and Sanin as the Other, 140; sport rejected by, 183
The Pornographic Element in Russian Literature (Novopolin), 62, 105-6
pornography, 10, 107-9, 228n49; anti-Saninism and rejection of, 138-42;

pornography (*continued*)
"depornographization" of work in Germany, 115; individuality and, 110; linked to social disintegration, 105–6; as political instrument, 105; vs. "principled" literature (*ideinaia literatura*), 104–5; Russian "pornography with ideas," 106; *Sanin* as pornographic work, 24, 62, 97–99, 107–11; 1001st statute and, 12, 97, 100, 102–4, 148

Potapenko, Ignatii, 39, 49, 56, 215n56

Potemkin, Petr, 121, 231n13

principled literature: as political or ideological, 105; *Sanin* as, 106–7

publication history of *Sanin*, 7, 14, 24; censorship efforts and, 101, 112; circulation statistics, 117–18; German translations and editions, 111, 113; reprints and the commercial market, 98; Revolution of 1905 and, 17, 51–52, 54, 99–100; serialization delays, 53–54; Stolypin coup d'état as context for publication, 17, 53; timing ("sign of the times"), 27

Racheev (character, "Not a Hero"), 43–45

Rakhmetov (character, *What Is to Be Done?*), 34, 121, 182

Rapgof, Ippolit (Count Amori), 83–90

Rasputin, Grigorii, 6

rational egotism, 33, 71

raznochintsy, 33, 36–37, 213n18

reader response criticism, as methodology, 19–23; and gymnasium students as readers, 117–19, 122–24, 125; reconstruction of reader's "horizon of expectation," 230n1; and university students as readers, 103–4, 107, 136–38. *See also* "average readers"; critical reception

readers: access to books, 101, 117–19, 130–31, 235n5; critics and profiles of "typical" *Sanin*, 24; female, 126–29; general readership, 21; "horizon of expectation" and, 230n1; journalistic exploitation of, 22; *Sanin* and asserted popularity with, 192; sensitization of the, 22; social class of, 8, 13, 84

reading behavior, 118, 120, 124–26

realism, 13; Artsybashev and realist school, 8, 15; in Artsybashev's works, 16; as context for reception of *Sanin*, 193; designation and, 21; "hedonistic," 106; and "hero of our time" character types, 28; hyperrealism, 109; objectivity and, 99, 103; pornography and, 108–9; *Sanin* as lacking in verisimilitude, 81; *Sanin* as realistic work, 99, 102–4; "sexual realism," 109; symbolism and, 10; Turgenev and, 35–36; typicality and, 28, 32

Red'ko, A., 73

Reitblat, Abram, 45

religion: blasphemy as cause for censorship, 100; Ecclesiastes, epigraph of *Sanin*, 16; negative reception of *Sanin* by the church, 14; religious connotations of *Sanin* scandal, 12

resistance: nonviolent, 90–92; radicalism and violent, 38 not 90, 42, 90, 212n7

the revolutionary, as literary or cultural figure, 68–69

revolutionary salvation, 5–6, 5–7; Hippius and, 73, 74; as master narrative, 191

Revolution of 1905, 5–6; as context for Hippius's *A Devil's Doll*, 70–71, 73; as context for reception of *Sanin*, 5, 17, 23, 129; as "failed" revolution, 51–52; freedom of expression and, 193; moral decay linked to failure of, 154–55

romantic idealism, 31

Roman Tsarevich (Hippius), 74

Rozanov, Vasilii, 6, 80, 128–29

Rubakin, Nikolai, 118

Rudin (Turgenev), 29–30, 38, 212n7

Rudin, Dmitrii (character), 29–30, 31, 35, 212n7

Russkaia shkola (*Russian School*, newspaper), 168

Russkoe slovo (*The Russian Word*, newspaper), 133

Rzhevskii, Mikhail (character, *A Devil's Doll*), 70

sacrifice, "superfluous man" and heroic martyrdom as, 29. *See also* self-abnegation

sadism, 111–12

salvation, moral, in Amori's *Sanin's Return*, 86, 88–89, 90. *See also* revolutionary salvation
Sanin: blasphemy in, 100–102; concluding scene of, 18–19, 76–77, 170; critical reception of, 54, 69, 95, 97–98, 98–99, 107–11; defenses of the book, 66–68; defenses of Sanin, 66–68; as derivative work, 20, 23–24; economic self-determination in, 178, 182, 189–90; as "Gospel" or "manual for living," 21, 81–82, 106, 117, 120–22, 192; *At the Last Frontier* and, 92–96; literary quality of, 8–11, 20, 112–13; objectivity debate regarding, 100–104, 107; popularity of, 131; as pornographic, 24, 62, 97–99, 107–11; as realistic fiction, 81, 102–4; rumors of free-love leagues as context for reception of, 144; synopsis of, 17–19; as tendentious novel, 54–58, 86, 99, 102–4; as trendy novel, 74–75; typicality and, 27–30
Sanin, Lida (character), 17–18, 170–71; as female role model, 82; as presented in film adaptation, 113–15; in *Sanin's Return* (Amori), 85–86, 88–89; in satires, 79–80
Sanin, Mr. Artsybashev, and Woman (anon.), 81–83, 128, 132
Sanin, Vladimir (character), 6; in Amori's *Sanin's Return*, 84–89; as character type, 23–24; and "The Death of Lande," 90–91; as employed or involved in physical labor, 171–72, 178; as former student, 170, 171–72; as healthy and vigorous, 179; as "hero," 23, 27, 106; as "new man," 23, 55–56, 64–65, 139; physical descriptions of, 64–65, 88, 179, 181; relationships with family, 170–71; as representation of the status quo, 33; as role model, 24–25, 33, 117, 137–38; as static character, 90; as wanderer "on the road" and changing identity, 91, 96
Saninism, 7, 21, 25, 81, 125; in Artsybashev's *At the Last Frontier*, 96; boulevard press and constructions of, 5; as class-bound phenomenon, 132; and collective self-image of youth, 25–26, 120, 137, 140–42, 150; emergence of myth of, 25; expunged from cultural memory, 7–8, 20; female naïveté exploited by, 81–82; as frame for interpreting juvenile debauchery, 193; hooliganism and, 133–34; as ideology, 4, 13, 56, 86, 88, 120–22, 131, 134, 137–38, 141, 193, 207n5; as interpretive framework for Revolution of 1905, 5, 74–75; as social/journalistic construct, 22–23, 134; as synthesis of discourses rather than ideology, 193; as trend or fashion, 74–75; women as Saninists, 126–29. *See also* free love leagues; *ogarki*
Sanin's Return (Count Amori, pseud. Rapgof), 59, 83–90, 96, 136
Savinkov, Boris, 59, 68–69
Secret Societies of Young People (Dobryi), 148–49, 168–69
self-abnegation, 6, 17, 43, 181; sport as egotistical rejection of, 189; as value of the intelligentsia, 172
self-deceit, as theme in Artsybashev's work, 13, 16
Semionov (character), 171, 179–81, 224n48
sensationalism: and appeal to moral indignation, 90, 224n47; commercial value of literary scandal and, 84, 92, 98, 111, 113, 132–36
sensitization of the audience, 22
sensuality, 11–12, 72, 94, 103, 109, 126–28, 160, 171, 178
sequels. *See* countertexts to *Sanin*
Sergeev-Tsenskii, Sergei, 92
serialization, 53, 118; censorship and, 19–20, 101; impact on critical reception, 53–54
sex, or sexuality, 5; as common theme in fin-de-siècle texts, 11–12; critical reactions to severing of love and, 109–10; female, 127–29; homosexuality in literature, 11; incest, 57–58; as pathologized, 127–28; in *Sanin*, 98–99, 127–28; sexual nonconformism, 13; as theme in Artsybashev's works, 16–17; vulnerability to sexual predation, 128–29, 185. *See also* free love leagues; pornography; sensuality

Sh., A. (wrestler), *185*, 185–86
Shelgunov, Nikolai, 40–41, 42, 212n7
Shtolts (character, *Oblomov*), 31–33
Shvarts, Aleksander, 143, 162–66
the Silver Age: as context for Saninism, 5–8; as period of moral degeneracy, 5–8, 191–92
Sinii zhurnal (*Blue Journal*, newspaper), 168
Skitalets (pseud. S. G. Petrov), 80, 151–54, 237, 237n36
Skvortsov, N. A., 174–75
"small deeds," theory of, 41–43, 46, 55
Smentsev, Roman, 74
Sologub, Fiodor (pseud. F. K. Teternikov), 10, 103, 133
Soloveichik (character), 18, 90, 94, 137, 139, 170
Solov'ev, Vladimir, 109–10
"Song of the Saninists," 134, 195–97
Sontag, Susan, 110, 228n49
sports: in Breshko-Breshkovskii's works, 25, 172, 184–87, *185*, 189–90; Lebedev and the "student wrestler" ideal, 187–89; popularity of sports novels, 184; as profession, 184; as rejection of self-abnegation, 181; as social trend, 75, 182–83, 189–90; and student wrestlers as ideal, 172, 184; as "unhealthy" preoccupation, 183–84
Spring Awakening (*Frühlingserwachen*, Wedekind, drama), 11
Ssanin (film adaptation, 1924), 115; advertisement for film adaptation, *114*
Stirner, Max, 11
Stites, Richard, 121–22, 223n26
Stoianovskii, 93
Stolypin, Piotr, 51; concerns and investigation of Saninism, 25, 51, 162–67; coup d'état as context for publication of *Sanin*, 17, 53; economic reforms as context for *Sanin*, 25, 52, 63–64, 66, 178
"struggle for life," 25, 52, 63–64, 66, 178, 193; the body as instrument in, 182; student culture and pressures of, 172–73, 175, 182–90; student wrestler ideal and, 25, 172, 182–90; as theme in Artsybashev's works, 15–16, 25, 189–90

Strunin, Dmitrii, 46
students. See gymnasium students; university students
style, of Artsybashev, 8, 11, 15, 69, 79, 108, 209n23, 211n41
suicide, 6, 15–16, 94–95; in Amori's *Sanin's Return*, 85–86; Artsybashev and, 15–16, 55, 92, 211n39, 225n60; boulevard press and sensationalized reports of, 135; heroic suicide as model for emulation, 154; in Hippius's *A Devil's Doll*, 71; in *At the Last Frontier*, 92–93, 96; perception of epidemic of youth, 135–36, 154, 168, 175; press reports on, 22; Revolution of 1905 as context for, 6; in *Sanin*, 18, 76; "suicide leagues," 168–69
"superfluous man": class and, 237n37; critics and construction of concept, 27–28; as devoid of agency, 29–31; in *At the Last Frontier*, 94; as literary type, 21, 23, 27–30, 47, 49, 52, 55, 213n9; vs. "new man," 36; Sanin as, 59; spiritual loneliness and, 36; uselessness and, 30
Svarozhich, Iurri (character), 18, 54, 56, 58, 67, 71–72, 136, 137, 171, 178–79, 181
symbolism, 10, 209n17

Tarnovskii, Veniamin, 127
"The Tattooed Wrestler" (Breshko-Breshkovskii), 186–87, 189
Tolstoy, Aleksei, 11, 12
Tolstoy, Dmitri (Minister of the People's Enlightenment), 155
Tolstoy, Lev, 3–4, 90, 110–11, 123–24, 125, 207n3, 239n81; as influence on Artsybashev, 209n18, 211n41
Trubetskoi, Evgenii, 109–10
Tsivian, Yuri, 84
Tur, Evgeniia, 35
Turgenev, Ivan: Artsybashev as indebted to, 8; Artsybashev compared to, 113; Bazarov (*Fathers and Children*) as epoch-making hero, 34–37, 52; Insarov (*On the Eve*) as "new man," 31–33; and "superfluous man," 29–30
Tynianov, Iurii, 8

Index

typicality: lack of social typicality in popular fiction, 87; popular fiction and lack of social specificity, 87. *See also* "contemporary types"

Uncle Vania (Chekhov), 46-47
university students: "American-style" model for, 25, 173, 176-77, 186-87; Artsybashev as preoccupied with student work ethic, 25, 171-72, 177-82; as characters in Artsybashev's works, 81-82, 90-91, 136, 171, 177-78; as characters in fiction, 43-44, 69-74; intellectual work and student identity, 173-77, 181, 184, 189; poverty of, 171-78, 188; Sanin as former student, 136, 170-71; sport as challenge to traditional student identity, 189; and "struggle for life," 25, 172-73, 182-90; student-wrestlers as literary type, 25, 172, 182-90
utilitarian function of literature, 30

vanity, human, 15-16, 18
Vaniushin's Children (Naidenov), 156-57
venereal disease, 81, 157-58, 168, 174
Verbitskaia, Anastasiia, 8, 10, 12-13, 84, 95, 127-28
Veresaev, Vikentii, 42
Vesti studencheskoi zhizni (*News of Student Life*, journal), 175
"Videant Consules!" (Evgenii, gymnasium student, poem), 158-60, 197-99
Villard, André, 111, 112
Vorovskii, Vatslav, 36, 46-47, 49, 55, 62
Vorshev (Privy Councillor), 101
Votsianovskii, Vladimir, 54
vulgarization: Artsybashev's works and, 8, 62, 122, 130, 159-60; of highbrow works for popular audience, 8, 20-21, 132; intelligentsia and concern over, 132
Vyrubov, Petia (character, "The Murderer"), 188-89
Vysotskaia, Evgeniia (character, "Not a Hero"), 43-45

wandering, 91, 96
Wedekind, Frank, 11
Weigand, Wilhelm, 113
What Is to Be Done? (Chernyshevsky), 13-14, 32, 33-34, 56, 57-58, 120-21, 149, 182, 214
Why Do Young People End in Suicide? (Dobryi), 135-36, 168-69
"The Wife" (Artsybashev), 16-17
Wings (Kuzmin), 10
Woe from Wit (Griboedov), 37
wrestlers: as embodiment of ideal, 172; "struggle for life" and, 25, 172, 182-90

Youthful Impulses (literary journal), 138-42
youth identity (collective self-image): free love leagues and, 145, 151-56, 161; "Lunatic Fringe" and definition of, 160-61; Saninism and, 25-26, 120, 137, 140-42, 150

Zanoza (pseud. of anon. young woman), 153-54
Zarudin (character), 18; in Amori's *Sanin's Return*, 85-86, 88-89; in film adaptations, 115
Zemlia (almanac), 92
Zhizn' (*Life*), 10
Zhukovskii, Iulii, 35
Zinov'eva-Annibal, Lidiia, 12
Zorkaia, Neia, 20

www.ingramcontent.com/pod-product-compliance
Lightning Source LLC
Chambersburg PA
CBHW070939230426
43666CB00011B/2493